Two Men in a Trench

Two Men in a Trench

BATTLEFIELD ARCHAEOLOGY - THE KEY TO UNLOCKING THE PAST

Tony Pollard and Neil Oliver

MICHAEL JOSEPH
an imprint of
PENGUIN BOOKS

To Jerry Newlands Hamer
1950–2001

To my family, with love – Tony
To Pat and Norma Oliver, with love – Neil

MICHAEL JOSEPH

Published by the Penguin Group
Penguin Books Ltd, 80 Strand, London WC2R 0RL, England
Penguin Putnam Inc., 375 Hudson Street, New York, New York 10014, USA
Penguin Books Australia Ltd, 250 Camberwell Road,
Camberwell, Victoria 3124, Australia
Penguin Books Canada Ltd, 10 Alcorn Avenue, Toronto, Ontario, Canada M4V 3B2
Penguin Books India (P) Ltd, 11 Community Centre,
Panchsheel Park, New Delhi - 110 017, India
Penguin Books (NZ) Ltd, Cnr Rosedale and Airborne Roads,
Albany, Auckland, New Zealand
Penguin Books (South Africa) (Pty) Ltd, 24 Sturdee Avenue,
Rosebank 2196, South Africa

Penguin Books Ltd, Registered Offices: 80 Strand, London WC2R 0RL, England

www.penguin.com

First published 2002
1

Copyright © Tony Pollard and Neil Oliver, 2002
Contemporary photographs copyright © Mark Read, 2002
The picture credits on pp. 350–52 constitute an extension
of this copyright page

Set in 10/14pt Rotis Serif
Printed in Great Britain by Butler & Tanner, Frome and London

A CIP catalogue record for this book is available from the British Library

ISBN 0-718-14474-0

CONTENTS

Introduction   6

SHREWSBURY   12
BARNET   74
FLODDEN   118
NEWARK   184
CULLODEN   240
THE FIRTH OF FORTH   286

The Battlefields Today   340
Acknowledgements   346
Further Reading   348

INTRODUCTION

Let's start by being completely honest about why we started studying battlefields in the first place: this stuff can be almost too exciting for words.

We're on Branxton Hill in Northumberland. We're where the Scots soldiers lined up in readiness to fight the English on 9 September 1513. It's raining and the wind is driving the droplets into our faces as we watch one of our metal detectorists check what he reckons is 'a strong signal'. We're cold and miserable and we're pretty sure it'll turn out to be just another chrome handle from a car door, or the clutch plate from a tractor, or maybe a shotgun cartridge – but we're wrong. Instead of another piece of junk to add to our growing collection, it's a lead cannonball. We take turns to handle it. It's about the size of a child's fist – not what you might think of at the mention of a cannonball – but it's so heavy! Mud-smeared and slightly battered though it is, it's unmistakable. The awful weight is mesmerizing. On that September afternoon in 1513 an English artilleryman dropped this ball into a cannon that then exploded into life at the touch of a smouldering taper. Perhaps it missed its target; perhaps it ploughed into a phalanx of Scots soldiers, passing through their bodies like a hot knife before embedding itself in the rain-softened ground. There it lay undisturbed for 488 years. Now we come along, and we're the first people to handle it since that dreadful day. Nothing separates us from the man who loaded it and the men it was blasted towards – except time. The battle of Flodden is alive for us again on that Northumberland hillside.

Archaeology can be a clinical, removed exercise, any sense of the individual being lost over the hundreds or thousands of years between an object being discarded and then recovered by an archaeologist. It is very difficult to put a face or an emotion to a person who made a neolithic pot 5,000 years ago, or dropped a cow bone on to a dungheap 400 years ago. This was normal life, the everyday round of social and domestic activity – the same things done by the same people day after day. That is not to say that archaeologists do not empathize with these people, and it would be very wrong to say that this type of archaeology is unimportant or boring. But there can be no denying that battlefield archaeology is different, the experience of doing this type of archaeology is very personal, even intimate. What we are sometimes looking at when we relocate objects dropped by soldiers – the arrowheads or bullets they used in battle, for example – are the movements and actions of a person who could have been in the last hours or even moments of his life.

Archaeology is the study of the human past through the recovery and study of the physical traces that people leave behind them. Archaeologists excavate the remains of houses, churches, temples, castles and tombs in their quest for evidence. These sites can tell us about the way people lived and how they treated their dead – graves are often excavated by archaeologists. Battlefields differ from all of these in that they tell us about where, when and how people actually died.

Our investigations are not framed within the secure walls of a house or even a castle. The battlefield is a broad canvas and a challenging one for an archaeologist. In order to make sense of expansive tracts of landscape and the other special demands of battlefield archaeology, a customized set of techniques has to be mobilized, in addition to those usually used in archaeological investigation. These include metal-detector survey to locate discarded artefacts and battlefield debris over wide areas, and ground-penetrating radar to search for mass graves. All the results are then tied together using state-of-the-art mapping and topographic-survey technology.

Everything people do leaves traces that an archaeologist can use to build up a picture of what's been going on. But while archaeologists have tended to concentrate their efforts on sites where people went about the business of living and dying for hundreds or even thousands of years – ritual sites like Stonehenge in Dorset, or settlement sites like Skara Brae on Orkney – we decided to look for traces of living and dying that had happened in the space of a few hours. A lot of the work of archaeologists is painstaking, methodical and time-consuming – even pretty mundane. But the basic premise of archaeology could hardly be more fascinating: it's about snooping around after people and seeing what they get up to. It's a licence to be nosy.

Historians study events by reading about them – everything from contemporary documents to books and articles written by scholars down through the intervening centuries. These written sources are often biased or inaccurate, and the axiom that history is written by the victor has no greater relevance than in the case of a battle. Most records are at least one step removed from the events themselves. Archaeologists are historians with the gloves off. We go to where the event happened and we find the remains the event left behind, rather like a forensic scientist at a crime scene. We may be able to use this evidence to piece together a more objective picture of the battle, which can then be used to augment or question historical records and thus provide a more accurate account of events. Historians read about James IV of Scotland

and how he died at the battle of Flodden on 9 September 1513. But we can uncover the landscape which that long-dead king actually walked on and we can find and touch the objects his soldiers left behind. From time to time, we find the things that killed those soldiers.

War is one of the defining characteristics of the human species. No other animals do what we do to one another with guns and bombs and knives. We are exploring the dark side of the human character, and for archaeologists this has been almost taboo. The past can serve as a flattering mirror, and we like to think the best of our ancestors. It is also very tempting to view the past as a halcyon period when people lived in harmony with nature and with one another. The archaeological study of human conflict – even the admission that such conflict has taken place – is often out of fashion. A good example of this can be seen in the study of Iron Age hillforts: even after the excavation of material directly related to warfare, these sites were interpreted as symbols of power and prestige rather than as defensive structures. A battlefield archaeologist, however, has little use for a pair of rose-tinted spectacles.

We decided that if archaeology is a way of studying people, then it was about time we found out what archaeological techniques could tell us about war and, more importantly, the people caught up in war. Soldiers do not flit across a landscape like shadows. Rather than blocks of colour on the map of a battlefield, they are ordinary, real people. But although they are ordinary people, by taking part in a battle they experience extraordinary emotions and exhibit extraordinary behaviour. As they go about

the messy, bloody business of killing and being killed, they leave traces in the ground. Buttons are cut or wrenched from clothing; coins fall from pockets and purses; bullets are fired and cartridge cases ejected; weapons are broken and thrown aside or dropped from dying hands as the action plays out like some horrifying dance. Many battles are fluid affairs in which thousands of men are choreographed across the landscape, usually over short spaces of time. Indeed, Wellington himself went so far as to say that a historian may as well try to write the history of a dance as that of a battle. But we are archaeologists, and as such take little notice of advice given to historians, even when it comes from great generals!

After the fighting is over, the dead are stripped and buried close to where they fell. This takes place in a very short space of time, but so much awful incident must leave its traces, and if we can find just a fragment of all that was dropped or buried, then we can bring those events back to life. Battlefield archaeology is a chance to reveal the past to the present.

Killing is one of the jobs that soldiers are paid to do. But away from the battlefield the same act is usually defined as murder and is therefore a crime. Over the past twenty or so years it has not been uncommon for archaeologists to be called upon by the police to 'help them with their inquiries', as the well-worn expression has it. The archaeologist is a skilled retriever and recorder of evidence, and many of the techniques developed for normal archaeological practice have been used at crime scenes, usually those where murder is involved.

Forensic archaeology has developed to the stage that it is now taught in some universities to archaeologists wishing to specialize after gaining a first degree in their subject. It is a strange and undoubtedly upsetting experience to be told by a detective to excavate the body of a woman recently murdered and then buried in her back garden. Death has an odour which you never forget – it is so strong that it is almost a taste – and when you have experienced it once, it will come back to haunt you at unexpected moments for years afterwards. When we walk over a battlefield today it is impossible to imagine what the stench of hundreds or thousands of corpses must have been like as it hung in the air like an invisible cloud for days or weeks after a battle. What must it have been like to have buried those dead?

Battlefield archaeology has much in common with forensic archaeology: it deals with death and the events that surround it. In today's unsettled world

forensic archaeologists are increasingly called into war zones to investigate the sites of mass graves, usually holding civilians slaughtered in the name of war. But there can be no denying that our work is a little less immediate; our battles were fought hundreds of years, or at least several decades, ago. When we do excavate the graves of the dead we are not confronted by flesh, nor by the smell. These dead are long dead.

We were sure that in every battle there had to be constant elements, identifiable in every case. With this in mind, we decided that we could build up a useful picture of the nature of 'the battle' by concentrating on six battlefields in the UK. We also wanted to examine the way weapons evolved over time and how tactics were developed to exploit and confound those weapons. For this reason we picked a set of battles spanning nearly 550 years of British history, to take in everything from classic medieval warfare through to the Second World War.

We were also painfully aware that battlefields are something of an 'endangered species' for archaeology. Other remains of our past have been preserved and protected by statute, while battlefields have often been left to the mercy of modern development and the rest of the machinery of progress. Clearly, battlefields are not self-contained sites like tombs or churches and range instead over wide areas. No one is suggesting that whole areas should be fossilized, but if something is not done, these scenes, upon which such telling moments of our history were played out, will be gone for good. Sites such as Tewkesbury in England and Bannockburn in Scotland have hit the headlines in recent years as battlefields at risk from development. It is partly in response to this situation that bodies such as English Heritage and Historic Scotland have begun to recognize the cultural importance of these unique sites. The sooner we can perfect the techniques of this new branch of archaeology, the better.

Like many scientific endeavours, archaeological investigations require a team effort. If this is true of an excavation of a Neolithic tomb the size of a living room, it is an absolute necessity in the face of, say, Flodden battlefield, which covers several square miles. Our team includes: topographical scientists, who make detailed contour maps of the battlefield and its place within the wider landscape; geophysicists, who use state-of-the-art machinery to analyse subsurface features otherwise invisible to the eye; metal detectorists, who cover wide areas of the battlefield and mark the locations of dropped metal artefacts; excavators, who carefully reveal sections of the buried landscape, keeping detailed notes, making scale drawings and taking photographs as they delve ever deeper into the ground; conservators, who preserve the artefacts recovered by the excavators and metal detectorists and make sure that they are damaged as little as possible by exposure to air; and physical anthropologists, who study any human remains and glean information about the age and sex of the people who died in the battle, as well as their physical health at the time of their death.

We are the first to admit that we are not historians. In dealing with the archaeology of historical periods, however, we have obviously had to read a lot of history books. Different versions of history are passed down from one historian to the next and sometimes the truth is blurred along the way, like in Chinese Whispers. We don't claim to replace historians – indeed, the information archaeologists recover would be meaningless without the framework that history provides. What we hope does come across, if nothing else, is that personal contact with the past through archaeological remains allows a unique and meaningful insight, making it something we can experience rather than just words to read on a page.

Lastly, we have looked at the troop formations for each battle (excluding the Firth of Forth) and the key below lends itself to the 'movement of troops' maps in each chapter.

A map of Britain showing the location of the six battlefields

Inverness ⊡ **+Culloden**

⊡ Oban

Firth of Forth+

Glasgow ⊡   ⊡ Edinburgh

Flodden+

Carlisle ⊡   Newcastle ⊡

N

⊡ York
⊡ Leeds

Liverpool ⊡   ⊡ Manchester

⊡ Chester

+Newark

Norwich ⊡

Shrewsbury+

Birmingham ⊡   ⊡ Coventry

Swansea ⊡   Cardiff ⊡

⊡ Bristol

Barnet+
⊡ London

Southampton ⊡

Exeter ⊡

SHREWSBURY 1403

SHREWSBURY

SHAKESPEARE MADE A CAREER OUT OF
DRAMATIZING THE CONFLICT WHICH ON
NUMEROUS OCCASIONS TORE AT THE
HEART OF MEDIEVAL BRITAIN, FROM
MACBETH'S DASTARDLY DEEDS TO THE
SCHEMING POLITICS OF HENRY VIII.
BUT THE REALITY OFTEN INVOLVED
MORE SPILLED BLOOD AND COMPLEX
PLOT TWISTS THAN ANY OF THE GREAT
BARD'S PLAYS.

News from the battlefield of Shrewsbury opens *King Henry IV, Part II*. Quizzed by the rebel Northumberland, Lord Bardolph gives the following account of the battle's outcome:

> As good as heart can wish.
> The king is almost wounded to death,
> And, in the fortune of my lord your son,
> Prince Harry slain outright; and both the Blunts killed
> By the hand of Douglas: Young prince
> John and Westmorland and Stafford fled the field;
> And Harry Monmouth's brawn, the hulk Sir John,
> Is prisoner to your son. O, such a day,
> So fought, so followed, so fairly won,
> Came not till now to dignify the time
> Since Caesar's fortunes!

When asked if he had been to the battlefield to gain this information first hand, Bardolph replies that he hasn't, but learned the good news from someone who had returned from Shrewsbury. As it turned out the reality was the opposite of the triumphant picture painted by Bardolph. The harsh facts are presented by a messenger who, with face as white as snow, tells his lord: 'I ran from Shrewsbury, my noble lord/Where hateful death put on his ugliest mask/To fright our party ... Brother, son, and all are dead.'

We have, therefore, two interpretations of the battle, the former learned second hand, celebrating victory and triumph, the latter telling of defeat and death. As with many of the battles we have looked at, the truth often lies buried beneath many layers of retelling, in both oral and written history, folklore and dramatization. This is why, as archaeologists, we place so much importance on seeing the battlefields for ourselves and using archaeological evidence, not just historical accounts, to come to our own conclusions about a battle. ❖

The truth often lies buried beneath many layers of retelling, in both oral and written history, folklore and dramatization

BACKGROUND

WHAT WERE THE EVENTS THAT LED UP TO THE BATTLE THAT OPENS 'KING HENRY IV, PART II'? IF WE WERE USING SHAKESPEARE'S CYCLE OF PLAYS AS A GUIDE, WE WOULD HAVE TO WIND BACK THROUGH 'KING HENRY IV, PART I' AND BEGIN WITH 'KING RICHARD II'. IT WAS DURING RICHARD II'S REIGN THAT THE GLOWING EMBERS OF JEALOUSY AND PERSONAL AMBITION BETWEEN THE HOUSES OF YORK AND LANCASTER WERE FANNED INTO THE FLAMES OF CONFLICT.

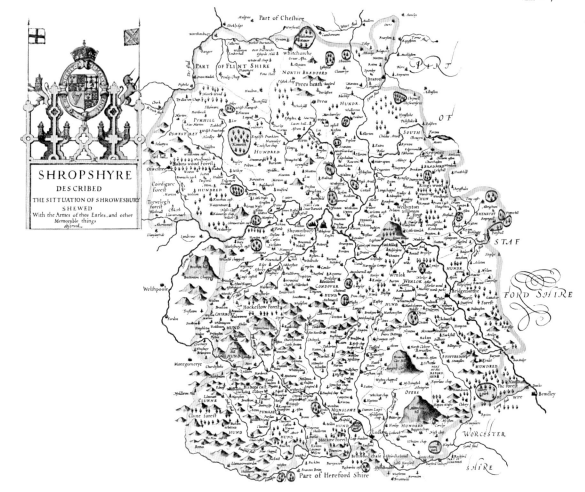

It was not, however, until the reign of Edward IV, some seventy years after Richard's downfall, that conflict erupted to become what we today know, partly thanks to Shakespeare, as the Wars of the Roses.

Richard II was the son of Edward, the Black Prince, and grandson of Edward III. He came to the throne in 1377 at the tender age of ten and was guided through the early years of his reign by a regency council of high-ranking nobles, the most influential of whom was his uncle, John of Gaunt, Duke of Lancaster. Although some of these men had the king's best interests at heart, others undoubtedly saw an opportunity to increase their own power and prestige. Richard's reign was destined to be an unhappy one. Trouble first came in the shape of the Peasants' Revolt of 1381, during which the young king showed impressive fortitude, crushing the uprising with a minimum of bloodshed. Unfortunately for Richard, he was unable to settle the conflicts he was to have with the regency council, and it was the nobles who were to bring about his downfall.

Opposite The coronation of **Richard II**

Above Map of Shropshire, 1610

Richard's reign was destined to be an unhappy one

These were

uncertain times: if

Richard were to

fall, who would

succeed him?

1403

As with any young man, the king preferred the company, and the advice, of a close circle of young friends to that of his elders. Seeing their power eroded by this young clique, the nobles became increasingly jealous and, bonding together as a group known as the Lords Appellant, stood up in open defiance of the king and called for these new advisers to be tried for treason. One of these rebel lords was Henry Bolingbroke, son of John of Gaunt and cousin of the king. Henry had proved himself a popular figure around the Court and had gained important experience as a soldier on the continent.

The crisis escalated into war, and Henry was given command of the Appellant army. It was just as his appointment was announced that he learned of the birth of his son Hal (later to become Henry V). Henry's army defeated the king's at Radcot Bridge near Oxford and very soon Richard found himself besieged within the Tower of London. Richard was allowed to retain the throne, but the rebel lords did everything they could to keep some hold on the reins of power. But these were uncertain times: if Richard were to fall, who would succeed him?

As Richard himself had produced no offspring we must turn back to his grandfather Edward III to make sense of the line of accession. Richard was the only son of the Black Prince, himself the firstborn of Edward III's four sons. The next in line would therefore be Edward's second son, Lionel, Duke of Clarence. He, however, died in 1368, and so the crown would go down through the line of his daughter Phillipa; but as she died in 1382 the heir would be her firstborn son, Roger Mortimer, the fourth Earl of March. Roger's sister Elizabeth was married to Henry Percy, the first son of Henry, the Earl of Northumberland.

The Percys were a very important family in the north of England. They were Marcher lords – holders of lands on the English borders with Scotland or Wales – and Henry Percy had been appointed by Richard as Keeper of Berwick Castle and Warden of the East March. The Percys were Marcher lords on the border with Scotland; the Mortimers Marcher lords on the border with Wales. Much of the lords' power and influence rested on their willingness and ability to repulse raids and protect England against full-scale invasion. The link between the Mortimers and the Percys was to play an important role in the events that led up to the battle of Shrewsbury.

Richard had alienated the entire population of London by levying extremely high taxes; even worse, he had managed mortally to offend the Percy family. The elder of the house, the Earl of Northumberland, was enraged when Richard granted the family's archrival, Neville, Earl of

Henry Bolingbroke enters London

Westmorland, the Penrith estates in Cumberland which adjoined Northumberland's own. Richard was to pay dearly for this poorly judged use of the royal prerogative.

In a clear demonstration of his refusal to bend to the will of others who claimed some part of his power, Richard took revenge on Henry Bolingbroke for his role in the Appellants' rebellion. In 1399 a feud between Henry and another lord, Thomas Mowbray, Duke of Norfolk, gave Richard an excuse to exile Henry to the continent, where he was to remain for six years. While Henry was overseas, his father, John of Gaunt, one of the wealthiest men in England, died and in Henry's absence the king immediately seized his huge estate. Understandably infuriated at this seizure of his inheritance and egged on by the Appellant nobles remaining in England, Henry made plans to return and take back his land by force of arms. There can be little doubt that the crown was also in his sights. Henry sailed from France with three ships and 300 men and landed in the north of England. Richard was in Ireland, having taken with him Henry's son, perhaps as a hostage. At Doncaster Henry swore an oath to the Earl of Northumberland that he would not seek the crown while Richard lived. Men flocked to the popular Henry's cause and he made his way west with a large army to intercept Richard on his return from Ireland. The king landed at Milford Haven in Wales on 25 July 1399 and holed up in Conwy Castle. Henry sent Northumberland and Thomas Arundel, the former archbishop, to Conwy to seek terms with the king. Northumberland, in a profound act of treachery, talked the king into leaving the castle to visit Henry under a flag of truce. Outside the safety of the castle walls, the king was promptly placed under arrest, and Henry Bolingbroke was crowned King Henry IV on 12 October 1399. While London echoed to the sound of coronation trumpets, Richard remained confined in Pontefract Castle, forgotten. Early in 1400 he starved to death – but his spectre was to haunt Henry for years to come.

Henry had no legal right to the throne; he was a usurper and as such was constantly threatened by rebellion from those who disputed his claim to the throne. Trouble was already brewing with the Percys. Although Northumberland had done Henry such good service in delivering up Richard, the earl's son, Henry Percy (Hotspur), was not as pro-Henry as his father and refused to attend the coronation banquet. Henry also had enemies in Wales.

Owain Glyndwr had become the figurehead of what is sometimes described as a nationalistic war against England. At the time the motives

Opposite **Richard II**

A scene from the wars between the English and the Scots

for revolt were somewhat more modest. Glyndwr had entered into a dispute with Reginald, Lord Grey of Ruthyn, another Marcher lord who was a close ally and friend of Henry IV. Grey was no friend of the Welsh, so his appointment as a Marcher lord showed some lack of judgement on Henry's part. It is said that Grey landed Glyndwr in hot water with the king out of sheer malice, failing to deliver a summons for Glyndwr to turn out for war against the Scots and thus making him appear a traitor.

The Welsh conflict worsened, and in 1400 Glyndwr proclaimed himself Prince of Wales, transforming the rebellion into something more like a national struggle against English domination. Once again the Percys were involved. Hotspur had been appointed by Henry Justice of North Wales and was therefore actively involved in the campaign against the Welsh rebels. In 1401 two of Glyndwr's cousins cleverly took Conwy Castle from the English, but the official Prince of Wales (Henry's son Hal) successfully laid siege to the castle, accompanied by Hotspur.

Elsewhere, things did not go badly for the Welsh. In 1402 Glyndwr captured his archenemy Grey, and during a battle at Pilleth, near

Knighton in Herefordshire, another of the Marcher lords, Edmund Mortimer, was also taken. Henry IV, suspicious that Mortimer might have gone over to Glyndwr, and aware that Mortimer's claim to the throne, as a grandson of Lionel, Edward III's second son, was stronger than his own, refused to pay the customary ransom for Mortimer's release. Henry's suspicions must have been heightened when Mortimer married Glyndwr's daughter, Katherine. Mortimer was furious at the king's refusal to pay the ransom, as was his brother-in-law, Hotspur. The king had also failed to supply Hotspur with money to pay his troops in Wales. Hotspur thus resigned his post as Justice of North Wales; once again Henry had failed to keep his allies sweet.

In 1402 Hotspur was back at the family home in Northumberland. Warfare with the Scots continued, as it always did, and things were going well for the Percys. The Scots had suffered at their hands at Nesbitt Moor after crossing into Northumberland, and their commander, Patrick Hepburn of the Hales, had been captured. In an effort to avenge this defeat a fresh force of over 10,000 men under the fourth Earl of Douglas crossed south of the border. With much of the English army fighting the Welsh, Douglas and his men made it as far south as Newcastle, leaving chaos in their wake. But on their return home, heavily laden with the spoils of war, they found their path blocked by the English, led by the Percys.

The Scots took up position on Homildon Hill while the English took the lower ground at Milfield-on-Till, just outside Wooler. Hotspur let the English archers loose on the Scots rather than attempt an assault. The archers, many of them from Cheshire, did their terrible work, and the Scots fell in their hundreds. Eventually the surviving Scottish troops surged down the slope, still under fire; it is doubtful whether they even got close enough to come to handstrokes with the English men-at-arms. The Scottish army scattered, and many nobles and knights were captured, among them Douglas himself. Milfield was littered with Scottish dead. The English army under the Earl of Surrey tried to coax the Scots army under James IV into fighting on this same ground 111 years later, almost to the day, but perhaps remembering this lesson of history the Scots refused to come to Milfield. The battle of Flodden was fought on Branxton Hill; the Scots lost again.

Henry should have been pleased with the Percys, who once more had kept things under control in the north – especially considering his difficulties with the Welsh. But the king again failed to grasp the fragile nature of his relationship with the family. Victors usually received

Owain Glyndwr

The Welsh conflict worsened, and in 1400 Glyndwr proclaimed himself Prince of Wales

Hotspur, Worcester, Mortimer and Glyndwr

ransom for their return of enemy prisoners, but the king ordered the Percys to hold their prisoners until further notice. Perhaps Henry wanted the ransom for himself, to top up the war chest, which was quickly being emptied by the war in Wales. Eventually Northumberland agreed to release his prisoners into the king's care, but his son Hotspur refused.

If any of the Percys were going to take on the king, it would be Hotspur, slighted in Wales and now refused his due for defence of the northern border. His father remained at home, apparently ill. Hotspur had formed an alliance with Douglas, the Scot; the other desirable ally would be Glyndwr, the Welshman, distantly related to Hotspur through marriage (his daughter had married Hotspur's brother-in-law Edmund Mortimer). Percy struck south and recruited heavily in Cheshire, the home of many of his archers at Homildon Hill. The memory of Richard's usurpation by Henry still fresh, there were many eager to flock to Percy's banner. There was even a rumour spreading that Richard was still alive and would join with Percy against the king – as unlikely perhaps as the tale that Henry's downfall had been predicted by none other than the Arthurian magician Merlin.

To feed on the latent sympathy for Richard, and to turn his cause into something a little more noble than personal antagonism and revenge, Hotspur made a proclamation. In it he railed against Henry for failing to honour the oath he had supposedly made to Northumberland at Doncaster in 1399 – that he would not take the crown while Richard lived but seek only what was rightfully his. His army now around 14,000 strong, Hotspur made his way to Shrewsbury on the Welsh border, where he hoped to be joined by Glyndwr and his Welsh army.

Henry got wind of Hotspur's intention at Burton-on-Trent on 15 July and, predicting the rebel force's movements, marched his army to Shrewsbury, just managing to reach the town gate before Hotspur. When Hotspur arrived to see the king's banner flying from the walls, he had no choice but to withdraw to a position a few miles north. There was no sign of Glyndwr, who in any case would have had to bring his army across the river Severn in order to join Hotspur's troops. Henry, his army superior in numbers, had taken the upper hand: in gaining Shrewsbury he had successfully prevented his two enemies from joining forces. Glyndwr was, however, later to excuse himself on account of delays caused by floods in Carmarthen.

If any of the Percys were going to take on the king, it would be Hotspur, slighted in Wales and now refused his due for defence of the northern border

THE BATTLE

ON THE MORNING OF 21 JULY HOTSPUR AWOKE AFTER TROUBLED SLEEP IN THE HOME OF THE BETTON FAMILY AT UPPER BERWICK. IT WAS EARLY WHEN WORD REACHED HIM THAT A ROYAL FORCE WAS ON THE MARCH TOWARDS HIS MEN'S ENCAMPMENT NEAR BY. PRINCE HAL, A YOUNG MAN OF SIXTEEN YEARS BUT A LEGENDARY KING-IN-WAITING, HAD BEEN PLACED IN COMMAND OF THE SOLDIERS OF THE GARRISON AT SHREWSBURY.

He approached from the south-east, and the initiative, for as long as the rebels idled at Berwick, was his and the king's. Hotspur needed to make his move – and soon.

There was a disorganized, even panicked, air in the rebel camp as orders were barked back and forth in the half-light. Commanders struggled to assemble the 10,000-odd souls into order, ready to strike out against whatever the day held in store. It was neither the hour nor the certainty of killing and dying to come that caused this atmosphere of disorder. The commanders, and no doubt not a few of the men, knew that the force camped near Berwick amounted to just one of three pieces of the rebel jigsaw. Where was the army from Northumberland – the force being raised on behalf of Hotspur's ailing father? And where were Glyndwr and his Welshmen, Hotspur's allies in this rebellion against the crown? Silently present in the camp then, as weapons were readied, animals loaded and men prepared to move, was the awful knowledge that the rebellion could now be tackled by the king piece by inadequate piece. If neither Glyndwr nor the force from the north joined them, these men alone would have to face the king, the prince and their combined armies.

As Hotspur was making his farewells to his hosts, the Bettons, one of them made a strange request: would he leave the family a souvenir of his presence there? Something that, in times to come, and when King Henry was overthrown and the young Earl of March was in his rightful place upon the throne, the Bettons and their heirs could point to and declare, 'And here is the proof that Harry Percy, Hotspur, spent that night under our roof.' Suitably moved by this, and despite his understandable haste, he rested one hand upon a wooden wall panel, fingers splayed. With a knife, he carefully traced the outline. Family legend later held that the loss of this panel would swiftly be followed by the Bettons' loss of both their house and their lands, and sure enough, sometime in the nineteenth century that same panel was misplaced during renovations – and soon afterwards the estate was lost to the family as well.

But the advantage seemed to belong to King Henry: Prince Hal was already in pursuit of the rebels and now he too was on his way. He had a pincer movement in mind. If young Hal continued his approach from the south-east, and the king took a line from the south-west, then, together, father and son could hem in the rebels and crush them before they could retreat northwards in the hope of reinforcements. Suddenly word came in from the scouts: the rebels were not seeking to flee – anything but. The mounted men coming back in from their early

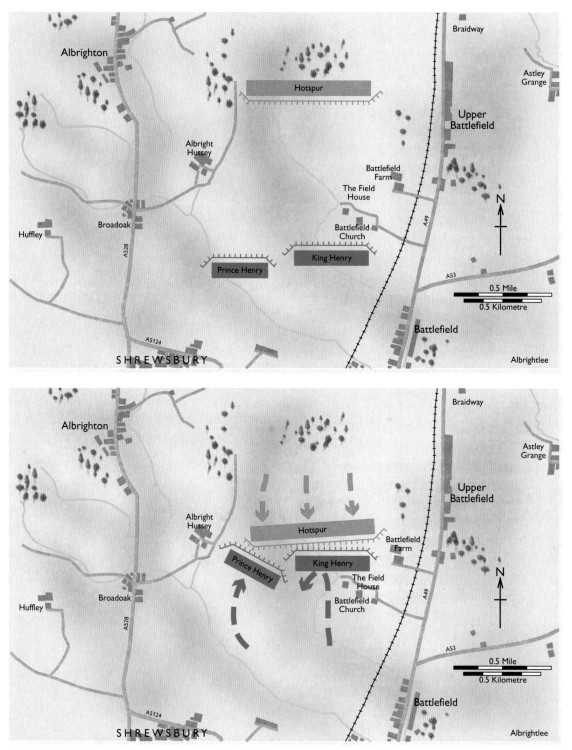

Movement of troops during the battle of Shrewsbury superimposed on a modern map

morning reconnaissance reported that Hotspur and his army were taking up a defensive position. The stag was at bay.

Henry Percy was as close to being a career soldier as anyone, including Henry IV, in the early fifteenth century. He had spent long, hard years at his father's side, and in sole command, in Northumberland and other places, by turns invading Scotland for land and to pillage, and then fighting to repel those same Scots whenever they made their forays south into Percy territory and beyond. Cross-border raiding – endemic in the fourteenth and fifteenth centuries – had made Harry Percy the warrior he was. Indeed, the nickname 'Hotspur' applauds his appetite for the fight. With this wealth of experience behind him, the battle-scarred warrior was not slow to recognize the defensive potential of the ridge of high ground before him as he led his men east past the settlement of Albright Hussey. His choices that morning, anyway, were stark: King Henry and the prince were hard on his heels, and he could either continue north and east in the hope of indefinitely forestalling any clash, or make a stand at a place and time of his own choosing. The instinct that gripped him was not flight but fight.

The ridge was made all the more prominent by the otherwise open and level landscape it dominated. This part of Shropshire was, in the fifteenth century, relatively clear of hedges and other boundaries; low, scrubby vegetation crawled across the plains, broken only by the rude tracks that passed for roads in that part of the world. Determined to fight, Hotspur drew up his rebels in a solid line, perhaps half a mile in length, along the crest and behind some fields of peas. As was the custom and practice of the day, the centre was composed of men-at-arms. This fighting heart of any medieval force – armoured and bristling with swords, bills and the rest of the murderous tools of chivalry – had at its front the dominant force of longbowmen. More bowmen formed the flanks. While the soldiers stood, sat and crouched in their positions, some whiled away the time by plaiting the pea-plants in front of them into matted tangles. Five hundred and more years before the barbed wire that added such horror to the battlefields of the First World War, the intention was the same: to impede the enemy advance at all costs and in any way possible.

King and prince came in sight of the rebels together, though from different directions. Prince Hal had the left, his father the right, and they remained as two separate fighting units for the duration. Like Hotspur's, the king's forces had men-at-arms at their centres and longbowmen to front and flank. The royal forces easily had the numerical advantage,

This fighting heart of any medieval force had at its front the dominant force of longbowmen

Massed clash of bowmen against bowmen at the battle of Agincourt

1403

with perhaps 14,000–15,000 soldiers, and they took up position downslope from the rebels and out of range of the bowmen. There was an uneasy stand-off. Efforts were made to find peace, and this stands as a testament to the king's forbearance. Despite having received a missive signed by Hotspur himself and the earls of Northumberland and Worcester, Hotspur's father and uncle, accusing him of oath-breaking, the murder by starvation of Richard II and the usurpation of the throne of England, Henry still sought to avoid bloodshed. He charged the Abbot of Shrewsbury with persuading Hotspur and his men to lay down their arms in return for a royal pardon. The Earl of Worcester lost his temper first, and this, coupled with the king's growing impatience to draw matters to some sort of conclusion, finally brought the situation to a head.

Realizing that blood would soon have to be spilt, Hotspur called out to have his favourite sword brought to him – only to learn that it was not to hand. In his haste to leave Upper Berwick, he had left it behind – this of all things! – and he saw in the oversight the signature of his own doom. He confessed to those close by him that before leaving his own lands he had been told by a seer that he would die 'at Berwick', and that it now seemed to him that the truth of the prophecy would out.

The Earl of Stafford commanded the royal front ranks and, at the king's order, he signalled the advance of the bowmen. Immediately this movement began, the rebel archers responded and let fly a lethal hail of arrows from their longbows – and the Royalists immediately released their own deadly rain into the sky. Here at Shrewsbury, the first massed clash of bowman against bowman took place. The sky darkened as wave after wave of arrows were exchanged. It was the king's men who took the worst of this opening exchange – bowmen were lightly armoured and horribly vulnerable to any concentrated dose of their own medicine. To make matters even worse, they were trying to make ground uphill through the tangles of peas and vetch recently prepared by the rebels. Buckling under the bombardment, Henry's archers recoiled, stumbling back into the path of their own men-at-arms, who, though better armoured, were obstructed by the dead and dying archers at their feet. It was there, on the lower slope of that knotted hill, that the royal army suffered terribly, and in these moments that the figures for their casualties rose into the thousands. Rebel men-at-arms, emboldened by the sight of fleeing royal troops, stepped forward in pursuit, clashing with bowmen and royal men-at-arms alike.

Hotspur took his cue from the bloodshed before him, from the retreat and near rout of the royal bowmen, and decided that his moment had come. The Earl of Douglas, his newly found Scottish ally, was by his side, and these unlikely comrades-in-arms made the king himself their target. Together with thirty or so others, they chopped their way forward through the retreating mêlée. Douglas felled men in front of him like lumber: twice he thought he had killed the king, only to learn that Henry had dressed the knights around him in garb that resembled his own. The Earl of Stafford and Sir Walter Blount were among the alleged *doppelgängers*, and it may well be that their deaths saved not just the king but, in the end, the war. Somewhere in the mass of fighting men, Henry was unhorsed, but he was promptly rescued and borne to safety by Dunbar, the Scottish Earl of March.

Despite these efforts and close calls, the tide turned in favour of the king. The greater numbers of his forces began to tell, and what might

The rebel archers responded and let fly a lethal hail of arrows from their longbows – and the Royalists immediately released their own deadly rain into the sky

have become a full-scale rout was checked by the stalwart bravery of the king's men-at-arms. Prince Hal, too, had a role in this, for it was the approach of his own troops that added to the rising royal swell. He took an arrow to the face for his trouble but refused to leave the field. While his father's men fought the rebels to a standstill – perhaps on ground known today as King's Croft – it was the prince's forces who actually made headway. A disciplined advance from the left gradually began to outflank the enemy, aided in part by the bunching of the rebels in their effort to join in the bloodbath at the centre. Now young Hal was pressing round to the rebel rear, forcing them to fight on two fronts, and still no quarter was offered or received.

In the end, it was a death foretold that broke the rebels' spirits. A momentary lull in the press around him prompted Hotspur to seek to steal a quick breath of cool air. Raising the visor of his helmet, he inhaled deeply. Perhaps his eyes were closed, then, when the arrow, nocked into the string and loosed by a most vigilant and opportunist royal archer, found its fatal mark in his open mouth. Perhaps this was bowman as close-quarter executioner, firing the deadly missile over the shoulder of the shielding, armoured men-at-arms who were holding Hotspur and his men at bay and providing openings for shots from point-blank range. In any case, seeing his enemy slain, the king cried out, 'Harry Percy is dead!' And so, too, was the rebel cause. They broke, turned and fled the field.

In the rout that followed, some 3,000 rebels were cut down. Their bodies littered the ground for three miles or more around the scene of Hotspur's death. Perhaps the same number of Royalists lay dead, too – felled in that murderous fight of bowmen against bowmen. The battle of Shrewsbury, greatest of the battles fought on English soil during the entire period of the Hundred Years War, and a bloody prelude to the Wars of the Roses, was over.

Despite these efforts and close calls, the tide turned in favour of the king

1403

Hotspur is killed at the battle of Shrewsbury

THE AFTERMATH

THOSE WHO CHALLENGE A KING CAN HAVE NO DOUBT ABOUT THE LIKELY FATE AWAITING THEM SHOULD THEY FAIL. AS THE BUTCHERY IN SHREWSBURY'S CLOSING STAGES WAS BORN OF ACCEPTANCE THAT DEATH IN BATTLE, NOT CAPTURE, AWAITED REBEL SOLDIERS, SO THE TREATMENT METED OUT TO THEIR LEADERS WAS SIMILARLY HARSH. SIR THOMAS PERCY, EARL OF WORCESTER, WAS BEHEADED ON 23 JULY AT SHREWSBURY HIGH CROSS.

CRIME AND PUNISHMENT

Worcester's head was displayed on London Bridge until late December before being taken down and sent back to Shrewsbury to be reunited with his already buried corpse. Rebel commanders Sir Richard Vernon and Sir Richard Venables were similarly dispatched, their heads being taken to Chester to be displayed there. Nor was Hotspur afforded a resting place directly after his death in battle. Initially buried at Whitchurch by his kinsman Lord Furnyvale, his body was dug up at Henry's orders and taken to Shrewsbury for public exhibition near the town pillory, the better to dispel any myth of his survival. It was kept there for some days, propped between two millstones and under armed guard, before being decapitated and quartered. His arms and legs, salted and in sacks, were sent variously to London, Newcastle, Chester and Bristol for display. His head was dispatched to York as gruesome decoration for the main gate into that city. Early in November, by order of the king, his head and the grisly four-piece jigsaw of his trunk were gathered together and delivered to his widow Elizabeth for a second, final burial. Percy senior, Hotspur's father, was spared the axeman's blade. The king accepted that, since the earl had been ill at the time and had taken no active role in the rebellion, he should be pardoned: 'the erlle of Northumbirlond ... cam to the parlement, and [King Henry] excusid him that he was not gilty of the bataille of Shrewesbury, and swoor upon the cros of Cantirbury befor the parlement, he sholde evir be trew to king Harri.'

Others who had fought and lived yet were spared execution suffered the ignominy of seeing their lands confiscated and distributed among Henry IV's supporters. The people of Chester, where Hotspur had raised his standard and proclaimed his intentions, and the men of Cheshire, too, had to wait until November before hearing that the king had issued a pardon, although levying a fine of 500 marks. Later the same month, the rest of Percy's supporters were similarly let off the hook.

The mass of the men who stood to at Shrewsbury on 21 July, for king or for Hotspur, who did not live to see the aftermath, are still there on the field. A huge grave pit was dug close to the scene of the heaviest fighting, apparently near the site of the church built soon after the battle for the thousands of battlefield dead. The remainder are doubtless close by in grave pits which the chroniclers failed to record.

Henry's victory at Shrewsbury secured the Lancastrian hold on the throne of England until the time of the Wars of the Roses. The challenge by the Percy family – their assertion that the Mortimer claim on the

His head was dispatched to York as gruesome decoration for the main gate into that city

Henry IV

throne was more legitimate than Henry's own – had been severely weakened. There is insufficient evidence to say with certainty that Hotspur and Owain Glyndwr acted in concert that summer of 1403. It is reasonable, however, to suppose both men were well aware that the one's efforts could only help the other. From Henry's point of view, he was being challenged from two directions. It would appear that he identified the Percy threat as the greater of two evils and so set about neutralizing it first, before turning his full attention back to Glyndwr and his pretensions to be prince of an independent Wales.

Glyndwr remained a problem after Shrewsbury – and a potent one at that, despite the setback caused by the removal of Hotspur and Worcester: Glyndwr's own son-in-law, the elder Edmund Mortimer, was uncle to the young Mortimer claimant to the throne, but without the two Percy firebrands to champion the cause, his voice was that much quieter. The tighter Henry Bolingbroke's grasp on the throne, the harder it would be for Glyndwr to prise his homeland from it, but even allowing for the

Percy disaster at Shrewsbury, Glyndwr was most definitely still in the fight. In 1404 France signed an alliance with Wales, in so doing making it clear that there was a recognition, within the wider European political arena, of Welsh independence under its self-proclaimed prince. More impressive still is the confidence and intent enshrined in the fascinating document known as the Tripartite Indenture. Signed early in 1405 by Henry Percy, Earl of Northumberland, Edmund Mortimer senior and Owain Glyndwr, it divides the whole of mainland Britain between the three men. Under the terms of the indenture, most of England was split between Percy and Mortimer. Glyndwr – and this is the clearest indication of the strength of his bargaining position nearly two years after Shrewsbury – was to have all of Wales, plus the whole of Cheshire and goodly chunks of Shropshire, Wiltshire and Herefordshire. Since no original copy of the document survives, the Tripartite Indenture should be considered with caution. That said, the tenor of those references to it that do survive show that, as late as 1405, Henry still had much to fear from Glyndwr.

In the event, however, the Welshman's dreams ended – and not with a bang but with a whimper. With the Percy threat diluted, Henry was able to focus his attention on the Welsh rebels. It was through gradual inroads, a steady attrition brought about by small-scale English victories (in battles that, alone, would seem to have counted for little), that the territory and credibility of Glyndwr were slowly but surely eroded. From 1406 until 1409 popular support for him waned steadily, in part due to the absence of any glories like Pilleth and that crucial capture of Edmund Mortimer. With the fall in late 1408 and early 1409 of the castles of Aberystwyth and Harlech – the only two castles that had been held by the rebels for any length of time – Glyndwr's rebellion was effectively at an end. However, the echoes of that dream could still be heard in the valleys, and a sense of Glyndwr's threat rumbled on. It was not until 1414 that towns throughout Wales were the scenes of ceremonies of communal submission to the crown and acceptance of fines for rebellion. By this stage, the rebellion really was over and done with. Glyndwr himself appears in the government records for the last time on 24 February 1416, with regard to an offer extended by the king to Owain and his son Maredudd, to accept their surrender. By this time, the leader was probably already dead. In 1421 Maredudd was formally pardoned for his crimes.

With the Percy threat diluted, Henry was able to focus his attention on the Welsh rebels

WHO FOUGHT HERE

'CAUSE PUBLIC PROCLAMATION TO BE MADE THAT EVERYONE OF THE SAID CITY [LONDON] STRONG IN BODY, AT LEISURE TIMES ON HOLIDAYS, USE IN THEIR RECREATIONS BOWS AND ARROWS ... AND LEARN AND EXERCISE THE ART OF SHOOTING; FORBIDDING ALL ... THAT THEY DO NOT AFTER ANY MANNER APPLY THEMSELVES TO THE THROWING OF STONES, WOOD, IRON, HANDBALL, FOOTBALL, BANDYBALL, CAMBUCK, OR COCK FIGHTING, NOR OTHER SUCH LIKE VAIN PLAYS, WHICH HAVE NO PROFIT IN THEM ... UNDER PAIN OF IMPRISONMENT.'

EDWARD III, 12 JUNE 1369

The battle of Shrewsbury is remembered, in terms of the evolution of military tactics at least, as the first clash on English soil of longbow against longbow. Each of those thousands of archers, facing one another across that Shropshire plain while their leaders bickered about a possible peace, had probably spent a large part of his life practising with this simple weapon. For that was the way of things in England once the use of the longbow had been established: all men were expected to keep a bow and arrows and to practise regularly. By the time of Shrewsbury, expertise – or proficiency at least – was commonplace. An outbreak of plague in the middle of the fourteenth century had cut huge swathes through the population of England – taking fighting men as readily as women and children – and prompt action was required to replenish the supply of archers for use at home and abroad. The statement by Edward III quoted opposite demonstrates the importance – the necessity – of having a male population skilled with the longbow. As a result, such knowledge was as common in fifteenth-century England as a driving licence is today. England was awash, too, with men who had seen service in the campaigns of the Hundred Years War, and many of these were longbowmen. They were accustomed to being paid for their skills as well; a proficient archer could expect and demand pay equal to that of any skilled craftsman of the day.

The battle of Poitiers

It is Edward I who is generally credited as the first English monarch to spot the military potential of the longbow. At Crécy in 1346 his grandson Edward III would consolidiate its status with his famous victory over the French; in 1356 Edward I's great-grandson the Black Prince would add fresh shine to the legend, again against the French, at Poitiers; and in 1415 Henry V would enshrine the longbow in English memory for all time with his triumph at Agincourt – the completion of a truly memorable treble. Edward I had noticed the value of the bow against his own mounted knights during the late 1270s when he was battling to assert his authority over the Welsh. Using guerrilla tactics, the Welsh archers, armed with an earlier, somewhat shorter bow, had successfully harried heavily armed and armoured men in a series of telling ambushes. Edward picked up on the idea but saw that the real effectiveness of such weapons, and such men, would come only when they were used *en masse* to disrupt bodies of cavalry and men-at-arms.

Against the Scottish army of Sir William Wallace at the battle of Falkirk on 22 July 1298 Edward deployed his contingent of Welsh archers in precisely this way, and to great effect. They succeeded in breaking up the hitherto immovable 'schiltrons' – the Scottish spearmen

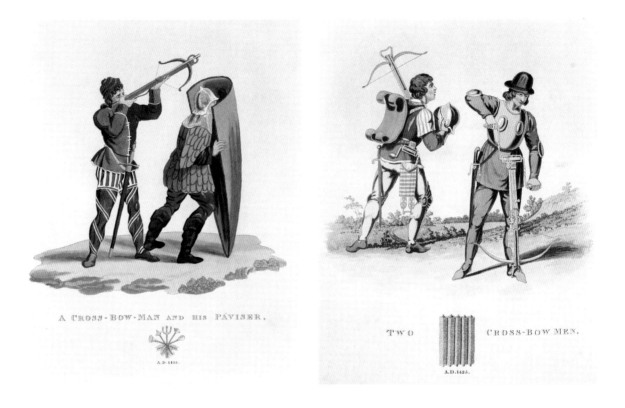

A CROSS-BOW-MAN AND HIS PAVISER.

A.D. 1453.

TWO   CROSS-BOW MEN.

A.D. 1425.

1403

who had stood like stubborn hedgehogs against the English heavy cavalry – opening them up for the final, conclusive cavalry charge. This, then, was the beginning; from now on the significance of the longbow would grow irresistibly.

Less than a year before Shrewsbury, at Homildon Hill on 14 September 1402, precisely the same tactic was employed. It is safe to assume that many of the Cheshire longbowmen who so mercilessly attacked those Scots schiltrons at Homildon would have turned out for Hotspur once again on 21 July the following year. At Shrewsbury, however, they would face their own countrymen, skilled in the same arts.

By the early fifteenth century, the longbowman was a constant in the English tradition of war. Lightly armoured, his defence lay in the weapon itself, in that it placed him out of range of cavalry and men-at-arms. Taking up his position, behind a defensive sharpened stake forced into the ground at his feet and pointed towards any advancing foe, he would stand side-on to his target, sighting over his shoulder. His bow was a gentle crescent of yew, often well over six feet long and, in the hands an expert, capable of accurately launching twenty or more arrows a minute

English soldiers with crossbow, artillery and longbow

at ranges of 300 yards and beyond. The skeletons of longbowmen recovered from the Tudor warship *Mary Rose*, sunk in the Solent in 1545, are of massively boned men, many over six feet tall. These bones show changes in shoulders and shoulderblades – changes which may well have been wrought by years and years of practice with bows that had drawn weights of up to 100 pounds and more. Their bowman ancestors of 150 years before were cut from the same cloth – tall, big-boned men with the massive physical strength and stamina required for their skills. Together with hundreds and often thousands of like comrades, the fifteenth-century longbowman was part of a lethal missile-delivery system which could stop any enemy advance in its tracks.

His great weakness and his great fear, however, was the threat of enemy bowmen – and it is precisely this that greeted him at Shrewsbury. Rather than advancing cavalry or footmen, he found himself in a fire-fight with men as capable of reaching and killing him as he was of killing them.

1403

KNIGHTS AND MEN-AT-ARMS

Use of the longbow was not the only tactic employed at Shrewsbury that had its roots in battles like Crécy and Poitiers. Biding their time while the archers performed their cruel duty were knights and men-at-arms. Those who could afford it would have been clad in the latest armour (armourers at this time were working constantly to contrive more and more effective defences against arrows); the rest had to make do with whatever protective gear was available from the family store or scavenged from battlefields abroad and at home.

Experience in those legendary battles in France had taught commanders and fighting men a valuable lesson: knights and men-at-

Far left **Neil as a knight clad in armour**
Left **Tony as a longbowman**

Knights and men-at-arms were often at their most effective on the ground rather than on horseback

arms were often at their most effective – not to mention safest – on the ground rather than on horseback. The rise of the longbow had already exposed the most notable weakness of the mounted man, namely the vulnerability of his horse. While armour for men was having some success in the face of arrow-shot, it was then, and always would be, impossible to protect a horse to the same extent. At Crécy and at Poitiers, while the crucial damage was being inflicted by the archers, the knights and men-at-arms swiftly learned the wisdom of dismounting and taking cover behind natural defences. Heavily outnumbered as the English were in both encounters, these new footmen also found they could maximize their own contribution to the fray by working in close cooperation with their archers. While contemporary illustrations show clashes of mounted knights at Shrewsbury, it is reasonable to imagine large numbers of their colleagues finding greater protection and doing a more worthwhile job by planting their armoured feet firmly on the ground.

MEDIEVAL MEDICINE

Of pumpkins and princes

We met up with Dr Carole Rawcliffe, Reader in the History of Medicine at the University of East Anglia, in the suitably medieval setting of St Chad's Church, in the heart of Shrewsbury. There, in the atmospheric gloom, she vividly described the skills and know-how of the fifteenth-century surgeon. From our twenty-first-century perspective, we tend to imagine scenes of clumsy butchery as men ignorant even of basic hygiene hacked and probed at their patients' wounds. In fact, medieval medical practitioners were thoughtful and often impressively learned men who had studied their craft for many years.

Medieval surgeons and physicians worked within a rounded philosophical approach. Illness was thought of as a disturbance in the balance of the body's 'humours': phlegm, blood, bile and black bile. These humours could be thrown off balance by unequal distributions of elements (earth, air, fire, water); qualities (heat, cold, moistness, dryness); and temperament (sanguine, choleric, phlegmatic, melancholic). A physician treating an illness that he had diagnosed as 'dry and hot' would apply medicine extracted from a plant thought to have 'moist and cold' properties. This approach may initially seem alien to us, but it has at its core a sense of holism that is not completely out of step with some modern alternative medicine.

We hadn't turned up at St Chad's empty-handed. We had spent an afternoon testing our skills with

A contemporary drawing of the arrow-extracting tool

longbows – and had shown a pumpkin-headed scarecrow a pretty thin time in the process! One particularly well-placed shot had penetrated deeply into the pumpkin itself and it was this we had carried along to show Carole. Mindful of the awful injury that the sixteen-year-old Prince Hal had sustained during his crucial attack on the rear and flank of Hotspur's army, we wanted to know how the royal surgeons would have removed an arrowhead from the flesh and bone of a living man.

The arrow had entered Prince Hal's face 'overwharte' – from the left side, burying itself deep into his cheekbone and reaching as far as the bone behind his nose. For five days after the battle, his doctors had fretted over how best to get the iron arrowhead out of the wound. The prince would have been treated initially with sedative extracts from plants and herbs, and prayers would have been recited at his bedside. Combined, and for a young man raised with an absolute faith, this may well have had a comforting, soporific effect.

The royal surgeon John Bradmor – a man with an already formidable reputation as surgeon to Henry IV – finally extracted the arrowhead. Using the

metalworking skills that were part and parcel of his craft, he designed a tool. With the aid of a somewhat painful-looking replica, Carole demonstrated how the head of the instrument was inserted into the wound and into the socket of the arrowhead itself. As a key-like screw was gradually tightened, the three sections making up the extractor's head gradually opened up inside the socket, rather like a Rawlplug, until they had a tight grip. Like Bradmor nearly 600 years previously, Carole successfully extracted the arrowhead from the 'wound'.

Hal would have borne a considerable scar, but such marks were expected of, and even desirable among, medieval soldiers. And he took something else from the experience of the wound he suffered at Shrewsbury. In the run-up to the Agincourt campaign of 1415, Hal, by then King Henry V, arranged for the surgeon Thomas Morstede and twelve others to tend his troops in France. We can see in this the foundations of the medical corps that supports armies today.

the dig

THE debris found on battle sites provides archaeologists with important raw material. Battles are messy: whether it be bits of a broken cooking pot, a buckle from a belt, a button from a tunic, a ring from a finger or coins from a purse, these untidy affairs leave their own particularly macabre litter in their wake. In short, a lot of things are dropped, lost or discarded, so battlefields should be good places for archaeologists to recover evidence.

When men are killed in battle, they fall carrying weapons and personal possessions. Although it was traditional for bodies to be looted by the victors, some objects always escape notice, and these eventually become part of what we call the archaeological record. Things are also dropped during hand-to-hand fighting: weapons knocked from hands; buckles and buttons ripped from clothing. Arrows or bullets often miss their targets and fall harmlessly to the ground. At Shrewsbury, as we have seen, the longbow played a crucial role, and thousands of arrows were shot by both sides during the early stages. Although this hail of arrows exacted a terrible toll, many of them must have fallen short of their targets or become embedded in open ground. The battlefield must have been strewn with arrows, sticking out of the ground like flowers. Most of these would have been collected afterwards so they could be used again, but some shafts may have snapped on impact or been broken under the feet of the enemy. These may have been left behind as junk or overlooked altogether as the impacted arrowhead lay out of sight. Over the centuries the wooden shaft decays to nothing, leaving only the rusted iron arrowhead behind.

On most battlefields, even those from relatively modern times, it is the metalwork that survives in the ground. The metal detector is therefore a uniquely

Modern replicas of medieval arrowheads

valuable archaeological tool. Confident that there were metal artefacts to be found on the battlefield, we gave some thought as to how we should best deploy our metal detectors and their operators in order to find them. In the time available we could not hope to cover the entire area over which the battle was fought. And in any case it is never our aim to remove *all* the metal artefacts from a battlefield. What we try to recover is a sample of material which will hopefully answer specific questions about the battle and also leave areas of the battlefield undisturbed for archaeologists working in the future. The search has to be a careful one, and since we have to know where on the battlefield we have found things, it starts with the mundane business of laying out survey grids. We looked at all the historical accounts available, both those that were written close to the time of the battle and those by later historians. Using these texts – along with maps, old and new, and most importantly our own observations of the landscape – we select areas we think might be likely sites of the battle. Then, like policemen carrying out a finger-tip search, the detectorists walk up and down within each of the survey grids, putting a pin flag in the ground to mark every 'bleep'. The pattern that gradually

forms – and which is allowed to build into a complete picture before we dig anything up – provides a clue to the way objects became scattered across the battlefield as the fighting played itself out. The people who moved across a landscape which we today call a battlefield are long gone, many of them killed during the few hours over which the fighting raged, but some of their movements have left a trace which time has not managed to erase.

Our first trawl through the literature about Shrewsbury concentrated on the general area in which the battle is thought to have been fought. It included archaeological reports on nearby road schemes and watching briefs around building projects, but it did not at first suggest that much in the way of artefacts related to the battle had been discovered. Perhaps there wasn't much to be found – maybe the battlefield had been picked clean by looters in the immediate aftermath of the battle. It was also possible that metal detectorists had been working here secretly and hadn't wanted their findings to be known. Precisely because battlefields tend to feature concentrations of interesting metal 'finds', they tend to be popular with metal detectorists. Just as a well-stocked trout pool increases a fisherman's chance of a catch, so the site of a battle increases the chance of a detectorist finding interesting metalwork. But an object found with a metal detector is meaningless unless it is excavated as part of a complete archaeological project. Each find is like a piece from a jigsaw, and any piece that is removed means there will be a hole in the picture the next time someone tries to put the jigsaw together. When metal

Opposite and above **Metal-detecting the battlefield**

detectorists work on their own without the disciplined recording techniques of field archaeology, every item they find, regardless of its individual value, is instantly turned into so much scrap metal. That object's part in the big picture is lost for ever.

However, despite the lack of clues in this literature, we know from the writings of none other than Charles Darwin, who grew up in Shrewsbury, that some battle-related artefacts have been found. He describes the discovery of arrowheads in a nearby farmer's field, and this was encouraging for us – even though we didn't have a clue where this 'field' might be. There are also one or two historical mentions of objects found through the years, including the head from a bill, and spurs from fields close to the church. ❧

THE SPIES WHO CAME IN FROM THE RAIN . . .

We had been driving through heavy rain for hours, and now it was getting dark. The news on the car radio did little to lift our spirits, full as it was of reports of the worst floods in the region for years. 'Shrewsbury's going to be under water!' lamented Neil, as he peered through the gloom at a road map. The windscreen wipers swept back and forth, back and forth, barely managing to keep the water at bay but simultaneously threatening to send me into a trance. We had an appointment to keep and, according to Neil's navigation, which makes up in drama what it lacks in accuracy, we were in grave danger of being late. 'There must be a road sign somewhere!' I cried, in semi-desperation. Neil turned the road map around in his hands, perhaps hoping for a new perspective on our plight. 'Just keep on this road, the A5, it takes us straight into town . . . I think.'

'There!' I cried, as the first road sign for ages loomed up out of the dark, 'Shrewsbury, five miles, we're going to make it.'

'Thank God for that,' sighed Neil, as he tossed the now-redundant road map over his shoulder on to the back seat.

But that was not the end of our troubles. The town was in chaos. It was like a war zone, with sandbag barricades and roadblocks everywhere. We couldn't get into the centre because the river had burst its banks. On more than one occasion men in vans with flashing yellow lights waved us to a halt and told us to turn round and go back the way we had come. We followed diversion signs which seemed to take us round and round in circles. Just as our patience and, more importantly, our petrol was about to evaporate, Neil saw it. 'There! The Boathouse Inn, we're here!'

The pub was almost empty. Most of the town's population were probably at home, manning the pumps and bailing out their living rooms. Half the bar was taken up with crates of bottles and chest freezers brought upstairs from the cellar, which was now totally submerged. We bought drinks and sat at a corner table.

'This is like something out of a spy movie,' said Neil.

'Yeah, *The Spies Who Came in from the Rain*,' I replied as I peered out of the window at the river below, which seemed to be rising even as I watched. Maybe there was something to Glyndwr not making it to the battle because of floods! I knew what Neil meant, though: coming all this way to meet two guys we didn't know from Adam in a pub was pretty weird. Every now and again some poor, soaked punter would come into the bar and order a drink, and we wondered whether they were one of the people we had arranged to meet. 'We should have asked them to wear carnations and carry copies of *The Times*,' said Neil.

Archaeology is very much a communal exercise, and Neil and I spend a lot of time working with a dedicated team of archaeologists: Iain and Jerry handle the geophysics; John and Olivia do all the survey and mapping work; and whoever we can bribe or blackmail into getting wet and muddy helps us out with the digging. But this more solitary exercise, with just me and him, generates its own sense of excitement. Before we do any fieldwork we always scout out the lie of the land, make local contacts and talk to people who have lived and worked in these places for years, including other archaeologists. This is what had brought us to Shrewsbury several months before we planned to start our investigations on the battlefield. Tonight we were going to meet up with Trevor and Alan, a pair of amateur metal detectorists who had been working on the fields around the battlefield for years.

Two guys walked in and looked around. They had a couple of carrier bags, and one of them had a document folder tucked under his arm. 'These are our boys,' I said, getting up to intercept them before they could pay for the round. Sure enough, they were the detectorists. We introduced ourselves, and I paid for their drinks. We explained to them what we were doing, how we hoped to investigate the battle using archaeological techniques. We said that while a lot of archaeologists viewed metal detectorists with suspicion, we didn't. We explained that as archaeologists we were not just interested in objects found with metal detectors but also where they had been found. We were delighted when they opened the folder and unfolded maps and drawings with their finds marked on them – these were people we could work with. They told us they had been working in fields on the battle site for quite some time, with the permission of the landowner, of course.

Neil couldn't wait any longer. 'Can we see what you've found?' he asked, eyeing the plastic bags expectantly. Trevor opened one of them and pulled out a smaller, clear plastic bag. 'Well, here are some buckles,' he said, pouring the contents on to the table. There were dozens of them, buckles and metal fittings made of brass and other metals. 'Wow!' exclaimed Neil and I in unison. We were no experts on buckles, but a lot of these certainly looked medieval and were therefore possibly related to the battle. We asked the guys whether they had ever found anything like arrowheads, but they said no. We asked them if they'd be interested in helping us out when we came down with the team in a few months' time. 'Oh, yes, please!' they replied. Now it was their turn to buy us a drink.

The spread of metal-detector finds from Hotspur's ridge down to the church

Swords out of ploughshares?

More than one person had told us we wouldn't find anything related to a battle fought 600 years ago. Our friendly metal detectorists in the pub had shown us their fine collection of buckles from the fields around Battlefield Church. But would there be anything left for us to find?

Most of the buckles that Trevor and Alan had shown us had been made from copper alloys. Buckles, the metal plates from the ends of straps, purse fastenings and buttons may relate to the battle – they may have been torn off as the battle became a vicious hand-to-hand struggle, when the fighting was close up and personal – but they are not the hardware with which the battle was fought, not the tools with which the killing was done.

The weapons themselves – at Shrewsbury, arrows, swords, spears, daggers and the like – were not made from these rather fancy metals but beaten from iron or forged from steel. Unfortunately, though, these metals decay more rapidly. Most iron is regarded by metal detectorists as junk, and they have some justification in thinking this: it is a rare field which does not contain a skipful of rusting iron bits and pieces which have fallen off tractors or broken off ploughs and harrows.

For the project we had called upon the services of the local metal-detecting club, and now had an eager team of volunteers. The detectorists were set to work under the able supervision of our surveyer, John Arthur, who had the onerous responsibility of recording all the finds so that we knew exactly where each one had come from. Like the geophysical survey, the detecting was carried out in measured grids, which tied down the detected ground for future reference and also ensured that we covered the entire area.

At first the detectorists were puzzled when we

asked them to set their machines on all metal, but when we explained to them what we were looking for they were quite happy to 'set their phasers on stun'. They set to work at several locations across the field, in order to get a sample of material from different areas rather than seek to find everything on the battlefield.

We set out a line of grids running from the top of the ridge on which the rebels were positioned down to the bottom of the hill, just opposite the church. Very soon there was a twenty-metre-wide corridor of the field covered in fluttering white flags, each one marking a buried metal object. More detector grids were put into the field behind the church, in the place once known as King's Croft, thought to correspond to the king's position. The other main area of interest was the field which runs down off the ridge where it comes to an end just in front of the Albright Hussey site. Again, these fields had very soon sprouted a healthy crop of coloured pin-flags. The process of excavating the finds and recording their position was a little more time-consuming – though it did not take long to recognize that we had a lot of junk: broken points from harrows, plough shoes, bits of chains from horse-drawn ploughs and other weird and wonderful objects related to the tillage of the soil.

It was only when we got our collection of finds back to the lab in the Archaeology Department at Glasgow University that we could begin to take a really good look at them. Many of the objects were just too far gone; some objects would be sent for X-ray photography to see whether the rust was hiding something recognizable within its ugly shell; but some objects were instantly recognizable as battlefield artefacts. Among these were prick spurs (curved pieces

of iron with a spike protruding from them), typical of those worn by mounted men in the medieval period. The curve nestled against the heel of the foot, where it was held on with a leather strap, and the spike was used to prick the horse when speed was required. What better battlefield on which to find spurs than the one on which Hotspur himself met his end! And what about the name 'Hotspur' itself? It probably relates to a spur which has been heavily used on a galloping horse and is hot with the animal's blood. Such was Hotspur's eagerness to get into battle!

We found prick spurs in small numbers across the field, but perhaps most interesting were those from the Albright Hussey field, and low down, towards the bottom of the hill, in the ridge field. These spurs were found not far from where the royal lines may have been positioned at that time, perhaps beginning to make their way up the hill, and it is tempting to imagine that they were pulled from riders as Percy and his retainers made their desperate charge into the royal lines in an all-or-nothing attempt to cut down the king. Those from Albright Hussey may not relate to a point of contact but are close to an area of dead ground at the end of the ridge which could have been used by young Prince Hal and his troops as they swung unseen around the enemy flank before crashing into the rear of Percy's lines. As they passed this way, the men, mounted and on foot, would have been very close to the small chapel next to the manor house. How many of them uttered a silent prayer as they passed by the church to enter the fight?

As for the weapons themselves, these were generally more difficult to pick out among the hundreds of pieces of heavily rusted metal. But the tip of a sword was so obvious that we spotted it before we left the field. Imagine how ferocious the hand-to-hand fighting must have been to cause the tip of a heavy medieval sword to come flying away from the blade! Another sword-related find was a copper-alloy chape. It would have been one of a pair attached to the end of a leather sword scabbard to reinforce the sheath against wear and tear, and as decoration.

Given the importance of the longbow at Shrewsbury we were obviously very keen to find arrowheads. Before Hugh had shown us the wide variety of designs available to the medieval archer, we had both imagined arrowheads to be triangular, with hollow tangs where the wooden shaft would have been attached. But, as Hugh explained, many of the arrowheads used at Shrewsbury were bodkins, which are not triangular at all but long and narrow, with strong points like drill bits to punch through armour.

We found a lot of objects which looked like nails in

Comparing the arrowhead we found with a modern replica

the fields, some of them quite old, even medieval. But as we went through them it became obvious that there was more to some of these 'nails' than met the eye. Rust is no friend of iron, and corrosion can transform the shape and profile of an object quite dramatically. There is sometimes not much difference between a rusted nail and a rusted bodkin arrowhead!

The problem is that some of the giveaway characteristics of the arrowhead disappear over time. Rust chokes the tube into which the wooden shaft would fit, and the narrowing of the head just before the tip corrodes. Despite these problems, we are confident that we have several examples of bodkin arrowheads. One was found just off the top of the ridge, where the rebel archers were positioned. Whether it was an arrow left unshot by a rebel archer or an arrow shot at their lines by a royal archer down below we shall never know, but this object places men here on the day of the battle. Finding it was one of those magical moments that makes all the hard graft worth while: you can almost feel time slip away as you handle the object and stand in the place where it has remained untouched by all others for 600 years. This is contact!

The maximum range of a longbow is around 200 metres. Assuming that the arrow had been shot by a royal archer from the bottom of the slope, we tried a little experiment. One of us stayed on the ridge where the arrow had been found and the other paced out 200 metres down the slope towards the church. This little exercise would give us some idea where the royal archers had been standing when they shot this arrow at the enemy. Only when we had paced out the full 200 metres did it really hit home what a devastating weapon the longbow must have been. From this distance we

Decorative silver fitting, possibly from a belt or armour

both looked like we'd shrunk to the size of a pin. It must have taken quite some time for an arrow in flight to cover that distance. We tried to imagine hundreds, thousands, of them airborne at the same time. What horror to face that! The 200 metres placed us right at the bottom of the slope, just before the holly hedge that divided the bottom of the field from the lane which ran along the north side of the church. Here were the king's men! ❁

The graves

As is often the case with British battlefields, Shrewsbury today exudes an atmosphere of peace and calm and looks as though it has never witnessed anything more upsetting than the infrequent funerals now indicated by headstones on the eastern side of the churchyard. But the church itself is really the focus for the awful events of the battle and its aftermath. The Christian calendar, full as it is of saints' days, unites for ever the battle of Shrewsbury and the church of St Mary Magdalene. Fought on 21 July, the killing and dying was on the eve of that saint's day. It was for this reason that Henry sought to commemorate what had been done there in his name by ordering that a church and college be built on the site and named for Mary Magdalene. While the genesis for the project would have come ultimately from Henry, the securing of land and the commissioning of the actual work was by Roger Ive, rector of Albright Hussey from 1398 until 1447.

The church existed for no other reason than to provide a conduit for prayers dedicated to the memory of those who had perished in the battle, and it was the duty of the small cadre of priests based in the college to ensure that these prayers were offered daily. Work on the church began around 1404, and the completed building was in use for services by 1408 or 1409.

There is a strong tradition that the church was built on top of the largest of the mass graves, and documents from the time of the battle certainly suggest that this is the case. One such, known as the Laud Manuscript, is in the Bodleian Library and gives dimensions for what was known as the 'great burial pit': 160 by 68 feet wide and 60 feet deep. The document also tells us that no fewer than 2,291 corpses were placed in the pit, both gentry

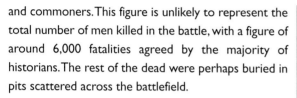

and commoners. This figure is unlikely to represent the total number of men killed in the battle, with a figure of around 6,000 fatalities agreed by the majority of historians. The rest of the dead were perhaps buried in pits scattered across the battlefield.

The document that relates to the granting of land for the construction of the church makes reference to a bank and a ditch enclosing the area occupied by the great grave pit. This feature, or at least part of it, was still clearly visible in 1855, when a plan of the church and its precincts was made by one S. Poutney Smith. The bank and ditch appear to have been created around the grave pit in order to mark it out in the landscape and keep the dead apart from the world of the living outside the enclosing moat. The moat and bank may have served as a monument to the dead, too, reminding people of what had taken place here, and as such it represents a very early example of what we would today call a war grave. This idea of a monument was obviously carried further and the memory cast in stone through the later construction of the church. Victory or defeat in medieval battles was regarded as God's will, and prayers acknowledging this were thereafter channelled to God through the church and perhaps amplified by the presence of so many of the battle's dead – the grave pit acting something like a spiritual satellite dish.

With the dissolution of the college during Henry VIII's reign, when the king broke away from the Catholic Church and adopted Protestantism as the national religion, the buildings fell into disrepair. The church itself was renovated in the late nineteenth century, but there is little or no trace of the college and its buildings other than the series of old fish ponds within the lands of the college on the southern side of the church. It was during that time that a number of bones were discovered on the north side of the church when workmen were putting in a new drain leading from the Corbett family vault. These were thought at the time to be the remains of men buried in the great grave pit.

An extract from a reproduction of the Laud Manuscript

Survey and excavation

The top of the church tower, which we reached only after scrambling up a very dark and confined stone staircase, gave us a really good idea of the lie of the land. Behind us, to the south, fields stretched out over a level plain, right up to the edge of the town of Shrewsbury, which at the time of the battle must have been quite a lot further away. To our front, on the north side of the church, was the ridge along which Percy's army had positioned itself. Its gentle slope was divided into fields by hedges but in our mind's eye we tried to take these away and imagine the slopes partially covered with ripening peas. Part way up the slope towards the east, we could see a low grassy platform in the middle of the field. We knew from our research that this was thought to be the site of a medieval fair that was held once a

year on St Mary Magdalene's Day to raise money for the college and church. It was strange to think that where sheep now grazed people would once have gathered to sell their produce and take the opportunity to catch up on gossip with their neighbours, perhaps even have a drink or two. But this picture of a rural past pales into insignificance when you consider that men once gathered across this slope in their thousands to kill or be killed.

Looking down at the ground immediately below us we could see the car park with our blue van and its rusty roof. If you walk from the car park through the lych-gate, towards the tower, you come into the churchyard, where you would normally expect to find gravestones. They were there all right, but they were confined to the eastern half of the churchyard, leaving the rest of the ground open and apparently undisturbed. You could have played a game of football on the rectangular patch of grass that spread out below us, just outside the entrance of the church. Why had no graves been dug into this ground?

We spoke to the vicar, Nick Todd, who told us that that part of the church's land had never had graves on it. It was, he said, believed to be the site of the great grave pit and so had always been avoided by the gravediggers. According to him, that piece of ground had always been a bit of a problem, because even though he didn't know for sure whether the grave pit was there, he couldn't allow fresh graves to be dug there, and it also meant that the ground could not be used for anything else which might lead to the disturbance of the grave pit.

Always eager to be of assistance, we offered Nick our help in resolving this dilemma by trying to find out

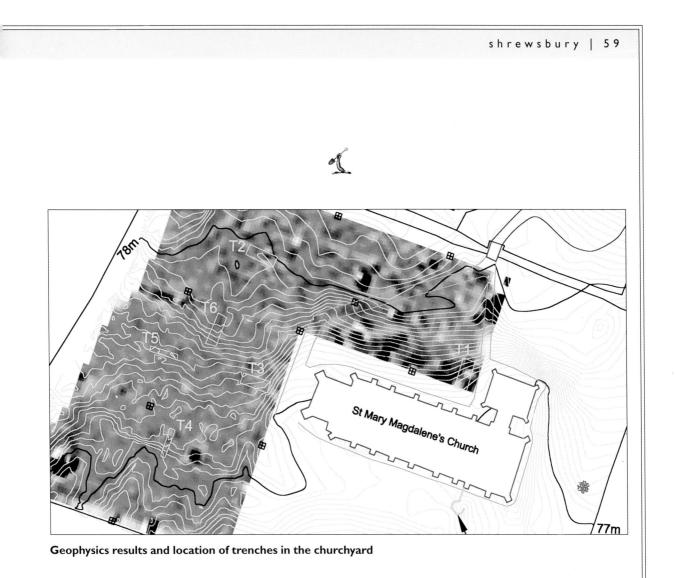

Geophysics results and location of trenches in the churchyard

for sure whether or not the grave was there and so we began our investigation.

The short grass and the level ground, give or take a hump and bump or two, provided ideal conditions for the ground-penetrating radar rig. Although it's a pretty high-tech bit of kit, you wouldn't know it just to look at it. Even to an archaeologist the contraption looks pretty much like a couple of tea trays slung under a home-made pram – very Heath Robinson. But the 'tea trays' are actually the radar transmitter and receiver units, and the signals they produce show up as wavy lines on a laptop computer strapped across the handlebars of the 'pram'. Jerry and Iain had gone to Shrewsbury a

week or so before us, so that the radar and geophysics results would be ready and we could start digging as soon as we arrived. Both the radar and geophysics were showing fairly strong anomalies in several places across the survey area, indicating where we should locate our trenches.

Our Scheduled Monument Consent, which by now had been granted by English Heritage, allowed us to proceed with the trial trenching. The most efficient way of getting down to the archaeology was to use a small mechanical excavator, known in the trade as a mini-digger, to scrape away the topsoil from trenches we had carefully positioned and measured out from the survey

plots generated by the computer. The first trench was as close as we could get it to the Corbett vault, which juts out from the north side of the church. It was here that nineteenth-century workmen putting in drains had come across masses of jumbled bones which they thought were part of the great grave pit.

Expectations were high: all the evidence, from contemporary historical documents to the eyewitness accounts of Victorian workmen, pointed to a mass grave somewhere in our area. Even if it was under the church, a grave of the size recorded in the documents must surely extend beneath the footprint of the building. As the mechanical arm of the digger pushed into the soft earth and dragged it back there was a definite tension in the air. This was nerve-wracking – all that forward planning and now here we were. It was the moment of truth. Would we find the mass grave?

We watched nervously. It wouldn't take much for the machine to damage fragile archaeological deposits and, to top it all, we were looking for bones, not the sturdiest of things after they've been in the ground for 600 years. But the first thing the digger encountered wasn't bones but bricks. Just under the topsoil was a pile of bricks, many of them smashed and broken. We signalled for the digger driver to stop and jumped into the trench. The bricks looked pretty old, more hand-made than mass produced, and they seemed to be sitting on a really nasty, sticky clay soil. We hoped that there would be something a little more interesting beneath. But no, all we encountered was more sticky clay, no sign of a pit or bones. Although our initial sense of excitement had begun to evaporate, we persevered and finished digging the trench with the machine before stepping in and cleaning it up with trowels. Only after this had been done would we get a good look at what we were dealing with. But there was still no burial pit to be seen. We did find an old drain, perhaps the one the Victorian workmen had been digging at the time of their encounter with the dead, but not a single bone.

We set aside our disappointment as the mini-digger

Far left **The trenches dug in the churchyard**
Left **Julie Roberts examining a bone fragment from the churchyard**
Above **Fragment of bone that turned out to be from an animal**

started on the second trench, just outside the door of the church, at its western end. No bricks this time, which was a relief, and there was a distinct change in the colour of the soil as it was scraped back. This contrast was just what we'd expect of a buried feature like a pit, the lighter soil representing the undisturbed natural soil into which the pit had been dug, the darker soil representing that which had been shovelled back into the pit. Our excitement grew further when a white smear flashed underneath the scraping bucket. We signalled the driver to stop working and jumped into the trench. It was a bone! We cleaned around it carefully with the trowel, exposing the edges and trying to define the shape. It was in poor condition, with yellowing splinters crumbling away from it. We are no bone experts – but we know someone who is. We phoned Julie Roberts, our forensic anthropologist.

While we waited for Julie to arrive, we set about opening more trenches. We looked at our geophysics and radar results again and targeted several other anomalies, all of which had the potential to be grave pits. A couple of them showed nothing, just undisturbed subsoil. The last two contained fragments of medieval floor tiles and even shards of green-glazed medieval pottery. Finds from more recent times included half a dozen clay tobacco pipes and large cow bones, which showed cut marks where the animal had been butchered for meat. This debris, along with the pile of bricks in the first trench, was left by workmen in the 1800s, when the ruined church was renovated and re-roofed. What we were looking at was really a Victorian building site. The tiles and bricks had been cleared out from the ruined building and used to make paths and fill up hollows in the ground. The animal bones may have been the remains of the builders' lunches – after which, if the clay pipes were anything to go by, they enjoyed a smoke.

This discovery of what were obviously animal bones had begun to ring alarm bells by the time Julie arrived to cast her expert eye over the bone we had thought to be human. At first she couldn't tell, because the bone was in much worse condition that those from the other trenches. But then it became clear that it was animal and not human, probably another cow bone. Foiled again!

We began to clean back the darker soil. It was in an artificial hollow all right, but it was very shallow and very obviously not a mass-grave pit. We found another, better preserved cow bone in the bottom of the hollow, which we had by now realized had been caused by a medieval ploughing system known as rig and furrow. There was evidence for this elsewhere in the churchyard, with the rig visible as low earth banks, raised just above the ground surface and separated from their neighbours by troughs known as furrows. These distinctive features had been created over time by the plough mounding up earth to provide a sowing bed for crops. The battle 600 years ago had been fought across medieval fields worked just like this, and the sloping field in which the rebels positioned themselves is reported to have supported a healthy crop of peas at the time.

Medieval field systems were all very interesting, but where on earth was the mass grave? Nick, the vicar, had been right: no individual graves had been put into this part of the graveyard – but there was no mass grave either! For as long as people had been buried in this churchyard the gravediggers had avoided this area, thinking there was a mass grave here. Could the grave be under the church? Building a church directly over a mass grave would surely make for poor foundations, but it *was* weird to have a medieval church of this size with no under-floor crypt or vault. Maybe the builders hadn't wanted to disturb the grave pit under the church

floor. Then again, if the grave was under the church, it's nowhere near as big as described in the early accounts, and having seen how difficult the clay soil was to dig even with a modern mechanical excavator, it is very hard to imagine such a deep hole being dug by medieval wooden spades.

A grave pit there may be, but neither huge nor deep. It seems more likely that the dead were buried in several pits, and any hole or hollow at hand may have been used. These pits may be scattered across the battlefield, and perhaps just one of them was chosen as the site for the church, but over time the churchyard itself has come to be identified with not just a few but with all the dead of the battle.

The home front

Battles are not fought in specially designed battlefields set aside for the purpose like football stadiums. They are fought across and within everyday landscapes, wherever the opposing forces come together, by accident or design. These pivotal moments in history were played out in someone's meadow, someone's upland pasture, someone's valley. Only after the fighting had finished and the dead had been buried did the area come to be identified and remembered as 'the battlefield'.

When we walk around these battlefields today, we often think how difficult it must have been to bring those warring armies together in the first place. In a time before modern means of communication (not to mention the kind of news-gathering industry we're used to – one that delivers live coverage of far-off conflicts directly into our homes) it must have been hard enough for rival commanders just to keep track of one another's forces in the field. In order to get everyone in the right place at the right time and get the battle going, one side or the other practically had to advertise its presence in some likely, visible spot, inviting the other force to join them there for a square go. In the medieval world – devoid of any surveillance techniques more sophisticated than men on horseback and word gleaned from the locals – whole armies could, and did, move unchecked and unmonitored through the countryside for days at a time. One of the armies for the battle of Shrewsbury may have lined up close by the homes and outbuildings of a little settlement some three miles north of Shrewsbury itself (and scarcely more than a mile or so, as the crow flies, from the site of what is also known as Battlefield Church). Here the people were probably just going about their normal morning

business on that long-ago 21 July, when an army arrived on their doorstep, ready for war. And up on top of that ridge, a location that afforded them some tactical advantage as well as making their presence clearly visible to the men looking for them, Hotspur and his army of rebels made their stand.

There would never have been much in the way of a population in this little place, still on the map as Albright Hussey – not by our standards. But in 1403 there was a well-established moated manor house here, complete with its associated farming community and a small chapel. The manor house is still there – at least its sixteenth-century incarnation is. This atmospheric listed building occupies the same site as the house known to have been standing at the time of the battle and is now the core of a hotel and restaurant complex. It is still easy to get a feel for what that fifteenth-century building must have been like, brooding behind its moat and stone revetments, parts of which still survive, and it does not take too much imagination to envisage the more modest homes and outbuildings that would have made up the farming community around it. A walk through the fields hugging close by the hotel reveals the humps and bumps in the grass that are all that remain of those long-since-demolished structures.

Albright Hussey was already old when Hotspur and his horsemen arrived here on their journey north, pursued by Henry IV and his bellicose son. Before the Norman Conquest, the land was owned by Siward, a freeman relative of Edward the Confessor. By the time the Domesday Book was written in 1086, it was held by Sheriff Rainald, from Roger of Montgomery, Earl of Shrewsbury. Rainald's descendants were the FitzAlans, and from the twelfth to the seventeenth centuries, the place that we know now as Albright Hussey was held by vassals of that family – the Husseys.

People have found ancient artefacts in these fields from time to time – in 1994, part of an Iron Age pin was turned up by a metal detectorist prospecting near by and two brooches have come to light, one Roman, in 1995, one Iron Age, in 1997 or 1998. We hoped that these would be a foretaste of the clues we would unearth ourselves.

Excavating the battle site: Albright Hussey

First impressions of the site at Albright Hussey, cheek by jowl with a modern hotel complex and a working farm, did not fill the team with much hope of uncovering archaeological riches. The field within which we had to concentrate our investigations sloped gently downhill from the comparative high ground upon which the hotel was located, and recent heavy rain had left the low-lying portion of the field a virtual quagmire. We resolved to give the 'deep end' as wide a berth as possible.

We were on the look-out for remains of the little settlement we were sure must have huddled around the fifteenth-century manor house and the chapel, and our geophysical survey had pinpointed some subsurface features we were keen to investigate. Some of these subsurface 'anomalies' conformed to humps and bumps that were visible on the surface. Others were in areas where not the slightest trace survived above ground. Resistivity meters, gradiometers and the like indicate areas where something – an unnaturally straight line perhaps – seems to be concealed beneath the surface, but only excavation can establish whether that straight line is the wall of a building within a medieval village or a rubble-filled drain dug twenty years ago by the farmer.

The real prize we were after was the little chapel dedicated to St John the Baptist. Knowledge of its existence is owed in part to the creation of Battlefield Church itself. The establishment of the new Collegiate Church superseded the need for the little chapel at Albright, and its steady demise was recorded as a result. Having found mention of the building on one of our old maps of the area, Iain and John used surviving surface features (the manor house and field boundaries) to help them position the trench we hoped would expose it to the air once more. If we could find the remains we could confidently put the chapel back on the map and reinstate it into the narrative of events of that long-ago day. And it wasn't hard to imagine the significance the

building would have had on the morning of 21 July 1403. Medieval soldiers were religious men and when they prepared for battle they needed to know that God was on their side. To die in battle and have one's corpse flung into a mass grave, without the prayers required for safe passage through purgatory and into heaven, was quite literally a fate worse than death. This last spiritual port of call, then, would undoubtedly have caught the attention of some of Hotspur's men as they prepared to turn and face the royal armies in pursuit of them.

Elsewhere in the field, trenches were laid out over some of the more interesting anomalies revealed by the geophysical survey. One by one, under the supervision of one of our archaeological team, they were opened up by a mini-digger, and each scrape by the metre-wide bucket was carefully scrutinized to ensure that no important remains were being damaged at the very moment of their rediscovery. Slowly and surely the archaeology began to appear and – in stark contrast to the initially uninspiring appearance of the field – the indelible traces revealed told us a story that had been 600 years and more in the making. When we'd arrived, a look at our surroundings had suggested that we'd encounter elements from at least the fourteenth- and fifteenth-century occupation of the village. We were right.

In a trench reaching as far as we dared into the quagmire, fragments of twelfth- and thirteenth-century pottery were found – green glaze still giving off its instantly recognizable leaden sheen and testifying to the domestic occupation of the site in the years before 1403. In a second trench, we uncovered evidence of many different attempts to stabilize muddy ground by the use of rough cobbling – traces of cobbled and cambered road, actually running parallel to the modern driveway leading to the hotel. Our third trench revealed even more of that long-forgotten road, a route that may have seen centuries of use. After much scrupulous cleaning with trowel and brush, we found deep ruts worn into the cobbled surface by year after year of wear by wooden and iron wheels. Fragments of seventeenth- and eighteenth-century pottery were uncovered within the matrix of a fourth trench – testament to continued domestic activity near by. Another accident in another kitchen, another broken cooking vessel tossed aside.

Piece by piece our excavations were disclosing the story of this area, glimpsed through the keyholes of our trenches. But where was the chapel? Iain and John's first attempt at revealing it had drawn a blank. Hopes had been high at first, and Iain excitedly reported the discovery of two parallel lines of rubble about six or seven metres apart. These suggested the remains of massively built walls and had the kind of dimensions we would expect in a small, medieval chapel. Between the 'walls', a roughly cobbled surface was dotted here and there with corroded pieces of nineteenth-century tools. We knew from the documents detailing land use in this field that concerted attempts had been made over the years to scour every last trace of the chapel from the land. Nineteenth-century maps had mentioned a 'chapel-barn' on the site, and anecdotal evidence suggested that long after its use as a church building had ceased, the structure had been incorporated into later farmyard buildings. The traces that Iain's trench had turned up fitted this narrative perfectly. It was with considerable disappointment and not a few blushes, then, that Iain confessed that he'd excavated to the bottom of one of the lines of rubble to reveal … blue polythene sheeting, covering gravel dumped over a modern pipe. Rather than wall foundations, we had uncovered a pair of rubble-filled field drains that had been dug through a patch of nineteenth-century cobbled yard in the last few years.

Undeterred, Iain and John went back to the old map and tried again. We knew that the chapel's remains had to be here somewhere – we could practically smell them. Tell-tale fragments of dressed masonry had been used across the field as covers for modern drains, and we were pretty sure we knew just what kind of building those carefully carved blocks had come from! Using John's best estimates – and when you're working with a topographic surveyor of John's calibre, best estimates are usually all you need – a new trench was opened close to the first. Taking no chances this time, Iain opened up an area twice as large as the first and once more set about the careful work of removing the topsoil and checking for the presence of archaeological deposits beneath. And sure enough, smack in the middle of this new trench, conspicuously squared stones were revealed. More trowel work, more brushing, and gradually there were more stones, their alignment suggesting a near-to-right-angled corner. No doubting it this time – it had passed the test of our archaeological scrutiny: here it was. Rough cobbles ran right up against the remains of the chapel walls, suggesting that the foundations had indeed finally seen use simply as part of the farmyard itself. We had uncovered proof of the chapel's continued survival in the landscape.

Here was all that remained of the little settlement clustered around the manor house of Albright Hussey: a few shards of pottery, spanning hundreds of years; an ancient cambered road rutted by centuries of traffic; a cobbled farmyard produced by year upon year of attempts to make good the soft ground. The remains of the chapel had been humbled by steady, deliberate destruction, but still a few of the stones that had been walked upon by that community and, briefly perhaps, by those soldiers, had seen the light of day once more. ❧

OF ORDINARY FOLK

Dr Philip Morgan, Senior Lecturer in History at Keele University, proved to be a man after our own hearts. Like ours, his abiding passion lies in trying to add colour and detail to the shadowy forms that ghosted across the battlefields of history. Hotspur left the family pile in Northumberland accompanied by just eighty mounted men and yet was able to confront the king with an army many thousands strong. Who were they in private life, these otherwise faceless characters who swelled the ranks, of both those armies? We know that among them were many men of Cheshire still faithful to Richard II, and many deserters from Prince Hal's force that had been fighting the Welsh. The great and the good – the royalty, the nobility – had their names and exploits faithfully recorded by the historians of the day. But what of the ordinary folk – the fathers, sons and brothers swept up into that awful maelstrom of 21 July 1403, and the wives, daughters and sisters they left behind?

Philip has spent years carefully picking his way through documents that list even the merest traces of these people – names, occupations, possessions, transgressions. In all, he has sketched in names and some details of around 2,000 ordinary soldiers. He has found evidence of rebels who fought for Hotspur and who were punished for their treason on their return home; of men of both sides who left home on foot and came back on horses looted from the battlefield, only to be hauled before local magistrates for their thievery.

Sitting in the Loggerheads pub in Shrewsbury – pints perched upon bleached tables so old and scored they almost looked as if they might date from Hotspur's day themselves – Philip described the life of Philip de la Hay, a 'salt ship' maker from Runcorn, who'd wound up in the fray on that July day. He painted a picture of an ordinary working man, spending much of his time toiling on the land of a large estate but also having an income as a skilled craftsman. 'This man was supplementing his income by making salt ships,' said Philip, 'basically hollowed-out logs that look a lot like prehistoric dug-out canoes, that were used at the time in the salt industry.' Then something had motivated this man to down tools, leave his home and set out to take part in the rebellion on the side of Hotspur.

Philip has uncovered other revealing glimpses of ordinary lives lived in an extraordinary time in claims made by widows for loss of income and valuables as a result of their husbands' deaths at Shrewsbury. Amazing though it may seem to us, these early-fifteenth-century folk were making the equivalent of insurance claims, and mechanisms were in place to record and to process such claims. In many ways, then, day-to-day life in the fifteenth century was surprisingly recognizable.

As for Albright Hussey and the lives lived there in the years prior to the battle, Philip admitted there was nothing to be gleaned from documentary evidence; this begins only with manorial settlement there in 1415. We know that it was Richard Hussey, the parish gentleman and landowner at the time of the battle, who made available the land upon which Battlefield Church was built. But of life in that settlement in 1403, no written evidence has survived.

Archaeological Techniques: Excavation

THERE can be little doubt that Shrewsbury's most celebrated son is Charles Darwin, best known for his book *The Origin of Species*, in which he explained his theory of evolution, famously making himself enemies in the Church by having the audacity to suggest that humans had evolved from apes. As a young man Darwin developed some of his ideas from observations he made while walking in the countryside around his hometown. It was during this time that he developed an interest in earthworms. While most boys' interest in this particular creature is limited to brief experiments with the earthworm as food, before moving quickly on to use them as fish bait (that's evolution for you), Darwin made them the subject of detailed scientific study. He went on to write *The Formation of Vegetable Mould through the Actions of Earth Worms*. It may not be the sort of thing you would choose for bedtime reading, but despite its rather offputting title, it is actually quite a fascinating book. We have already noted Darwin's observation that iron arrowheads, from the battle of Shrewsbury, were found in a field north of the river Severn. But just as relevant here is Darwin's interest in the role of worms, and the soil they manufacture and move around, in the burial of ancient buildings, to which he devotes an entire chapter. It was around Darwin's time that the basic principles of archaeological stratigraphy were being developed, largely through an increased understanding of geology.

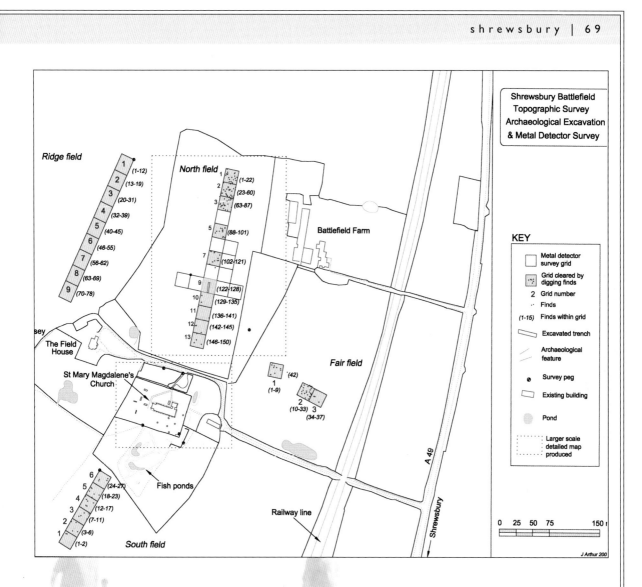

Shrewsbury Battlefield
Topographic Survey
Archaeological Excavation
& Metal Detector Survey

Ridge field

North field

Battlefield Farm

KEY

	Metal detector survey grid
	Grid cleared by digging finds
2	Grid number
··	Finds
(1-15)	Finds within grid
	Excavated trench
	Archaeological feature
⊙	Survey peg
	Existing building
	Pond
	Larger scale detailed map produced

sey
The Field House
St Mary Magdalene's Church

Fair field

Fish ponds

Railway line

South field

A 49

Shrewsbury

0 25 50 75   150 r

J Arthur 200

People like William 'Strata' Smith realized that older rocks lay under more recently formed rocks, and that archaeological deposits adhered to these same rules of stratigraphy, with remains relating to human activity from the distant past underlying remains from the more recent past. It is to these rules that archaeologists refer when they excavate archaeological sites and try to understand the meaning of the remains they uncover with their trowels. The process is rather like eating a layer cake, removing one layer to reveal the layer beneath, which, according to the basic principles of stratigraphic law, should be older than the layer just removed.

Excavation is what most people think of when they think of archaeologists, but it is only one technique available to the archaeologist in his/her endeavour to explore and understand our human past. Over the past 150 years or so excavation has developed from a way for the landed gentry to spend a pleasant weekend digging holes in the pursuit of antiquities to a scientifically controlled means of investigation. Excavation and the analysis of the results of excavation call on a multitude of skills and fields of expertise, including surveying, artefact conservation, physical anthropology, botany, entomology, geology and, as

Paul recording his trench

Katinka makes a find

Darwin recognized, soil science, to name but a few. The process of digging involves detailed recording, with each archaeological context recorded by photograph, record sheet and notebook, all of which are later put to use in the interpretation of the results of the excavation and the all-important writing of the excavation report.

It takes many years of training and experience to create a skilled excavator, but this does not mean that people new to archaeology cannot take part in an excavation. Most areas have archaeological societies, which usually invite archaeologists to give talks and organize excavations and field trips. Amateur societies do a great deal of important work and have become increasingly valued by professional and academic archaeologists. Anyone wishing to find out more about their local archaeological society should contact either the Council for British Archaeology (England and Wales) or the Council for Scottish Archaeology (Scotland). These organizations will also provide information on archaeological excavations in which people with little or no experience can take part. ✿

Conclusion

SIX hundred years is a long time. The world has moved on and much has changed since the battle was fought on that hot summer's day. It is perhaps this chasm of time which provided the greatest challenge in our archaeological investigation of the battlefield. Would there be anything left to find? A number of people, some of them archaeologists, had said we didn't stand much of a chance. But you never know until you try.

It has to be admitted that things didn't quite work out as we expected, but that's archaeology for you. We were quite confident that we would find some evidence for the great grave pit in the churchyard. Everything pointed to the grave being there – the historical accounts of the time, the Victorian workmen's testimony and the absence of more recent graves in half of the churchyard. But our intensive investigation did not provide us with a single scrap of evidence to

suggest that the grave was in the churchyard, at least not in the part we investigated. The grave may be under the church, but if so, it would have to be quite small – otherwise the church would be prone to subsidence and the grave would extend out beyond the edges of the church itself. If nothing else, we have proved that the belief that the grave is located in the empty space to the west of the church has no basis in fact.

Our investigations at Albright Hussey did recover evidence of activity at the time of the battle. Although we did not find proof that the village was occupied at the time of the battle, most of the deposits relating to the later use of the site, we did succeed in locating the site of the medieval chapel. Now represented by nothing more than a few stones, these walls must have echoed to more than a few prayers both before and after the battle.

But perhaps the greatest surprise was the success of the metal-detector survey. We only looked at a small part of the battlefield, but we found enough to give us some idea of where the various forces were arrayed. It seems less likely now that the fighting raged around Albright Hussey, but the hollow in which the site sits, at the end of the ridge, may well have served as dead ground through which Prince Hal's troops could pass undetected as they outflanked Percy's rebel army. Once we had got our eye in, we even came across arrowheads, and there out on the field we could not help but be awed at the bravery of men prepared to present themselves as targets to such terrible weapons. Yes, 600 years have passed, but the ghosts of the battle of Shrewsbury are still there for those who choose to look for them. ❧

A sword tip

Possibly a war hammer

BARNET 1471

BARNET

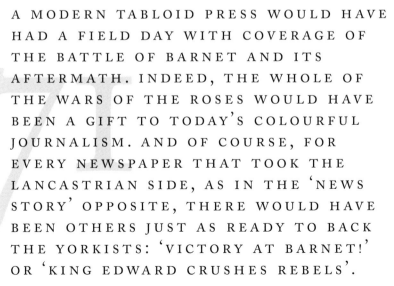

A MODERN TABLOID PRESS WOULD HAVE
HAD A FIELD DAY WITH COVERAGE OF
THE BATTLE OF BARNET AND ITS
AFTERMATH. INDEED, THE WHOLE OF
THE WARS OF THE ROSES WOULD HAVE
BEEN A GIFT TO TODAY'S COLOURFUL
JOURNALISM. AND OF COURSE, FOR
EVERY NEWSPAPER THAT TOOK THE
LANCASTRIAN SIDE, AS IN THE 'NEWS
STORY' OPPOSITE, THERE WOULD HAVE
BEEN OTHERS JUST AS READY TO BACK
THE YORKISTS: 'VICTORY AT BARNET!'
OR 'KING EDWARD CRUSHES REBELS'.

THE LANCASTRIAN

14 APRIL 1471

KINGMAKER WARWICK SLAIN!

Lancastrian champion cut down in Barnet clash

Yorkist sympathizers murdered Richard, Earl of Warwick, in the aftermath of a disastrous battle outside Barnet early this morning. Eyewitnesses said the Lancastrian champion was attacked by Yorkist thugs as he attempted to reach his horse.

One Lancastrian archer, who asked not to be named, told *The Lancastrian*: 'They surrounded him before he could mount up. There were so many of them that I didn't see the fatal blows being struck – thank God. There was nothing I could do.'

It is believed Warwick was seeking to rally the Lancastrian forces when he was set upon. The battle had gone badly for the House of Lancaster. Unconfirmed reports suggest poor weather – notably a heavy fog – had made fighting conditions particularly difficult.

John, Lord Montagu – Warwick's younger brother – was missing at the time of going to press and fears for his safety are growing.

Edward of York is once again attempting to seize the throne of England by deposing our own King Henry VI. The Earl of Warwick has been instrumental in coordinating efforts to thwart the usurpation in recent months.

See pages 2, 3, 4, 5, 6, 7, 8, 9, 17, 18, 19 and 20.
Queen Margaret steps ashore: souvenir pull-out, centre pages.
Editorial comment: page 21

News coverage today seems almost like a game: whatever your standpoint, you can find a newspaper that seems to share it. How accurate, then, is the picture painted by *The Lancastrian*? The alleged facts within the hyperbole might seem reasonable enough, but they are almost drowned out by the force of opinion that colours the whole piece. One of the closest things we have to newspaper coverage of events at Barnet is *the Historie of the Arrivall, of Edward IV*, written soon after the campaign by 'a servant of the king's'. Like a modern journalist, that fifteenth-century writer understood that he had to tailor his account to suit his target readership: 'Here aftar foloweth . . . how the moaste noble and right victorious Edwarde . . . Kinge of England and of Fraunce . . . aryved in England; and by his force and valliannes . . . reconqueryd the said realme . . . '

A pinch of the cynicism with which we regard today's press must also be applied to the contemporary or near contemporary coverage of the Wars of the Roses that has come down to us. As archaeologists, however, we have the opportunity to look for information that is completely unbiased: the remains that survive in the ground. Our responsibility is to ensure that our interpretation of those archaeological remains is, as far as possible, similarly unbiased.

As archaeologists we have the opportunity to look for information that is completely unbiased

BACKGROUND

THE TROUBLES BEGAN IN THE BED OF KING EDWARD III. TWO PRODUCTS OF THE UNIONS MADE IN THAT BED WOULD TWIST AND ENTWINE LIKE TWO COMPETING VINES AND DO THEIR UTMOST TO THROTTLE THE LIFE OUT OF ONE ANOTHER. BY THE 1440S AND '50S, IN THE TROUBLED REIGN OF KING HENRY VI, THOSE STRANDS WERE PERSONIFIED IN TWO MEN: EDMUND BEAUFORT, DUKE OF SOMERSET, AND RICHARD PLANTAGENET, DUKE OF YORK.

Somerset was descended from Edward III's third son, John of Gaunt, Duke of Lancaster. Richard drew his line back to Edward III's second and fourth sons, Lionel, Duke of Clarence, and Edmund, Duke of York. As such he was Henry VI's heir apparent – and if Henry were to die childless it was York who would succeed him.

Of great wealth and the holder of vast estates, York was a powerful man in his own right. But while Somerset was not in the same league in terms of material possessions, he had one thing that York's money could not buy – the ear of the Henry VI. It is impossible to read the accounts of the struggle between these two men – Somerset striving to remain at the king's side, York working furiously to replace him there – without a palpable sense of their mutual loathing seeping out of the pages. Add to this the manipulative personality of Henry's queen, Margaret of Anjou, and her single-minded pursuit of power for her family, and a fuse was well and truly lit. Tragically for England, and for generations of England's sons, it was a loathing that would not die with the fathers.

Humiliating defeat for the English at Castillon in 1453 ended the Hundred Years War. Unable to bear this final defeat, Henry VI suffered a mental breakdown – the first manifestation of a hereditary mental illness that was to plague him for the rest of his life. This was York's moment. Henry had been declared unfit to rule and York, as his heir apparent, was appointed England's Protector. Somerset was imprisoned – no doubt without his feet touching the ground. In the north of England, two noble families, the Nevilles and the Percys, were vying for supremacy. Richard Neville, Earl of Warwick, bore grudges against Somerset over territorial disputes and he became the ally of the new Protector. The Percys threw in their lot with Somerset. The lines were being drawn between York and his Yorkists, and Somerset and his Lancastrians.

For York, the path of ambition never ran smoothly. With impeccable timing, Queen Margaret gave birth to a son, Edward, Prince of Wales. Henry VI made one of his brief visits back to sanity, long enough to bless his son and heir and to release his old ally, Somerset, from prison. York was no longer heir apparent and, fearing for his life, he decided that more remained to be done to secure the destiny of his bloodline.

Riding out with his supporters in the direction of London, he got as far as St Albans before encountering the king's army. In this first battle of St Albans, in 1455, his victory was sweet. His forces set about killing any Lancastrian nobles they could find, including the Duke of Somerset. Henry's return from illness was brief: the death of his old friend and

Opposite **Choosing the red and white roses**
Above **Richard Neville, Earl of Warwick**
Below **King Henry VI on horseback**

Opposite **The battle of Barnet**
Below **'The Sun in Splendour'**

1471

counsellor set him back and he was once more unfit to rule. York was returned as England's Protector.

One scuffle followed another for the next five years. The battle of Northampton in 1460 was a disaster for Henry: his artillery was wet and failed to fire, and in the end turncoats led the attackers through the defences to capture the king. To the horror of his supporters, York now claimed the throne 'by right of conquest' and forced the exclusion of Edward, Prince of Wales, from his inheritance. This was not what the majority of the Yorkist lords wanted: they were happy to maintain Henry as a weak monarch while strengthening their own local positions. At the same time, by excluding Edward Richard had made a permanent enemy of the boy's mother.

By December Margaret had gathered an army in the north of England. She then arranged for a second force to march south from Scotland to free her husband. Lancastrians targeted Richard's lands in Yorkshire, and the Yorkists travelled north to crush what they believed was just a local rising. For York it was to be his final act. Together with many of his supporters, he died at the battle of Wakefield on 30 December 1460.

His eldest son, Edward, now inherited the dukedom of York and crushed the Lancastrians at the battle of Mortimer's Cross, on 3 February 1461. Before the fighting started, he took advantage of an occurrence of the natural phenomenon of a parhelion – the seeming appearance of three suns low on the horizon. In a telling stroke of genius, he told his men it represented the Holy Trinity and that God was on their side. Thereafter 'the sun in splendour' was to feature in his livery badge.

Then came a setback for this latest son of York: on 17 February Warwick's Yorkist army was defeated by Margaret's forces at the second battle of St Albans. Their blood up, the Lancastrians marched on London. But the inhabitants had been forewarned of the advance and, terrified, barred the gates. Even Henry was refused admittance. Edward arrived soon after and was acclaimed as king, but he postponed his coronation until he could take care of his foes once and for all. His army marched north out of London and split into three groups, thus maximizing their opportunities to recruit more men.

In freezing weather they approached Towton, where they found the massive Lancastrian army on high ground between the villages of Saxton and Towton itself. On Palm Sunday, 29 March 1461, the bloodiest of all English medieval battles unfolded: 28,000 soldiers lay dead when silence finally fell upon that field. It was said that heaps of bodies lay

over an area measuring six miles by three. On 28 June the Duke of York was crowned Edward IV at Westminster Abbey.

Edward married Elizabeth Woodville, from a prominent Lancastrian family, in 1464. Warwick, a man remembered by history as 'kingmaker' because of the influence his great wealth gave him during these dynastic struggles, disapproved of the match. Worse, he was embarrassed by it, since he had been planning with his ally the French king, Louis XI, to marry Edward off to a French princess and so add more power to his own elbow. By 1467 Warwick had switched his attentions to Edward's brother George, Duke of Clarence, who married Warwick's daughter at a ceremony in Calais. Faced by a Lancastrian force under Warwick and his brother, Montagu, Edward fled to Burgundy in 1470. Henry VI returned to the throne for the last time.

In March 1471, however, accompanied by his younger brother, Richard of Gloucester, and others, Edward returned to England to fight for his throne once more. A chastened Clarence, too, skulked back to his elder brother's side. Edward entered London unopposed in April and took the luckless Henry with him towards the north. On 14 April the Yorkists and Lancastrians clashed at Barnet.

THE BATTLE

THE KING AND HIS ARMY OF AROUND 10,000 MEN LEFT LONDON AND HEADED NORTH ON A WAVE OF POPULAR SUPPORT. HE AND HIS MEN HAD ONE AIM: TO CRUSH WARWICK AND HIS CAUSE AT THE EARLIEST POSSIBLE OPPORTUNITY. HE WOULD NOT HAVE LONG TO WAIT BEFORE HIS RESOLVE WAS TESTED. THE YORKIST ADVANCE GUARD SOON MADE CONTACT WITH WARWICK'S MEN AS THEY LOITERED IN BARNET. EDWARD ORDERED HIS MEN FORWARD, PUSHING SMALL BODIES OF THE ENEMY OUT OF THE TOWN AND THEN MOVING OUT TO MEET THEM.

Warwick had little choice but to prepare for battle and so he took position on the high ground to the north of the town. Instead of waiting until morning, the two armies deployed in darkness on the evening of 13 April with only a vague idea of their enemy's disposition. Warwick's army, which numbered some 15,000, straddled the main north road and apparently used a hedge running east–west to mark their line.

Eager to gain an advantage, Warwick ordered his artillery to open fire and the guns belched cannonballs out into the night. But because the Yorkists had manoeuvred so close to the Lancastrian lines, the cannonballs arced harmlessly over their heads to land impotently behind the lines. Edward, however, gave orders that the Yorkist guns were to remain silent, and it must have taken great discipline for his gunners to let their charges sleep as, all night long, the enemy poured fire over their heads.

When dawn broke on the morning of the 14th, a heavy fog covered the battlefield in a thick blanket. Nevertheless the two armies made their final preparations for battle, and following the custom of the time each army was divided into three divisions. Normally, each would face its opposing number directly, but in the confusion of, first, the night and then the fog, the two armies overshot on the flanks. The Yorkist right extended well beyond the Lancastrian left, which on the one hand gave an advantage in that they would be able to outflank the enemy, but on the other meant that they were equally disadvantaged on the opposite end of the line. But the error can only have been recognized as the two sides advanced towards one another.

The attack began around four or five o'clock in the morning, with Edward the first to give the order. His men must have been eager to go forward, having lost a night's sleep at the hands of the enemy's gunners. The Lancastrians were not about to stand around, and along their line too men stepped forward from their cover. Through the mist the armies advanced – even the nobles moved on foot and left their horses at the rear, a decision which for one commander in particular was to prove fatal.

The Yorkist right, under the command of Richard, Duke of Gloucester, later King Richard III, drove forward and many men passed around the extreme left of the Lancastrian line led by Warwick himself. This inadvertent outflanking brought Yorkists crashing into the Lancastrian left and rear. But at the opposite end of the line the Yorkists were suffering heavily for much the same reason. The Lancastrian right, under the command of the Earl of Oxford, had outflanked the Yorkist left under Hastings, and immediately began to drive them back. In fact, the entire line was turning on its central axis.

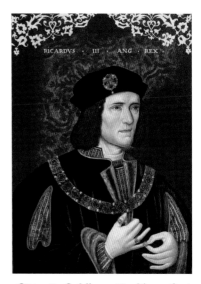

Opposite **Soldiers attacking a fort**
Above **Henry VI**
Below **Richard III**

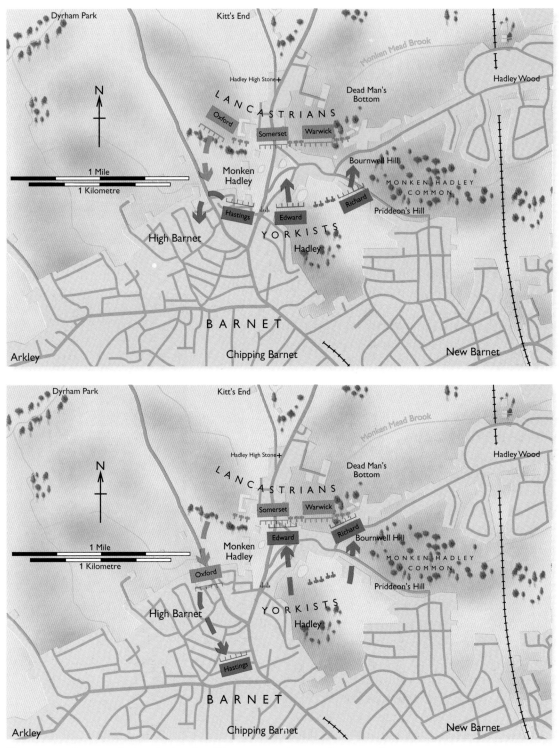

Movement of troops during the battle of Barnet superimposed on a modern map

But the Lancastrians pushed hardest and Oxford's men went crashing through Hastings's division and didn't stop until they had entered the town. Here it appears that discipline broke down, and some accounts record that the Lancastrians fell to looting while the battle behind them raged on. Although the shattering of Hastings's division had put the entire Yorkist line in peril, as so often in battle fortune was soon to turn the other way. Oxford eventually managed to get control of his men and encouraged them to return to the fray, but this turned out to benefit the Lancastrians little. Because of the confusion caused by the fog, Oxford's return to his own lines from what had been the enemy's position was seen as a Yorkist advance. In the centre, Somerset's men, although hard pressed in hand-to-hand fighting with the king's division, turned their attention to their own men as they loomed out of the gloom and began to cut down Oxford's troops. Today we call such tragic accidents 'friendly fire', but in those less than friendly times when fragile alliances and shifting allegiances were so easily broken, a cry of 'Treason!' went up and Oxford's men fought back. Soon, however, they tired of the fight and began to leave the field once more, this time for good.

Edward must have been overjoyed at his good fortune as he realized that his foes had turned against one another, and he was not slow to take advantage. The Yorkist reserve was brought forward and very quickly the balance was irretrievably tipped in the king's favour. When Warwick realized that all was lost, he made his way to the rear to retrieve his horse. The Lancastrian line began to crumple and fold, and men in their hundreds and then thousands began to fall back from the fight, their minds, perhaps like Warwick's, now fixed on survival rather than victory.

The rout had begun, and with it the slaughter so characteristic of the later stages of medieval battles. To this day the low-lying ground where much of the killing took place is known as Dead Man's Bottom. Warwick was just one individual among the great tide of humanity that now wanted nothing more than to be away from this dreadful place. He had a considerable distance to cover on foot, and he had to do it with the encumbrance of heavy armour. But man and horse were not to be reunited: Warwick was spotted by a group of marauding Yorkist men-at-arms and quickly overpowered. In the struggle his visor was lifted and a needle-sharp dagger thrust into his eye. Warwick the Kingmaker was dead.

The battle had lasted no more than three hours, yet when the fog finally lifted it revealed a scene of carnage, with around 500 Yorkist and 1,000 Lancastrian dead littering the field.

Red rose of Lancaster

White rose of York

WHO FOUGHT HERE

ACCORDING TO THE HISTORIAN
A.W. BOARDMAN, 'THE OVERALL
PICTURE IS CERTAINLY NOT ONE OF A
COUNTRY OF WELL-TRAINED,
MILITARY-MINDED AND BATTLE-
HARDENED VETERANS. IN FACT IT IS
CLEAR THAT THE MAJORITY OF
NOBLEMEN WHO FOUGHT IN THE WARS
OF THE ROSES WERE ENTIRELY THE
OPPOSITE.'

Certainly, England had no standing army at this stage in its history

Fifteenth-century bowmen

Certainly, England had no standing army at this stage in its history. What it had instead was an age-old system that enabled monarchs – and the nobles beneath them in the political hierarchy – to demand paid military service from those who lived on their land and by their leave. Feudalism had shaped the relationship between landowner and tenant in England since Anglo-Saxon times. By the fifteenth century, however, it was being abused. Where once it had simply delegated the process of raising an army in time of royal need, empowering nobles to play their part in drawing together fighting men loyal to the crown, now rich families were using that same system to back up their personal political ambitions with private armies. Often these aims would be regardless of – or even in direct opposition to – the aims of the king. In the most extreme cases (and the treachery and disloyalty permeating the Wars of the Roses were indeed extreme), this corruption of feudalism enabled the most ambitious men directly to challenge the king and the throne he sat upon.

MEN-AT-ARMS

Despite the absence of a standing army, and the trained soldiers implied by the term, medieval kings were not drawing their forces from an entirely unskilled population. Far from it: all men between the ages of sixteen and sixty were well aware of their duty to turn out for active service whenever called upon by their sovereign or lord. They also had a legal obligation to practise archery with the longbow. And while it is undoubtedly true that there was no professional army as such, there were many who had made the military tradition their chosen way of life. Many of those born of landed families had been trained in the ways of war from the time when they were old enough to stand and hold a weapon. It is not too much of an exaggeration to suggest that their principal aspiration in life was the chance of combat and the opportunity to prove themselves in battle – like actors hovering in the wings awaiting their cue.

English kings of the period had, with varying degrees of success, been obsessed with trying to take – and keep – the throne of France. Inevitably, this had produced war veterans from all the social classes. Those who had 'come safe home' from such adventures were a valuable commodity, and of particular value were those among the nobility who had been successful commanders. At any given moment during the Hundred Years War, English ports could be full of men gilded with victory or bitter in defeat, but nonetheless equipped with skills that would lie redundant only until the next fight. Edward IV, the victor of Barnet, has gone down in history as one of the most able generals of his time. But much of his success was a product of his sage preparedness to exploit the skills of the grizzled, battle-hardened veterans he had at his disposal.

For medieval English kings, there were further sources of able warriors and leaders: titled men – especially those holding land and estates on the always unstable borders with Scotland and Wales – had obligations to go along with their privileges. In return for the power and lands they held from the monarch, they had a duty to help with the defence of the realm. Together with the men under their command, they had to be ready for times of trouble when would-be invaders might

Longbow archers

1471

A painting depicting the Earl of Shrewsbury presenting a book to King Henry and his queen, Margaret of Anjou

storm across into England in pursuit of booty or perhaps the throne itself. Often they had to find and finance the necessary manpower themselves, and so the more successful of these nobles grew experienced in the ways of raising and training garrisons of men. Here in the far-flung outposts of the kingdom, then, were commanders and soldiers who were no strangers to the realities of war and the tactics and strategies that might be applied in the face of an enemy. Mercenaries too were available to those warlords who could afford their services, and professional warriors willing to fight for cold, hard cash could be found throughout Europe.

Of course, the same calibre of men was available to the commanders of both sides at Barnet. But while the 'rightful' king and his supporters could legally call upon the nobles and common men of the kingdom to turn out and fight in defence of the realm, a rebel leader during the Wars of the Roses, such as Richard, Duke of York, could make no such honest demand. They had therefore to rely upon their ability to inspire, cajole or force men into their service, or else pay for the services of professionals from elsewhere.

Tony dressed in the armour of the period. At the time a 'suit of steel' like this would have cost the equivalent of a Ferrari sports car

1471

KNIGHTS

So this was the stuff of which the armies on both sides at Barnet were made: common men largely self-trained in the use of weapons, led where possible by captains raised to the military life since childhood. Both groups – the leaders and the led – would probably have been schooled and bloodied in the continental wars. These veteran soldiers (mercenaries among them) – and the commanders, in particular – were at a premium during battles like Barnet. It was the prowess of these captains, these leaders of men, that was so often to prove the crucial element determining success or failure. For when those armies finally met in combat, the skills and bravery of individual foot-soldiers might count for nothing among the awful, bloody reality of hand-to-hand medieval warfare if there were no skilled leaders within the mêlée with some sense of tactics and the art of war.

It is in this period that the classic 'knightly' armour of our Hollywood-inspired imaginations takes centre stage. In place of the chain-mail costumes that had gone before, men who could afford the fearsome costs were covering themselves in whole suits of steel. These ensembles often bristled with protective spikes, the shoulders bearing the extra protection of 'pauldrons' (steel plates designed to reinforce those parts of the body vulnerable to downward strokes of sword and bill and to arrows raining out of the sky) while still permitting an impressive ease of movement.

Elsewhere on the field, the men-at-arms – with less money to spend but no less keen to defend their bodies as best they could – wore leather smocks reinforced with metal plates and pauldrons. Archers, who were responsible for the awesome victories at Crécy, Poitiers and Agincourt, protected their skulls with helmets called 'sallets' and their trunks with leather 'jacks'. Less effective, and certainly cheaper, than a nobleman's armour or a man-at-arms' steel-plated smock, they nevertheless offered a degree of protection against sword and arrow, and had the additional advantage of allowing greater mobility – particularly if it was necessary to escape during a rout!

It is important to be aware that battles such as Barnet had little to do with the near-mythical code of chivalry, which, in earlier times, was essentially a set of rules to permit war but limit its scale and level of violence. Whether or not anyone had ever really obeyed the code is a moot point. It may well be the case that chivalry was always an aspiration, seldom a reality. Explicit in the code, however, was the responsibility to preserve the lives of fellow knights, including those

Left Soldiers in 'suits of steel'
besiege a castle with handcannons
Above Neil with a modern replica
of a poleaxe, the favoured weapon
of the knight when fighting on
foot

fighting on the opposing side. Thus medieval knights could set out to cover themselves in glory on the field, secure in the knowledge that their opponents – their brother knights – were duty-bound to stop short of killing them. But by the time of the Wars of the Roses, there was no room for half measures. If chivalry had been a Geneva Convention of its time, then the desperate demands of battles like Barnet left no room for such courtesy. Indeed, by the time of Barnet it was the noblemen who were the targets for the worst excesses. Throughout the Wars of the Roses, the turning-point in a battle was traditionally met with a cry from the winning leaders of 'Spare the commons! Kill the lords!' Thus the ordinary folk were supposedly allowed to return to their humble lives while the opposing nobility, conspicuous in their expensive finery, were hunted down and slaughtered. Whether this is true is clearly hard to say. It is hard to imagine that in the slaughter at Barnet the common man fared any better than his social betters.

As archaeologists, then, we approach the battlefield of Barnet in the expectation that the level of violence meted out there, the descent into out-and-out savagery, will have left a resonance. On a field where it seems likely that few were spared, from the lowest common foot-soldiers to the most powerful lords in the kingdom, we would hope to find the physical residue of those events, like evidence at a crime scene that has long since been allowed to grow cold.

THE AFTERMATH

AT THE END OF A BATTLE THAT HAD
LASTED PERHAPS THREE OR FOUR
HOURS, THE YORKISTS HAD COMPLETED
A HIGHLY SUCCESSFUL MORNING'S
WORK. CASUALTIES HAD BEEN HIGH ON
BOTH SIDES, BUT MOST OF THE
YORKIST TOP BRASS HAD LIVED TO
FIGHT ANOTHER DAY. ONLY LORDS
CROMWELL AND SAYE AND SIR
HUMPHREY BOURCHIER HAD BEEN
KILLED. BUT FOR THE HOUSE OF
LANCASTER IT HAD BEEN A DISASTER.
NOT ONLY WERE WARWICK AND HIS
YOUNG BROTHER, MONTAGU, DEAD, BUT
MOST OF THEIR SENIOR COMMANDERS
HAD BEEN CUT DOWN TOO.

Significant though this victory undoubtedly was for Edward – the first of the great triumphs underlining his return from the continent and from exile – it was only half the battle. For while Barnet had removed Warwick, Edward's most tactically talented opponent, an enemy just as bellicose and just as driven had, that same day, stepped back into the fray.

Henry's queen, Margaret of Anjou, had landed in England on 14 April with her own army, accompanied by her son, Edward, Prince of Wales, the sole surviving hope for the Lancastrian line of descent. Margaret's plan had been simple: having crossed from the continent, supported by French troops, she was to have met up with Warwick prior to confronting Edward with a combined force. But her crossing had come too late, and she arrived at Cerne Abbey to hear the awful news from the Duke of Somerset and the Earl of Devon. Although greatly upset, she was persuaded to continue and her spirits lifted as more followers were recruited to the cause at Exeter, the south-west being a stronghold of Lancastrian support.

Edward, meanwhile, was back in London and fresh from his success at Barnet when news reached him of Margaret's arrival. With barely time to catch his breath, he set the wheels of war in motion once more. Orders were sent out to the shires for men-at-arms to be recruited (victory at Barnet had been a close-run thing and there were many gaps in the ranks that now needed to be plugged). Once his army was back to fighting strength, Edward set out in his pursuit of Margaret in a chase that was to last for fifteen days.

His progress was slowed by his wagons and the large amount of artillery that followed in his wake, much of it captured from the Lancastrians at Barnet. He sent scouts to shadow the queen's movements as she made her way northwards in the direction of the upper reaches of the river Severn. It must surely have been her intention to cross the river in order to link up with the Lancastrian Earl of Pembroke, Jasper Tudor, who had raised an army in the Welsh borders. Edward had at all costs to intercept her before she crossed the river, but he also had to be wary lest she try to advance on London and the south-east, where she might find additional support among the rebellious men of Kent. A game of cat and mouse ensued, and several times Margaret skilfully gave him the slip by making him believe that the Lancastrian forces had formed up for battle when in fact she and her army were putting as much distance as possible between themselves and Edward.

Although she was gaining many recruits from towns in the south-west, Margaret's fortunes took a turn for the worse at Gloucester, where

Edward IV

1471

she was refused entry. With the bridges of Gloucester denied her, Margaret had no choice but to strike north again, this time to Tewkesbury, where there was a ferry. Edward was in hot pursuit and he arrived at Tredington on the evening of 3 May, just three miles away from the Lancastrian encampment that lay within the protection of hedges, lanes and ditches on ground known locally as the Gastons. The race was run and Margaret the loser. Denied the opportunity to cross the river, her army had now to stand and fight without support from their Welsh allies.

The encounter at Tewkesbury on 4 May was more decisive than Barnet. The Prince of Wales, just seventeen years old, was among those cut down in the final, bloody rout, and his death severed the direct line of descent of the house of Lancaster. He was among more than 2,000 men on both sides who fell.

Somerset was among those who sought sanctuary in Tewkesbury Abbey, and for a time it seemed like they would live to tell the tale. Edward initially entered that sacred place on a wave of victorious goodwill and pardoned all the Lancastrians he found there. A local writer claimed, however, that on learning the abbey could not legally provide sanctuary, Edward had his enemies hauled out in a brawl so vicious that

Seeking sanctuary in Tewkesbury Abbey

the bloodied church had later to be reconsecrated. Subsequently, and after what must have been little more than a kangaroo court, Somerset and several other Lancastrian knights were executed in the marketplace at Tewkesbury. Margaret was captured the day after the battle in a nearby house of religion, and was imprisoned in the Tower of London. Her incarceration lasted for four years until Louis XI of France bought her freedom.

Edward made yet another triumphant return to London on 21 May, by which time the hapless King Henry was dead. It is said by some chroniclers that he died of a broken heart on hearing of his son's death. More likely is the suggestion that he was put to death by Edward's supporters. Some accounts tell of blood dripping from Henry's body and pooling on the floor as it lay in state in St Paul's Cathedral and again at Blackfriars. Examination of his exhumed remains in 1910 revealed traces of blood on surviving head hairs – evidence of a violent end?

For Edward the campaign that culminated in the battles of Barnet and Tewkesbury marked the end of the war. He had commanded his troops at five notable victories, and he would never need to take to the field again. The next twelve years, until his death in 1483, were peaceful and secure ones for the house of York.

Edward made yet another triumphant return to London on 21 May, by which time the hapless King Henry was dead

the dig

TODAY, Barnet lies on the outskirts of London and has changed dramatically from the small town and open fields of the late fifteenth century. But it is surprising how much green there is still to be seen.

Hadley Green is very much in the centre of things. It forms a large grassy triangle with ponds and trees, and although bordered by houses it appears to have been relatively untouched by modern development. To the west of the green is the huge expanse of Old Fold golf club. Although golf courses are obviously man-made, with earth moved to create bunkers and greens, older elements such as hedges appear to have survived and greens and fairways roughly follow the original contours of the natural landscape.

To the east are the remnants of Hadley Common and Enfield Chase, which include both open spaces and deciduous woodland. The common was open to all during the medieval period, as it is now; the chase, on the other hand, was wooded and rich hunting grounds for the wealthier members of society.

To the north the ground slopes down into Dead Man's Bottom, its name a lingering reminder of the battle.

Medieval hedges

There has been much excited debate in the past about how and where the Yorkist and Lancastrian armies lined up. It has been suggested that the hedge behind which Warwick's army was arrayed ran north–south along the edge of the Barnet–Hatfield road, but most modern scholars place the lines in an east–west orientation.

One of the earliest maps of the area is Rocque's, dated 1754, and it shows the area of Enfield Chase, to the east of the Great North Road (now the A1000), as entirely unenclosed other than by the boundary hedge. However, the land to the west of the road, now covered

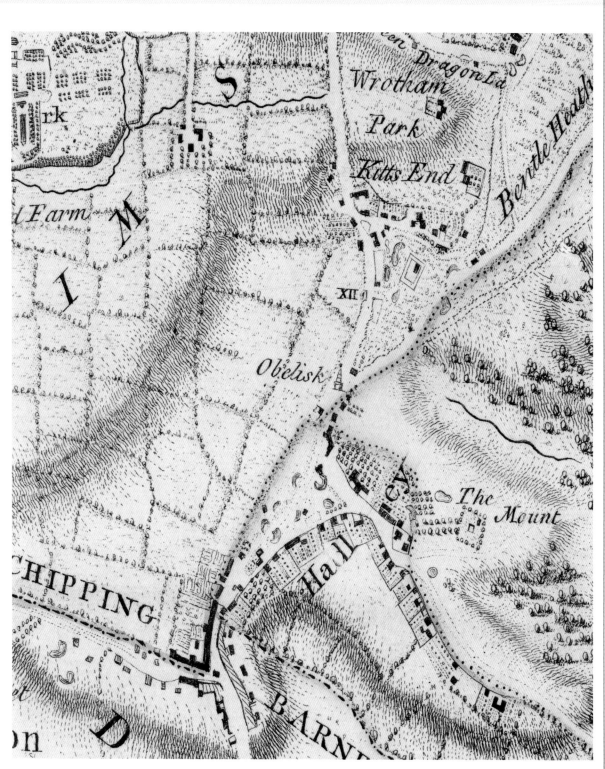

A detail from John Rocque's map of the County of Middlesex, 1754, showing the area of Hadley Wood

Fighting with poleaxes

by the golf course, was by that time parcelled up into small regular fields, typical of post-medieval agricultural improvements. At the time of the battle the landscape probably bore more resemblance to the eastern side of the road than the western – open, and broken by only a few hedges.

Rocque's map also shows areas of woodland on the Chase, and some remnant of this can be seen today on the common at Monken Hadley. The presence of woodland at the time of the battle would have curtailed the movement of troops and limited the space available for the disposition of both armies. As Gloucester moved around the left flank of the Lancastrian army, he must have been crossing open ground. This would suggest that the left wing of the Lancastrian army did

not extend much further east than Hadley Church. This movement would still have required the Yorkists to pass through the southern edge of the Enfield Close hedge. There is a tradition that parts of the hedge were hacked down immediately prior to the battle to allow freedom of movement by the warring armies. If we are to believe the contemporary accounts, then the Lancastrian army stood close to a hedge at some point along its line. If the Lancastrian soldiers were arrayed east–west and facing south, then the most obvious portion of the hedge would be that which runs from behind Hadley Church to the Great North Road. We have to consider, too, that any remnants of hedges dating from the battle may well have been incorporated into later, post-medieval hedge systems.

Having looked at the maps, our next tactic in trying to understand the hedges called not for mattocks and shovels, but the expert eye of a botanist. We were lucky enough to secure the services of a man whose work with dating ancient hedges is so respected that he has had a rule named after him! Dr Max Hooper was investigating the steady disappearance of bird-life from English hedgerows in the 1960s when he hit upon an interesting pattern: he noticed that species of trees and bushes die and are replaced within hedges about every 100 years or so. By counting the numbers of species in any given 30-metre stretch of hedge, he can then estimate its age in centuries – 6 species = 600 years; 9 species = 900 years; and so on. This is the basis of what has become known as Hooper's Rule.

Always keen to take advantage of any labour-saving device, we invited Max to take a stroll with us and give us his expert opinion of the likely age of the hedges cutting across the golf course. He began with the stretch lining the first fairway from north to south, where the presence of two different species of hawthorn and one each of oak, wild rose, sycamore, holly and elm enabled him to cautiously estimate the hedge's age as 700 years. If he was right, then that hedge could well have been in place at the time of the battle of Barnet.

Fascinated and encouraged by his findings, we moved on to the hedge line running east–west and separating two other fairways. Here the shrubs and bushes had long since been grubbed out, leaving only established trees dotted along its length to suggest the hedge line. Although the absence of plants made it impossible for him to apply Hooper's Rule, Max was impressed by the overall shape of the hedge line and its accompanying bank and ditch. He said that while more modern hedges tended to follow straight lines, medieval and earlier hedges took more sinuous paths across the landscape, as farmers then would have lacked the tools to easily remove large trees and other obstacles; instead, they would simply have used the irregular line created by the existing trees to mark the boundary of their ploughed fields. Since our hedge line followed just such a classic, lazy S-shape, he suggested that it might well prove to be 1,000 years old – or even older! 'If I was going to put in a trench to check the age of any of these hedges,' Max said, 'I'd concentrate my efforts here.'

With this advice securely in mind, we opened up two trenches across the east–west ditch and bank and just one across its north–south neighbour. With shortage of time as our main limiting factor, we could only open fairly narrow slices – just a metre or so wide – across the hedges. Our results, as it turned out, were less than conclusive. The trench across the north–south hedge – which Max had suggested could be around seven centuries old – revealed modern pottery and medieval roof tiles all mixed together. We had to accept that the day-to-day upkeep of the golf course had inevitably led to constant digging out of the ditch and piling of material on to the bank. It was quite probable that this was essentially a later hedge with all medieval remains long since scalped away. The same was true of our trenches on the east–west hedge which Max thought could have been 1,000 years old. However, the profile revealed in one section, in a portion of the line within a stand of trees, was satisfyingly substantial. The combination of ditch and bank created an obstacle suggesting that this had once been a considerable boundary marker, but there were no artefacts to enable us to date its construction. Despite Max's help, we had been unable to establish – at least to our own satisfaction – that either of our hedges had played a part in the battle.

It was then that we turned our attention to Hadley Green, where we had found a geophysical anomaly running roughly east–west, next to the golf club. What was really intriguing was the fact that this anomaly ran roughly in line with the east–west hedge on the golf course. Could it be a long-lost section of the battlefield hedge and ditch?

Using the computer plot of the geophysical survey as a guide, we marked out a long trench. Although we removed the turf by hand so we could put the ground back together like a jigsaw once the work was finished, we used a small mechanical excavator to remove the upper layer of stony soil. Again the going was tough and was not made any easier by the rain which turned the clay soil into mud. Below the upper layer, which contained building rubble, we came across an undulating layer of dark, greasy soil. This was actually a turf layer which at some point had been buried. The undulations were the result of rig-and-furrow agriculture and probably pointed to the green being used for cultivation sometime between the seventeenth and nineteenth centuries, if the pottery we found was anything to go by. Below the rig and furrow we found yet more disturbed ground, with the odd roof tile and bits of pottery.

Despite earlier high hopes, we were having great trouble finding our ditch. Eventually we came across a smelly layer of green clay, with a ceramic roof tile stuck in its upper surface. It was now obvious that the entire area had been heavily messed about with in the past, and had not after all escaped disturbance and change by human hand. We just couldn't find the edge of a ditch, and every soil layer we investigated was found to contain pottery or building rubble. Where was the natural soil that a medieval hedge ditch would have been cut into?

After much head-scratching and discussion we began to understand what we were looking at. Our green slime was probably the bottom of a pond which had long ago been filled in. Although no pond is shown here on any of the early maps, it is highly likely that at some time there were many more ponds on the Green than are visible at present. Until the nineteenth century Barnet played an important role in the movement of livestock into London, located as it is on the Great North Road. Ponds would have provided vital watering holes, and over time new ones may have been dug and old ones filled in. Our trench appeared to be on the edge of one of these old ponds. This did not explain our linear geophysical anomaly – there may still be the surviving remnants of a medieval ditch on the Green, but it will take much more work to investigate it properly.

Although we hadn't turned up definite evidence for the battlefield hedge, we had learned just how unpleasant and troublesome an obstacle a well-maintained hedge could have been. We'd spent days hacking our meagre trenches through the hawthorns, brambles and holly, and our tempers had become exceedingly frayed as we fought our own private battles. And the hedges we encountered were a poor imitation of what confronted the soldiers who fought at Barnet. For them, a deep ditch and bank would have

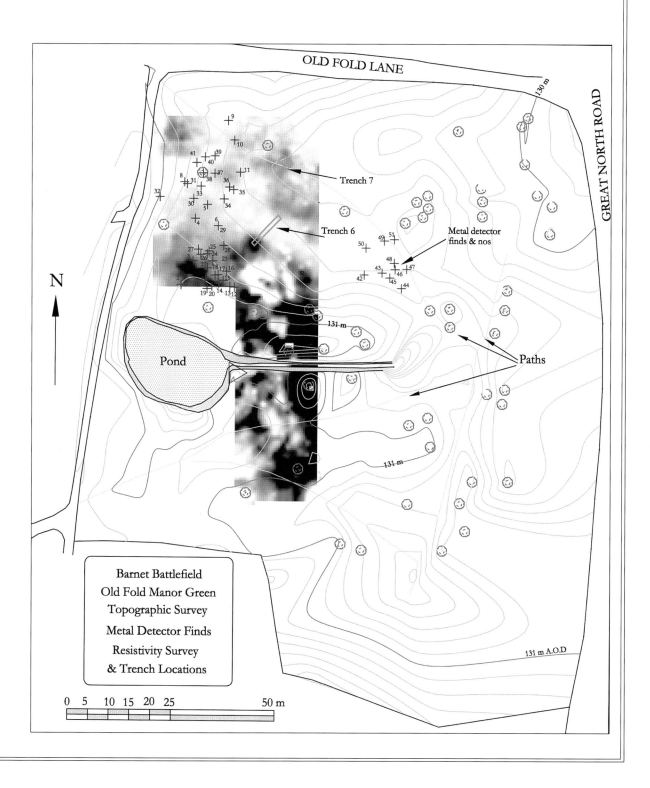

OLD FOLD LANE

GREAT NORTH ROAD

130 m

Trench 7

Trench 6

Metal detector
finds & nos

N

Pond

131 m

Paths

131 m

131 m A.O.D

Barnet Battlefield
Old Fold Manor Green
Topographic Survey
Metal Detector Finds
Resistivity Survey
& Trench Locations

0 5 10 15 20 25   50 m

placed them on the wrong side of a growth of trees and bushes perhaps six or eight metres thick. A heavily armoured man, having slashed his way through such an unyielding obstacle, would surely have been in a murderous temper by the time he emerged to face his enemies!

The Moated House

The accolade of the most impressive surviving feature must surely fall to the site of the moated house known as Old Fold Manor. Although the manor lands are mentioned in documents in 1271, the house itself is first recorded in 1310, when it was owned by the Frowyk family, and it is included in a painting illustrating the battle in the Ghent manuscript version of the *Arrivall*. Today, the site is occupied by Old Fold golf club, with the ground inside the three surviving arms of the rectangular moat now covered by the green of the eighteenth hole and the club car park, along with the clubhouse buildings. Most historians writing about the battle have placed the Lancastrian line either directly across the moated site or just to its front, on the south side, and it is generally accepted that the moated site played a role in the battle as either a landmark which influenced the alignment of the troops or as a Lancastrian strongpoint.

As part of our project at Barnet, we set ourselves the challenge of finding traces of the medieval occupation of the site, and hopefully some evidence for the use of the moated complex during the battle itself. But from the start we knew that this was a bit of a tall order, as previous small-scale excavations on the site had shown that demolition had removed earlier remains. We were also handicapped by the very small area available for our trenches: we obviously couldn't dig through the car park or areas already covered by buildings, and the members of the golf club wouldn't be too happy to find trenches appearing in the manicured

The moated house: Old Fold Manor

Aerial photograph of Hadley Green and surrounding area showing locations of investigation

grass on the eighteenth green! All that was left was a thin strip of ground that separated the green from the car park and was covered by a bank of earth which had probably been left over from building operations.

So this was where our mini-digger was brought in to remove the earth bank and get us down to the archaeological layers. We didn't have to wait long for our first surprise. As soon as the shovel was brought into action, the little machine began to buck and judder under the strain of digging into solid ground. It was only then we realized the bank was made not from soil but from clay, which had set really hard after it had been dumped. Eventually hydraulic brawn won over geological gloop and the shovel broke through to the next layer: at one end of the trench it took the form of a smooth concrete floor with the remains of a red brick wall along one edge; at the opposite end was a surface marked by rounded stones and fragments of old building rubble. Between this roughly cobbled surface and the red brick wall was a layer of hard-packed flint nodules, which may have been a path skirting the building now represented by the red brick wall and the concrete floor behind it. As we explored we kept finding plastic golf tees – a dead giveaway that this layer was not very old, and was probably an earlier car park.

The clock was ticking, so we abandoned our mattocks and pickaxes and brought back the mechanical excavator. It soon exposed a deposit formed from concentrated building rubble. This was a bit more like it! There wasn't a single golf tee to be had as we began to explore this layer. Instead, we found the odd sherd of medieval pottery – which was a good sign because it meant we were dealing with medieval rubble, but not so good in that it suggested our medieval

buildings had been demolished. The rubble, which was bound together in stiff brown soil, consisted largely of heavy ceramic roof tiles. We didn't find any intact examples, but they appeared to have been rectangular with a slight curve, and some pieces showed a square hole at one end. This is where the tile would have been secured to the roof with a nail or peg. Ceramic roof tiles were not uncommon on high-status buildings from the fourteenth century onwards, and so these may well have come from the rooftops of the buildings which stood on this site at the time of the battle.

As about one third of the trench was occupied by the concrete floor, we had little option but to blast it out and look underneath. We set to work with a sledgehammer, and after half a day's graft we had cleared a good portion of the floor and unearthed some more concentrated building rubble. We could also see the foundations of the red brick wall which extended quite a way beneath the level of the floor. The red brick wall was part of a Victorian building, probably

Opposite The trusty mini-digger
Above Neil has a tea-break

related to the farm which occupied the site before it was turned into a golf course in 1910. The concrete floor was a later addition and may even have been associated with an anti-aircraft battery located here during the Second World War.

The rubble beneath the concrete floor and the Victorian wall footings was made up of roof tiles very similar to those at the other end of the trench. It was carefully removed in the search for intact building remains, but none were found. Underneath the rubble layer, which was about a metre deep, we uncovered a hard-packed surface formed from mortar. This was probably the interior floor of a building, possibly medieval in date, and its roughness suggested an outbuilding rather than the house itself. A similar story emerged from the other end of the trench, where the removal of the medieval rubble revealed a rough cobbled surface, this time probably part of the original courtyard rather than the inside of a building. As time was limited we didn't dig through the middle part

of the trench where the flint nodules were, which was a shame as we might have found a medieval wall underneath this, separating the interior mortared floor from the exterior cobbled courtyard floor.

We had found evidence for medieval buildings, but only in the form of demolition rubble. There was nothing to tell us when these earlier buildings were demolished, but over time the medieval manor house and its buildings gave way to later development on the site, which included a Victorian farm complex and then the golf club car park. Unless other parts of the site can be excavated, we must content ourselves with the limited picture we have.

Possible mass graves

Unlike battlefields such as Shrewsbury, Flodden and Culloden, Barnet has no history of human bones being dug up by drain diggers or farmers' ploughs. This makes the location of the graves which must have been dug after the battle to accommodate the slain even more of

a mystery than usual. A number of low mounds are reported to have been located on Hadley Green and around the common, but many of these were removed some time ago. An elderly man who was interviewed by local historian Jenny Cobbam recalled that when he was a child these mounds were known as soldiers' graves. However, a local builder also recalls that one of these mounds was composed of nothing more than bricks and builders' rubble.

A large mound was once located in the grounds of the Mount House, which sits on the northern edge of the common and today is a private school. The mound had a legendary association with the battle and was thought to be the site of a mass grave. But investigations on several occasions – the last in 1925 by the then owner of the house, Mr Dove – failed to reveal any evidence for a mound relating to a mass grave. A deed for the house dated to 1584 states that a windmill was present on the land and it is possible that the mound was constructed to accommodate it.

As previous observations made during the removal of mounds in the grounds of the Mount House and on Hadley Green suggested, they consisted of nothing more than rubble, the site of the graves still remains a mystery. We may just have been looking in the wrong place. Indeed if much of the killing did take place in Dead Man's Bottom, which was unfortunately out of bounds to us because of the foot-and-mouth crisis, then the corpses of men slain there are also likely to have been buried there rather than moved to another site. There are probably other graves scattered across the battlefield, but these may be quite small, each containing just a few bodies, and being unmarked by mounds have thus far evaded accidental or archaeological discovery.

Archaeological Techniques:
Archaeological metal-detecting

THE metal detector is a descendant of the simple mine detector developed by the military to locate buried landmines during the Second World War. It seems particularly fitting that a tool invented in wartime has become one of the most important pieces of equipment to be used in the archaeological investigation of battlefields. However, it is only relatively recently that archaeologists have come to regard metal detectors as serious tools.

Despite the image portrayed in films like *Indiana Jones*, archaeologists do not excavate archaeological sites in the hope of retrieving valuable objects to add to their personal collection or sell for a profit. The archaeologist is a social scientist, interested in the story that objects have to tell and the contribution that they can make to our understanding of the human past. For archaeologists, the ultimate destination of artefacts recovered through excavation is a museum, where they can be further analysed and appreciated by the general public. Indeed, an artefact is considered to be next to useless unless we have full information on its context – that is, exactly where it was found and what it was found with. This information is recorded with great care on an archaeological excavation but, sadly, some amateur metal detectorists remove artefacts from important sites without bothering to inform anyone.

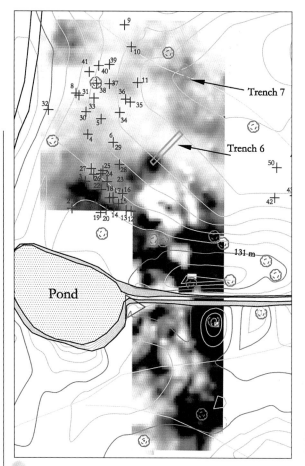

Map showing metal-detector survey and location of two of the trenches on Hadley Green

Fortunately, though, this bleak picture of metal detectorists is changing, and many now work in co-operation with archaeologists, usually as members of clubs and societies. It also has to be said that there has been a tendency for some archaeologists to be rather condescending towards metal detectorists, many of whom simply share their fascination with the past.

One of the most obvious legacies of a battle is the large number of metal artefacts dropped in its wake. Depending upon the period in which the battle was fought, these objects may include arrowheads, spearheads, swords, musket-balls, cannonballs and bullets, not to mention the buckles, buttons and badges torn from clothing and equipment during hand-to-hand fighting. Any archaeological study of a battlefield must therefore include the recovery and recording of this material, and the most practical way to do this is to use a metal detector. This is true of all the battlefields included in this book, and in many cases it was the amateur detectorist who located the artefacts and the archaeologist who recorded its position. The detectorists worked in grids, which ensured that all the ground to be surveyed was covered evenly – if one spot is favoured, it may provide a totally biased impression of how objects are distributed across the battlefield. Signals from metal objects were marked with small flags whose location was mapped using the total station electronic distance measurer (EDM). Only then were objects removed by careful excavation, and in some cases only a sample, perhaps 20 per cent, of the objects detected underground were actually removed. The objects were studied and, when required, cleaned and conserved by a specialist from a museum to prevent further decay.

The metal-detector survey

We positioned our first two 'corridors' – areas divided into grids with the help of our EDM – on the land at Hadley Green, on either side of the Great North Road. We knew from our historical research that an advance party of Edward's army had encountered Lancastrian outriders in Barnet on the day before the battle. They had chased them out of the town, possibly along the line of the road and all the way back to the main Lancastrian force, which was taking shelter up here on the plateau. On Hadley Green, then, we hoped to find traces of where that great Lancastrian army of 15,000

Probably one of our most exciting finds: an old brass finger ring

men had spent the night – and where, perhaps, some of the fighting had taken place the following day.

Our party of local metal detectorists made an unlikely sight as they set to work, and within minutes their multicoloured flags, each marking a positive signal from their machines, were filling the area of investigation. We were in no doubt that many of these finds would prove to be modern – after all, this area is popular with random strollers and families passing quiet afternoons – but we had our fingers crossed that we would uncover some historical treasures too.

Sure enough, as they began to investigate the signals – carefully removing little plugs of turf and soil with their customized spades – possibly medieval remains were present among the modern coins, silver-backed paper from cigarette packets and other detritus. One of the earliest and most exciting finds came from the corridor west of the road. It looked, even to the untutored eye, like an old finger ring. Dull brown in colour though it was, the outer surface bore a clearly visible pattern of incised lines in what looked like sunbursts or perhaps flower designs. We dispatched it to a Museum of London expert specializing in personal effects from the medieval period.

Also from this area came a number of tiny iron balls. About the size of peas, they were heavily corroded and already crumbling in the ground. We could see for ourselves that they were too small to be musket- or even pistol-balls, and anyway we would have expected such projectiles to be made of lead. We turned to Andy Robertshaw, of the National Army Museum, to solve the mystery. He explained that it was quite possible that these were iron shot of a very early kind. Andy said that in the early days of artillery, cannonballs were often made of stone or iron. During this same experimental period, in the fourteenth and fifteeth centuries, primitive hand guns were often loaded with iron shot just like the little brown 'peas' we had found, and they were used in much the same way as a modern shotgun, with a charge of gunpowder blasting out a handful of little iron pellets. This type of gun was called an arquebus, and several hundred of them were deployed at Barnet.

We also discovered a tiny, flattened, copper-alloy band, which looked like a crushed thimble from a doll's house. Once again we called upon Andy's expert eye to see through the damage and corrosion. Not a thimble, he said, but possibly the reinforcement around the handle of an eating knife, the part that stops the blade shaft splitting the handle into which it has been inserted. In his opinion it was of medieval date – perhaps fifteenth-century. We had no way of being sure, of course, but an eating knife would have been a vital element of a man's travelling kit in the period we were interested in.

Our corridors lay in the vicinity of Enfield Chase – what had once been extensive woodland used for the hunting of game – and one find evoked some long-ago hunting party. One of our detectorists turned up what, at first glance, looked like a fishing weight. It was about the size of ping-pong ball, with a loop at the top, but rather than the whitish colour we would have expected of a fishing weight, it was the dull green of copper alloy and had two holes punched into its sides with a slit clearly visible on its bottom end. Andy quickly solved the mystery: it was a decorative bell of the kind likely to

A light round of golf wearing some very heavy armour!

be worn by horses or hunting dogs. When a valuable hunting dog is in the undergrowth searching for game, it is vital that no hunter mistakes it for quarry and shoots it. For this reason, dogs often wore bells on their collars so that they could be quickly identified even when they could not be seen. Horses too would have had bells on their harnesses to add to the general splendour of their appearance, and Andy reminded us that the horses of mounted men-at-arms and knights would have carried such decorative items around the time of our battle. Possibly dropped from a hunting dog, yes − but not impossible that it had been ripped from the bridle of one of our warriors' mounts.

Finest of all our finds from the common, however, was the ring. The Museum of London expert identified the material as a copper alloy − possibly brass − and brass, he said, was popular for finger rings of the late fifteenth century. Furthermore, the band was D-shaped in cross-section, a further indicator of great age. It was possible too that the brass had once had a thin coating of gold leaf to make it look more impressive. Rings were very popular with men and women in the medieval period, and were often worn on every finger and both thumbs. It was impossible to say if it had been for a man or a woman − but not unlikely, in our context, that it came from the hand of a combatant. This, then, was the kind of find that makes all of our searches worth while: was this a ring torn from the hand of a foot-soldier in the hellish fighting at the battle of Barnet? Our expert's opinion certainly made it a possibility.

We also investigated the expansive grounds to the rear of St Martha's convent, a ten-minute walk to the east of the Green. The seventeenth-century house is set just back from Hadley Green Road, in the shadow of trees that look at least as old as the building. But the elegant frontage of the house gives scant hint of the huge and beautiful grounds to its rear. Carefully tended vegetable gardens and a cluster of greenhouses give way to paths lined with apple trees. Beyond these orchards, sunken paths wind out of sight towards allotments and patches of ground given over to bramble bushes and wild grasses. These largely untended slopes were as close as the foot-and-mouth restrictions would allow us to get to the hollow named on the maps as Dead Man's Bottom.

However, our detectorists found slim pickings. Heavily corroded and hopelessly unidentifiable scraps of iron added nothing of value to our story of the battle. In all, careful metal detection of selected areas of the open ground in the vicinity of what we believed to be the seat of the fighting had revealed much in the way of modern disturbance. This, coupled with the acidity in the soils around Barnet that rendered modern coins scarcely recognizable, had severely denuded what traces had been left in the ground in the aftermath of the battle. ❧

Conclusion

THE battlefield at Barnet reminded us of the truth of an old lesson: don't be fooled by appearances. While we were seduced by the peace and quiet of Hadley Green, the common, the chase and even the golf course – and had hoped our battlefield was safely entombed in these apparently undisturbed pockets – our experiences here showed us that the areas of greenery were every bit as 'false' as the tarmac of the roads and the bricks and mortar of the buildings. The urbanization of Greater London has affected these places as profoundly as any covered by streets and by shops, and the disturbance and destruction it has left in its wake has had an effect on the Barnet battlefield.

The many hundreds of years of human activity at Old Fold Manor, culminating in the present golf club, have left little trace of the original buildings, other than the debris of demolition. The creation of the golf course has changed the landscape more dramatically than may first appear, and any evidence for medieval hedge ditches and banks has been scoured away. Even the Green, which provided promising geophysical results, has been profoundly altered by the digging and filling of ponds.

We may perhaps have had higher hopes for our metal-detector survey, but even here the pickings were meagre, one of the few notable finds being the finger ring, which may have been torn from the hand of a combatant during the battle. The acid soil did us very few favours here: how could we expect 500-year-old

Teeing off towards the Yorkist line

iron arrowheads or sword blades to survive in soil where even twentieth-century coins were so badly degraded they were barely identifiable?

On the basis of all this it would obviously be foolish to say, 'There is no archaeological evidence for the battle, so it must have been fought elsewhere!' We did not cover all the ground we would have wished to in a perfect world. The tantalizingly named hollow of Dead Man's Bottom may well have yielded evidence of fighting and even graves, but at the time of our investigation this farmland, like much of rural Britain, was out of bounds thanks to foot-and-mouth disease. Though we gave the battlefield of Barnet our best shot, at the end of it all we have to admit that it succeeded in keeping many of its secrets intact. ❧

Barnet succeeded in keeping many of its secrets intact

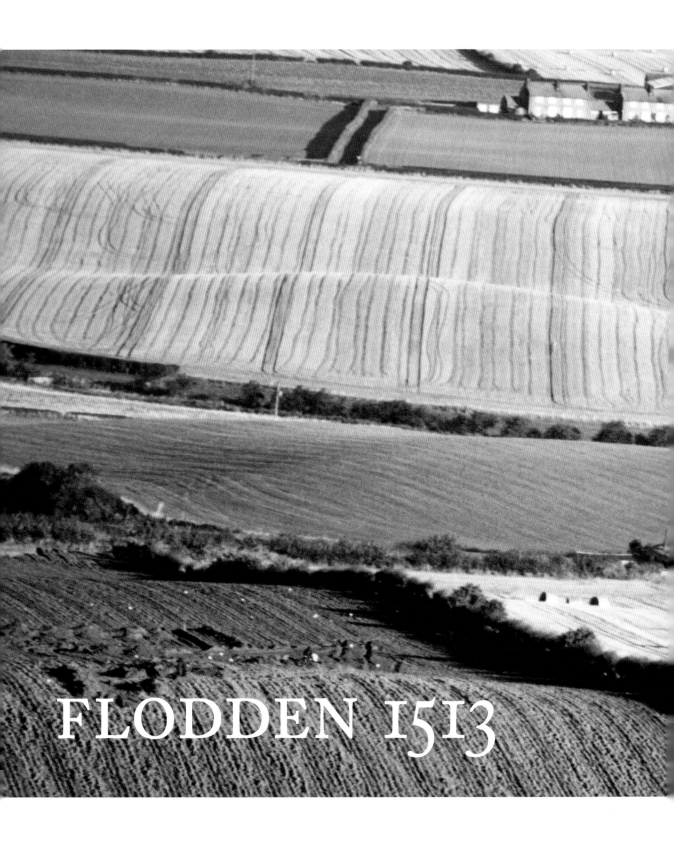

FLODDEN I5I3

FLODDEN

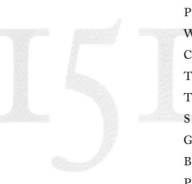

DAY AFTER DAY, YEAR AFTER YEAR, PEDESTRIANS HAVE WALKED ALONG WOOD STREET IN THE HEART OF THE CITY OF LONDON. DRIVERS HAVE SAT IN THEIR VEHICLES, ENGINES IDLING, AS THEY WAIT FOR THE TRAFFIC TO MOVE SLOWLY ONWARDS. FEW CAN HAVE GIVEN MUCH THOUGHT TO WHAT LIES BURIED BENEATH THE TARMAC AND PAVING STONES. AFTER ALL, IS NOT ALL OF LONDON BUILT OVER THIS OR THAT BIT OF HISTORY?

Opposite **James IV**
Left **Sixteenth-century map of the British Isles**
Above **Henry VIII**

Soon archaeologists will come here, as one of the buildings is due to be demolished. Before the foundations of these modern Standard Life of Edinburgh offices were dug, the site was occupied by the remains of the medieval church of St Michael. It was there right up until 1897. The church tower itself survived until 1965. Somewhere in the old churchyard, among the ordered graves, there was once a pit which we know contained a pile of bones. Church records tell us they were dumped there by a sixteenth-century sexton. He had cleared out the crypt beneath his church and needed a final resting-place for the jumbled remains. He threw something else into that pit, something given to him by a man living near by.

If we'd had the chance to excavate in that churchyard before its destruction, we might have found the pit. There, among the old bones, we might have found a skull bearing evidence of a terrible wound to the face. And that would have been all that remained of the head of a king – King James IV of Scotland, who was struck down, so the story goes, by an English bowman's arrow, fired into his mouth as he battled to within a spear's length of the Earl of Surrey on Flodden Field. We could have held in our hands a man's severed head, a person just like us – and yet not like us, for he was a king. He lived and died in our history books. His face stares balefully at us from a few portraits that hang in our museums and art galleries. But for us, as archaeologists, what an experience it would have been to make physical contact with the remains of a king who had died a violent death nearly 500 years ago.

The story is a strange one. After the battle, fought on 9 September 1513, James's body was carried from the field by the victorious English. Although King Henry VIII originally promised a burial fit for a king, it never happened. Taken to Berwick, the corpse was disembowelled, embalmed and sent first to Newcastle, then to Durham and on to the Carthusian monastery of Sheen, in Surrey, which became lodgings for the Duke of Somerset following its dissolution. There James's embalmed body remained above ground until workmen found it, cut off the head and, according to the legend, used it for a football. This battered object, apparently still bearing red hair and beard, became the property of one Lancelot Young, master-glazier to Elizabeth I. He kept it as a curio and a conversation piece: 'Look!' he could say, 'there is the head of the King of Scotland!' It was said to give off a 'pleasing' scent. Young held on to it for years. Maybe his conscience finally got the better of him, or maybe its scent was no longer so pleasing, but in any case he eventually saw to it that the head was handed over to the sexton of St Michael's church for burial in a common grave. Uneasy indeed lies the king's head!

1513

News of Flodden

BACKGROUND

WHEN THE ARMIES OF SCOTLAND AND
ENGLAND CLASHED AT FLODDEN ON
9 SEPTEMBER 1513, IT WAS IN A WAR
THAT BOTH JAMES IV AND HENRY VIII
COULD WELL HAVE DONE WITHOUT, BUT
NEITHER SEEMED ABLE TO AVOID.
JAMES INVADED ENGLAND IN SUPPORT
OF THE AULD ALLIANCE WITH FRANCE,
A PACT OF MUTUAL DEPENDENCE THAT
HAD EXISTED BETWEEN THE TWO
COUNTRIES SINCE THE END OF THE
THIRTEENTH CENTURY.

Henry VII   James IV

The scale of the disaster that was to befall the Scots at Flodden, however, would draw the value of that alliance into serious doubt.

The sixteenth century had begun on an altogether more hopeful note. James married Margaret Tudor, daughter of Henry VII, in 1503. The offer of his daughter's hand was a bold move by Henry – and a clear indication of his desire for peace rather than war – and it brought James and his descendants into the English line of succession. Since it followed the signing by both monarchs of the Treaty of Perpetual Peace the year before, the marriage might have seemed to underline their joint determination to avoid conflict. The treaty required Scotland and England to settle their differences by diplomacy, and a papal guarantee promised excommunication to the first monarch to breach the terms.

But while history reveals Henry VII to have been generally more in favour of diplomacy than violence, his son and successor was of a rather different hue. Henry VIII came to the throne in 1509, just before his eighteenth birthday. Although he quickly renewed the treaty, the rest of his behaviour set him on a collision course with his brother-in-law. Early offence was caused when Henry refused to hand over jewels left to Margaret in their father's will. This slight was compounded in 1511 when James's master-sailor, Andrew Barton, was killed in a naval

The offer of his daughter's hand was a bold move by Henry – and a clear indication of his desire for peace rather than war

The warning before Flodden

battle at the hands of Edward and Thomas Howard, sons of the Earl of
Surrey. James called upon Henry to bring the Howards to account – in
line with the terms of the treaty – but his appeal was dismissed out of
hand.

By now James had good cause to fear for the safety of his throne,
not because his brother-in-law refused to hand over some jewellery or
because of an act of piracy, but on account of wider political intrigue
unfolding across the Channel. Louis XII of France and Pope Julius II –
once allies against the economic and military power of Venice – had
more recently fallen out over French influence in Italy. Julius, a warrior
pope, formed the Holy League against France, and was supported in this
by Ferdinand of Spain and his former foes the Venetians. Seeing an

excuse to resurrect England's designs on the French throne, Henry willingly threw in his lot with Julius towards the end of 1511. James could be in little doubt about the threat now posed to France, and if this distraction – this buffer – were to be removed, what then would stand between his own kingdom and the ambitions of his young brother-in-law? His problem was relatively simple, even if its solution would have required the wisdom of Solomon. The Treaty of Perpetual Peace and the Auld Alliance could co-exist only while France and England were at peace. With these two on the brink of war, James might be forced to choose one or the other.

Still smarting from the death of his master-sailor, James wrote to Pope Julius expressing his belief that since Henry would offer no redress for the English attack upon his ships, the Treaty of Perpetual Peace must now be null and void. Julius did not reply – but it was James alone who would die excommunicated under the terms of the treaty.

TO WAR

At first, James attempted to walk a tightrope between France and England: on the one hand he renewed the terms of the Auld Alliance on stronger military terms than ever before, while at the same time he tried to unite Louis and Julius against what he argued was a common threat for all Christians – namely, the steady rise in power of the Turks in the east.

James was effectively knocked off that tightrope at the end of 1512 when the Emperor Maximilian joined the Holy League. Louis was caught between a rock and a hard place: he needed to keep his armies in Italy if he was to maintain his power base there, yet this left England and the Imperial forces free to threaten northern France. Now he needed James, his ally, to stand up and be counted.

Louis duly asked James to march an army into England in a bid to discourage Henry from sailing for France. Nevertheless, in June 1513 the English fleet set sail for Calais and for war. Henry planned to follow soon after, but before he departed he entrusted the defence of the northern marches of his kingdom to the old war-horse the Earl of Surrey.

By the time Henry joined his army in Flanders some weeks later, James could procrastinate no longer. He summoned his countrymen from all quarters of the kingdom, and the response was overwhelming. Thousands flocked to the muster at the Boroughmuir, in Edinburgh; thousands more made for a second rallying point at Ellem, in

Etal Castle

1513

Berwickshire. Estimates of the size of the force vary enormously – no doubt the romantic work of chroniclers who came later. But when James finally crossed the river Tweed into England on 22 August, it was at the head of a host numbering at least 30,000 and perhaps as many as 40,000 men. This was the largest force ever assembled in Scotland till then, and was almost certainly the equal of anything likely to be brought to bear upon it by the Earl of Surrey.

The Scots infantry were armed with eighteen-foot-long pikes, and had been hurriedly trained in the close formation fighting strategy required by such a weapon by a contingent of French captains loaned to James by Louis. James's force also comprised several units of light cavalry and 5,000 French regulars under the command of the Comte d'Aussi.

For a time James indulged himself by taking the English castles at Norham, Wark, Etal and Ford, but for little real tactical gain. Gradually the resolve of his army seems to have weakened. Many of the soldiers had local ties and knew all too well the reprisals that would probably follow these violent actions. In their hundreds and then in their thousands they drifted quietly away, arriving in Edinburgh in such numbers that the City Fathers issued a proclamation urging them to leave as soon as possible.

Meanwhile, the seventy-year-old Earl of Surrey, furious at being kept from France, had assembled his force at Newcastle by 1 September. Three days later he was joined by his son Thomas, Lord Admiral of England, and his 1,200-strong force. At full muster, the English army probably consisted of something in the region of 30,000 men.

An ominous warning of the disaster to come – the so-called 'Ill Raid' – had already been visited upon the Scots. An advance force of English troops under Sir William Bulmer, dispatched by Surrey to counter the Scottish raids in early August, successfully ambushed Lord Home's Borderers at Milfield in Northumberland on the 13th. English bowmen inflicted great slaughter on the Scots, and a cavalry charge mopped up the remnants. Home and his survivors fled, leaving their booty and rustled livestock behind them, along with some 500 dead and the same number taken as prisoners.

By the beginning of September, however, Surrey was running out of time. His supplies were dwindling and he had to either provoke a fight at once or face a humiliating withdrawal. He challenged James to a battle on 9 September, and the king accepted. James, we can be sure, felt confident, both in the size and equipment of his army and in the position he occupied on Flodden Hill. His men were encamped on high ground within a natural horseshoe of low hills, and the sole line of approach towards them was defended by entrenched cannon and men. Surrey, wily and experienced soldier that he was, had no intention of attacking the Scots uphill, and when he failed to persuade James to come down on to the low ground, he set about outmanoeuvring him.

James's master-gunner, Robert Borthwick, appealed to his master for permission to fire upon the English soldiers during this manoeuvre. Despite his sage advice that the enemy should be bombarded as they attempted to cross the river Till – within range of his cannon and before they could complete their march to a position north-west of the Scots – James refused.

Flodden memorial

THE BATTLE

BY THE TIME THE BATTLE BEGAN –
WITH THE SCOTTISH CANNON FIRING
TOWARDS THE ENGLISH LINES BETWEEN
FOUR AND FIVE O'CLOCK ON A
MISERABLY WET AND WIND-BLASTED
FRIDAY AFTERNOON – JAMES HAD BEEN
COMPLETELY OUTFLANKED. PREVIOUSLY
HE HAD DOMINATED THE HIGH GROUND
OF FLODDEN EDGE, BUT SUBSEQUENTLY
HE HAD BEEN FORCED TO COME DOWN
HURRIEDLY FROM THERE AND MARCH
THE MILE OR SO NORTH TO
NEIGHBOURING BRANXTON HILL.

It was the custom of Scottish camp followers of the time to set fire to the piles of rubbish strewn around the encampment, and they followed this practice here. Historians have from time to time suggested that the palls of smoke rising from the smouldering waste and drifting across Flodden and Branxton hills would have helped to conceal the Scottish army's movements. Whether or not this was the case – and surely the valley between those two gentle hills would have provided all the necessary cover – the air of menace and impending violence blanketing the landscape on that awful day must have been intensified by those slow-moving, grey-black clouds of stinking smoke.

Part of James's bid to beat the English to the nearby high ground of Branxton Hill required the movement of his cannon from their dominating position on Flodden Hill and into a hastily chosen and far less favourable location. Powerful and numerous though they were – and secure behind a ridge and up-slope from their enemy – the cannon were more suited to bombarding castle walls than to targeting mobile bodies of men. When they began their barrage, the guns did little more than make a loud noise as the cannonballs arced over the English heads. By contrast, the English artillery was positioned to catch its targets in silhouette against the skyline. This is what the English gunners had trained for, and what their lighter and more manoeuvrable weapons were eminently suitable for. Using the gradient to its best effect, they sent their roundshot bouncing and skipping up Branxton Hill, inflicting withering damage on the Scottish guns, men and morale alike.

The Scots were deployed in four large blocks along the slopes of Branxton Hill. Lords Home and Huntly commanded the left; the men of the earls of Crawford, Errol and Montrose formed the next group, with the king's column on their right and the men of the Highlands and the Islands under the earls of Argyle and Lennox on the extreme right. The Comte d'Aussi's force and the Lothian men under the Earl of Bothwell formed a reserve to the rear, behind the king's position and out of sight of the English. Military tactics of the time demanded a bowshot's worth of distance between each column, making the Scottish front line over a mile long, strung out in rank after disciplined rank along the entire length of the hill.

The English, now across the river Till, were in plain view. The men under the Lord Admiral Thomas Howard, son of the Earl of Surrey, took up position first, facing Home's massed Borderers and the rest of the Scottish left; Thomas Howard's younger brother, Edmund, was in command of the wing on the extreme right of this column. Quickly

When they began their barrage, the guns did little more than make a loud noise as the cannonballs arced over the English heads

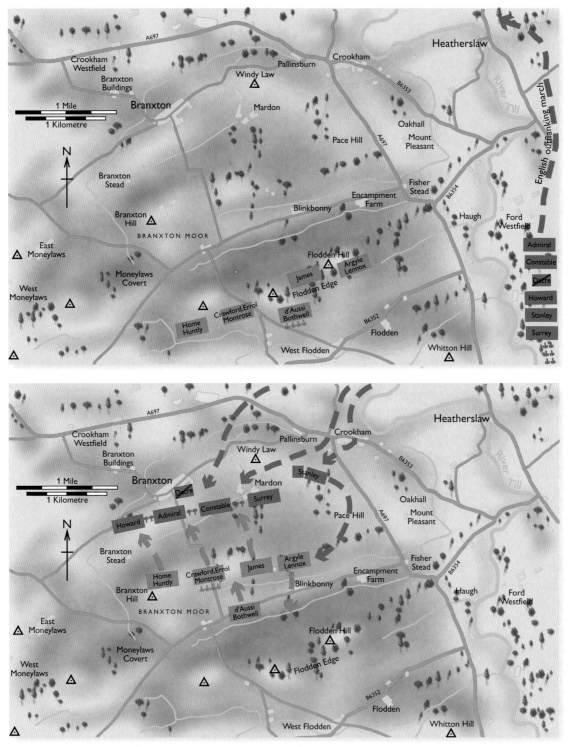

Movement of troops during the battle of Flodden superimposed on a modern map

realizing that he was facing the enemy with less than half of the English force in position, Thomas sent urgent word to his father, requesting him to move forward with all possible haste to fill the yawning gaps in the line.

Two hours later – and one has to ask why James failed to take the initiative and attack while his enemy was desperately being deployed – the English were ready for the fray, with Edmund Howard then in command of the extreme right, the Lord Admiral together with Marmaduke Constable in the centre, and the Earl of Surrey on the left. A cavalry of 'prickers' – a highly mobile mounted force led by Lord Dacre – lay in reserve at the rear. By the time the battle commenced, Lord Edward Stanley was still making his way with his men to a position on the extreme left of the English line. Whether this delayed arrival was due to unforeseen problems in fording the Till, or was part of a carefully timed plan designed to surprise the Scots at the height of the battle, history does not record. In any event, when Stanley did make his entrance on to the stage, he created an impressive impact.

The English gunners had the best of the artillery duel, silencing the Scottish guns. Home's Borderers and Huntly's Highlanders, no longer willing or able to tolerate the losses being meted out to them by roundshot punching into their ranks, were the first to take the fight downhill. They advanced in silence, concentrating on their formation and listening intently for orders, with hardly a sound other than the clank of armour and weapons. For Edmund Howard's men it must have been like watching a giant machine making its inexorable progress, its front and top bristling with pikes. The Englishmen broke and fell back in panicked and demoralized disarray – for there was nothing else to be done in the face of a pike phalanx advancing in good order. The Scots on the left of the line must surely have felt they were having the best of the battle – as indeed they were – and that the day would be theirs.

Edmund Howard was lucky to be alive, having been unhorsed three times in this savage clash. His standard-bearer had been cut to pieces, his standard was lost and his men were scattering all around him. Luck and tenacity in equal measure enabled him to fight his way to the relative security of his brother's column, and the English organized a stubborn regrouping and counterattack on their right. Perhaps seeing the dire personal straits of Howard, Dacre too entered the fray and brought his horsemen to bear upon Home and Huntly's troops, helping to check the Scottish advance. If indeed it was a rescue attempt aimed at saving Howard, the success came at a high price: some 160 of Dacre's men were cut down in the thick of the fighting.

The Englishmen broke and fell back in panicked and demoralized disarray

Rather than press home their advantage – and this loss of momentum would affect the whole course of the battle – the Scots stopped in their tracks. Home and Huntly's men took no further part in the battle, and when the Scottish centre, under the command of Crawford, jogged downhill in support of the action, they found the Borderers and the Highlanders were not fighting but pillaging the fallen. With the momentum of the left lost, the Scottish centre too was brought to a standstill, both by ferocious cannon- and arrow-fire from the English and by Home and Huntly's failure to roll up the English line. Had the Scots maintained the force of their forward drive and turned upon the Lord Admiral's flank, they might well have carried the day. Whatever the reason for their failure to fight on, Huntly is reputed to have urged Home to rejoin the fray while nearby Crawford's men were faltering in the face of the English defenders. Apparently unmoved, Home replied: 'He does well that does for himself. We have fought their vanguards and won the same; let the rest do their part as well as we.'

History and its chroniclers may have been unkind to Home, with selfish words and deeds attributed to him by contemporaries with political axes to grind. In any event, the disaster at Flodden had less to do with the behaviour of individuals than with the choice of weapons and terrain. For despite the early success of the Scottish left, elsewhere on that bloodied field the doughty English defenders who stood their ground found renewed hope. What had once looked like a mighty, steel porcupine gradually dissolved into a confused mass of men bogged down in heavy ground and armed with cumbersome weapons that were of little use in a straight fight. The great majority of the English infantrymen bore halberds or, as they are otherwise known, bills. Eight feet in length, these weapons combined the best elements of the axe and the spear. Englishmen confronting individual pikemen could easily lop off the business ends of their opponents' weapons. Instead of wielding eighteen-foot-long pikes, the Scots found themselves carrying sixteen-foot-long poles . . . then twelve-foot-long poles . . . then nothing. Forced to resort to their swords, the attackers were at the mercy of those viciously swinging bills.

Flodden was a battle on such a scale – sweeping so many men and horses into its whirling midst – that it is all too easy to forget that many hugely significant events were happening simultaneously. While Home and Huntly were grinding to a halt on the Scottish left, and Crawford's centre was fighting itself to a disorganized standstill under a hail of arrows and roundshot, the king himself had already engaged the enemy.

The legendary death of James IV – the most popular and, perhaps, most likeable of the Stuart kings – is impossible to place accurately. Maybe he was encouraged by the efforts of his soldiers on the left and was keen to move in support of them and of the centre. Perhaps the men he commanded were so fired up by what they had already witnessed that it was impossible to hold them back any longer. Among what little we know for sure is that he led his own attack, from the front, towards Surrey, and that he was cut down by the earl's defenders. One of the legends of that day placed him within a spear's length of Surrey before he succumbed to his wounds – a near-severed hand, no less than five bill strokes to the body and an arrow in the face. Whatever the truth concerning his injuries, he was fighting shoulder to shoulder with his men and his bravery, unlike so much on that day, was not in doubt. The men around him displayed great valour, falling, wrote the chroniclers, by the hundred and then by the thousand.

Over on the Scottish right, the Highlanders under Argyle and Lennox seem to have been mesmerized by the action below them and to their left. It is possible that the undulating lie of the land between their position and that of the left made it impossible for them to see everything that was happening. They were not pikemen, after all, but were conventionally armed with sword and targe and dirk and were not intended for the main thrust of the Scottish attack. In any event, when Lord Stanley – arriving later than the rest but with perfect timing – took his men into the dead ground on the Scottish right flank, he had all the initiative and element of surprise that he needed. His archers strafed the stationary Scots, forcing them back on to d'Aussi and Bothwell's men, who were struggling to come to the aid of the king. The Highlanders broke, harried beyond endurance by the archers and with no room to manoeuvre or regroup, and the English achieved the decisive breakthrough.

By six o'clock the fighting was over. The Scots survivors withdrew in good order, their departure from the field protected by well-disciplined remnants of the Scottish left under Home and others. They were not pursued in any comprehensive fashion. Perhaps Surrey himself was unaware at this time of the scale and completeness of his victory and therefore prudently held his forces in reserve. By the end of the day, though, between 5,000 and 10,000 Scots – including twelve earls, thirteen lords of parliament, many clan chiefs, the Archbishop of St Andrews, the Dean of Glasgow, the abbots of Kilwinning and Inchaffry and the Bishop of Caithness and the Isles – were, according to traditional accounts, dead. Some 1,500 English corpses lay tangled among them.

Armour, c. 1520, fluted in the 'Maximilian' style

WHO FOUGHT HERE

IN BRITAIN TODAY WE TEND TO REGARD
WAR AS A PROFESSIONAL AFFAIR, WITH
THE BRITISH ARMY COMPOSED OF
HIGHLY TRAINED AND RELATIVELY
WELL-PAID SOLDIERS WHO HAVE
CHOSEN TO FOLLOW A MILITARY
CAREER. HOWEVER, WE NEED ONLY LOOK
AT SOME OF THE BLOODY ETHNIC
CONFLICTS THAT HAVE CAUSED SO MUCH
ANGUISH IN MANY PARTS OF THE WORLD
TO SEE THAT NOT ALL WARS ARE
FOUGHT BY PROFESSIONAL ARMIES. IN
THE BALKANS, FOR INSTANCE, PEOPLE
FROM ALL WALKS OF LIFE, FROM
FARMING TO PHARMACY, CHOSE TO TAKE
UP ARMS FOR A CAUSE WHICH FOR
BETTER OR WORSE THEY BELIEVED IN.

In Britain we have to look back at least to the Korean war and the Malayan insurgency in the 1950s for a time when civilians became soldiers through no choice of their own. But these conflicts differed from later ethnic wars in that, by and large, civilians had no choice but to fight as they had been drafted into the army during the period of conscription known as National Service.

Despite the obvious changes in the 450 years or so which separate the Korean war from the battle of Flodden, the general concept of National Service may provide some sort of common thread between these two bloody conflicts. There was no such thing as a professional army in England or Scotland at the time of Flodden. When war threatened or was declared on an enemy, an army was raised simply by calling men to arms. Medieval society was based on the feudal system: at its most basic level, this meant that most of the land was owned by a noble élite, all of whom were either related to the crown or owed their privileged status to the crown. This élite comprised barons, earls, dukes and the Church, with the lowest levels of this ruling class made up of knights. Everyone else owed allegiance to a member of this select band, who owned not only the land their tenants farmed, but also the houses in which they lived. This allegiance manifested itself in a number of ways, including the payment of rents and taxes, and also service under arms. Depending on their status, each member of the nobility would be expected to raise a given number of men for service in the king's army. Although the feudal system was well on its way out by the time of the battle of Flodden, the power of landlord over tenant remained a strong one, no more so than in Scotland, as will be seen in the case of the battle of Culloden. At a moment's notice men would be expected to leave behind their ploughs and take up their longbows.

It was enshrined in the law of the land that men had a duty to maintain their proficiency with that most feared of medieval weapons, the longbow. Every village had an archery range at which men would be required to practise for so many hours each week, and we know from the archaeological examination of male graves of the time that many men had overdeveloped right arms as a result of constant drawing of the bowstring. Thus the majority of men who fought at Flodden probably had no choice in the matter, they were merely doing service for their lord. But by this time various towns were also raising their own bands of troops, with the town coffers opened to allow expenditure on equipment and supplies. This development may point to an eagerness to fight that went beyond the requirements of servitude and obligation,

There was no such thing as a professional army in England or Scotland at the time of Flodden

and it appears to have been especially acute on the Scottish side, where the chance to get even with the 'auld enemy' in the service of a popular king created an enthusiasm and nationalistic fervour perhaps not too dissimilar to that which swept Britain during the early days of the First World War. Such jingoism may have swelled the ranks of the army well above the number actually called upon to do service, but outside the tavern or bedchamber it would only carry a man so far: there are many reports that the Scottish army suffered numerous desertions once the campaign had begun.

Desertions were at their highest not in the face of battle as one might expect, but after the battle was over. The army was by and large unpaid (this was especially true of the Scots), except for the foreign mercenaries, and so an important incentive to fight was the promise of loot and booty, with the purses and pockets of the fallen traditionally picked clean by the victors. At Flodden there are even stories of soldiers looting the dead while the battle continued to rage around them. There was obviously a problem in keeping men in the field after they had filled their pockets with loot, as they were naturally keen to live long enough to enjoy the benefits of this hard-earned windfall.

FORTRESS FLODDEN

King James IV has gone down in history as a rather rash character: after all, it isn't every king who against all sound advice rushes into battle and gets himself killed. And on top of all that was the huge loss among his nobles and clergy, for which he must be held at least partly responsible. But there is evidence that this devil-may-care attitude may have become a little overworked as the story of the battle was told and retold down the years. One of the clearest indications of this was his apparent refusal to descend from his strong position on Flodden Hill to face the English army on the level ground provided by the Milfield Basin. It is documented that this refusal angered Surrey, the English commander, as it contravened the chivalric code that still governed warfare at the time; James IV's sense of chivalry was well known and Surrey may have hoped to take advantage of it. Whether killing on a massive scale could ever be regarded as a noble deed with fair play ensured by noble rules is a moot point, but it is clear that Surrey was not prepared to throw his force against a naturally strong position that gave the Scots a clear advantage.

There is some disagreement among scholars as to the nature of the Scottish army's position on Flodden Hill. Some writers infer that it was

THE HORROR OF BATTLE

A conversation with military historian Niall Barr, drinking pale ale in the Red Lion pub in the village of Milfield, reminded us why we were drawn to this stuff in the first place. Something Niall said about the likely impact of the battle of Flodden on the minds of the men who were there made the 500 years from then until now just disappear.

'The first day of the first battle of the Somme saw 20,000 men killed and 40,000 wounded,' he said. 'But that death toll was happening along a front that was tens of miles long. Participants would have had no sense of the scale of what was going on because they simply couldn't see it all.'

Niall said the difference at Flodden was that the killing and dying was all contained within a relatively small area – the Scottish front was just over a mile – and carried out with sword and axe amid scenes that would have made a busy butcher's yard look like the proverbial vicarage tea party. And insignificant though the numbers of dead are when compared to the Somme, the horror was much more intimate, much more personal and 'in your face' for those men who stood to on that day in 1513.

'In some ways,' he said, 'the experience at Flodden may well have been worse – more damaging psychologically for individual soldiers – than what happened on 1 July 1916.'

strongly fortified, with the guns placed behind purposely constructed entrenchments, while others merely state that the hill itself was like a natural fortress, which apparently required no further modification. An almost contemporary account, by Halle from 1550, states that

> the king lay upon the side of a high mountain called Flodden on the edge of the Cheviot where was but one narrow field for any man to ascend by the said hill to him and at the foot of the hill lay all his ordnance. On the one side of his army was a great marsh and composed with the hills of Cheviot so that he lay too strong to be approached of any side: except the Englishmen would have temerariously come on his ordnance . . .

Although there is no explicit reference to defensive trenches in Halle's description, most writers have mentioned these features. An Italian poem entitled 'The Rout of the Scots' was composed not too many years after the battle and includes this passage: 'the battle is fixed for the following day. Each of the camps [English and Scots] is well fortified so that they are able to sleep in safety.'

Later writers, such as MacKenzie in 1931, continue to refer to fortifications:

> The Scots were in an unassailable position. Their camp was on Flodden Hill. The plain below on their right was a morass with

Typical Scottish armour worn at Flodden

Typical English armour worn at Flodden

patches of mire and belts of reeds. On their left was the River Till as it emerges from the hills: behind them, cliff and copse. The only approach to the position was by the gentle slope on their front, and across this at the foot a ditch had been dug over the scarp of which appeared the Scottish cannon.

As recently as 1999 Gervaise Phillips wrote:

The naturally strong defensive position along the crest of Flodden Edge was enhanced by field fortifications, in which was located the powerful Scottish artillery . . . The flanks of the Scottish position were protected by treacherous, broken ground, a marsh to one side, steep slopes on the other. The only viable approach to the Scottish position was across a narrow field to the front of Flodden Edge. But any assault by that route would have been delivered straight into the teeth of the Scottish artillery.

If these later sources are correct and defences were built for the Scots artillery, then there appears to be little agreement as to their location. Phillips describes an entrenched position running along the crest of Flodden Edge, presumably quite high up, while MacKenzie mentions a trench dug across the foot of Flodden Hill. Providing yet another location, Ridpath writes in the late nineteenth century that 'the Scots had erected a battery of cannon, near the eastern declivity of Flodden Hill, bearing full on the bridge of Ford'. A footnote to Ridpath's text goes on to say that remains of these entrenchments were still visible at the time of writing. Whether some or all of these statements are incorrect cannot be assessed without some sort of archaeological investigation.

After Flodden

the dig

WORK in the library and in the office is one thing, but as archaeologists we know that our real work happens at the site itself. The historical sources, the maps, the aerial photographs – all had been considered but none had offered us anything real, anything tangible, to bring this story back to life. Places change over time. By dusk on 9 September 1513 the battle of Flodden was over, but life on the landscape continued. And so by the time we come to look for the echoes of that day, five centuries of daily life have had their inevitable effect. Open ground has been enclosed; the fields have been ploughed, seeded, harvested and ploughed again; forests have been planted; tracks have become tarred roads; farms have become villages; villages have become towns.

One clue from the maps was a farm at the foot of Flodden Hill called Encampment, and it was here that we made our first port of call and which we decided to take as our base of operations. Several things – the name of the farm, the fact that we knew the Scottish army had camped here or hereabouts (not to mention a friendly farmer!) – persuaded us that this was a great spot for our own camp. Tent pitched, we took one last look at our maps before setting out to make our discoveries.

Our tent was on the low ground, where the wheat had not long before been harvested. The well-ordered fields with their hedges and fences rose gently up the hill, until they were brought to an abrupt halt by the edge of a dense stand of trees. The entire summit of Flodden Hill was covered by tall conifers, a plantation which we knew from our research was no older than the 1920s. The fields held out little promise for upstanding remains, the plough being no friend of the earthworks we were seeking. True, the planting of trees also takes a heavy toll, but woodland, once established,

causes less disturbance than harvested fields which are ploughed once or even twice a year, every year.

We climbed the hill, stopping every now and again to take in the view: to the east was Ford Castle and running below it, from north to south, the river Till, both of which played a part in the events of 500 years ago. Green hills rolled gently to the north, where just within sight lay the border between England and Scotland – one-time troublesome neighbours now thankfully at peace. This was a landscape that still retained the feeling of openness that must have characterized it at the time of the battle.

But that changed as soon as we entered the wood. The light dimmed – filtered through leaves to an eerie green – and the view was instantly obscured as the trees closed in around us. We found a muddy track and followed it for a while before striking out again into the thick of the trees, our footfalls echoing to the sound of snapping twigs. We put distance between us so as to cover more territory, our eyes scanning the ground for suspicious lumps and bumps. Truth be told, we had no concrete idea of what we were looking for. There was little to take as a yardstick: when last we had checked, medieval artillery defences were not exactly common.

In the wood, without a compass and with our landmarks hidden from view, our sense of direction quickly became confused and we had to judge our position as best we could. Higher up the hill the spaces between the trees were overgrown with waist-high bracken, making it impossible to see the ground. But even bracken could not obscure a couple of deep quarry scoops from where the hard igneous rocks from which the hill is formed had been chipped away to build walls and roads. We walked on, sometimes retracing our steps before realizing our mistake.

Then it appeared. All of a sudden the forest floor dropped away in front of us, down into a hollow where the trees were more widely spaced. The slope was regular and in places surmounted by a lip, an earthen bank which immediately told us that this was no quarry scoop. Down below we could see another bank, running parallel to where we stood at the back of the hollow, and in front of that was the same track we had walked along earlier. We were not far from the edge of the wood, the light was better here and we could make out the fields between the trees just beyond the track. Our excitement rose as we dropped down into the hollow, which we could now see was some sort of enclosure, not quite rectangular, as one of the banks ran off at an angle. There was a gap in the bank at the front, just where it ran closest to the track, and as we talked about what we were seeing we wondered whether the bank there had been moved when the track was created. We had found an earthwork, sure enough, but was it a Scottish gun emplacement?

On the ground it was difficult to see what shape the thing was – we would need a topographic survey, a map to make sense of it. Eager to get the ball rolling, we crossed the track and stepped back out into the daylight. It was only when we were in the open again that we realized that, without the trees, anyone standing in the earthwork would have had a great view of the castle at Ford, the river in front of it and the low, flat ground below, upon which our tent now stood.

If this earthwork did turn out to be an artillery defence, it would imply that James IV was far from rash during this campaign: the effort required to dig these defences would demonstrate that he was cautious and

careful. James clearly wanted to fight the battle on his terms, and in maintaining his position on Flodden Hill after Surrey's challenge he displayed absolute common sense. After all, Lord Home had suffered defeat at the hands of the English at that very place only a month before, losing many men and all of his plunder during the 'Ill Raid'. However, in the light of the surest device in the strategic armoury, hindsight, we now know that James might have been better off if he had joined battle on the level ground. Although he had refused to come down off the high ground, he did agree that the fight would take place on 9 September. This combination of factors forced Surrey to take the initiative, his only other option being to disband his by now poorly provisioned and overstretched army, so he decided to march his army around the back of the Scots position. On 8 September the English army moved away from its camp at Wooler, crossing by Weetwood Bridge and Doddington Bridge to the eastern side of the river Till, where it camped just south of Barmoor Castle. Choosing a route which denied the Scots full knowledge of its movements, the English army then marched in two columns back towards the Till. The vanguard, commanded by Thomas Howard, the Lord Admiral, included 11,000 men and artillery, all of which crossed back over the river by Twizel Bridge. Surrey commanded the main column of 15,000 men and, not being encumbered with artillery which would have necessitated using a bridge, may have crossed at a ford, possibly at Castle Heaton one mile downstream.

The English army's manoeuvrings did not go unobserved, and it has been argued by one historian that James's Highland scouts reported the English were heading for the border and an invasion of Scotland. At

IN SEARCH OF LONG IRON NAILS

We arranged to meet Dr David Caldwell, an archaeologist specializing in medieval ordnance, at Edinburgh Castle. Mons Meg, greatest of the medieval cannons and so massive she seems unreal (surely someone's idea of a nightmarish joke), now lurks in a spotlit underground vault of the castle like the sullen, spent old lady she is. It was in her gruesome shadow that we chatted about the artillery known to have been in action at Flodden. David described the labours of Hercules that were heaped upon the gunners charged with manoeuvring the Scottish guns.

In just five days, those gun crews hauled and pushed their impossibly unwieldy cargo along what passed for roads between Edinburgh and their first destination, Norham Castle. Each of the biggest guns would have had its own wagon, cumbersome and awkward to move even when unladen, and pulled by anything up to thirty-six oxen when fully loaded. Strung out for miles across the unforgiving hills of southern Scotland, James's artillery train must have been quite a sight – the ultimate medieval Bank Holiday traffic jam!

It was while we talked about the possibility of a specially constructed entrenchment for the Scottish guns, however, that David provided a fascinating clue. He was at pains to stress how much effort was needed to operate such weapons in the field. Given their massive size and value – and these, after all, added up to one of the finest artillery trains in Christendom – such guns had to be treated with care. They would have worked best on pre-prepared platforms, and it was also likely that James would have wanted such prize possessions to be well protected from any enemy fire. For these reasons, David readily backed the thought that we had entertained for a while: if the Scottish gun crews had had the time, they would have constructed mini-forts on Flodden Hill both to protect the weapons themselves and to provide the kind of level surface that would have best suited their use in action.

'And if you're looking for a platform for guns,' he said, 'be on the look-out for long iron nails.'

Now this was the kind of information we could use – but why nails?

David explained that ideally the guns would have been placed on level platforms constructed from large planks of wood – each probably the size of a modern railway sleeper – and that these would have been nailed together.

'In my opinion,' said David, 'if you're searching for those platforms, your best bet is to use metal detectors to look for characteristic long, hand-made, iron nails. I found them scattered behind an earth rampart when I excavated a fort at Eyemouth, just ten miles or so north of Berwick, and those defences were built not that long after the battle.'

He was right, of course. After 500 years, it was improbable that much, if anything, would have survived of any timbers. Far more likely was the survival of any iron used in the overall construction. And how many explanations are there, we would have to ask ourselves in the event of such a find, for large numbers of long, hand-made iron nails lying in regimented patterns on a hillside in Northumberland?

another point James's master of artillery is said to have pleaded for permission to bombard an English column as it crossed the river, but James refused, preferring instead to fight the enemy in open battle. Now in great danger of being outflanked, with his retreat to Scotland possibly blocked, James ordered his soldiers to leave their position on Flodden Hill and turn to the north-west, where they were to form up on the edge of Branxton Hill, facing north. The camp was put to the torch, which appears to have been the standard practice at the time, while the cannon were dragged and slowly manhandled to the new position where their barrels overlooked the English army as it formed up along the foot of Branxton Hill. As Howard joined forces with Surrey, so the stage was set for the bloody struggle.

To start our survey, John Arthur set the total station electronic distance measurer (EDM) up on its tripod at the back of the earthwork, the high ground providing him with the best line of sight to the banks stretched out below him. Helen McQuarrie moved between the trees with the staff, stopping at regular intervals so that John could get a reading off the prism mounted on the end of it. With every press of the button the EDM fired an invisible beam of light, like a laser, towards the prism. The reflecting lens then returned the beam to the heart of the machine, where its chips and circuits turned light and distance into a measured point fixed in space. This data was collected in a small electronic logger and then at the end of every day hundreds of readings were dumped into the laptop computer, where the software made sense of them and recreated the earthwork as a contour plan.

With the topographic survey finished and its results processed on the computer, we could now see the

shape and appreciate the scale. 'About half the size of a football pitch,' said John, referring to the area enclosed by the earthworks. The contours on the computer screen, just like those on a map, clearly showed the steepness of the slopes and banks, but John also picked out a series of lumps and bumps inside the enclosure, some of which we had noticed when we first wandered around it. Having established it on the map, we now had to prove it was a gun emplacement, and the only way to do that was to excavate and search for evidence that would place it at the time of the battle.

Obviously we couldn't dig the entire enclosure as it was much too big, and anyway we didn't want to cause too much disturbance to what could prove to be a really important historical site. We agreed that a couple of well-placed trenches might be all we'd need to give us the answer, one way or another. With our plan freshly printed out from the computer, we visited the site once again to select areas for trenching. It was important that we understood the construction of the earthwork itself, so, using string, we marked out a trench running across one of the banks and also took in an area inside the earthwork. A second, smaller trench was placed over an internal bank whose right-angled shape suggested it might have been the remains of a small building inside the enclosure.

While the hard work of removing the leaf mould and topsoil from the trenches was going on, we began a metal-detector survey of the entire area within the earthwork enclosure in order to locate metal artefacts and plot their position on our plan. This was important because the type of things we found would add a further dimension to the story that excavation would tell us. David Caldwell had already told us to expect nails from the timber platforms of the gun emplacement – the gunners certainly wouldn't have wanted to sit those monsters on the soft earth we now found ourselves digging through.

Very quickly the area we mapped out had sprouted a healthy crop of colourful pin flags – plastic flowers of the forest, each fluttering bloom marking a metal object under the ground. With mounting excitement we began to excavate at the first flag. We may call what we do science, but that doesn't stop us feeling the thrill of discovery and the buzz of testing our ideas against the evidence in the ground. But our excitement began to wane as the first few flags turned out to mark the site of old shotgun cartridges. We should have expected them – people shot pheasants in the woods, and there were hundreds of specially reared young birds on the hilltop.

Resisting the temptation to pull on our plus-fours and reach for the 12-bore, we pressed on with our search. It was not long before our perseverance was rewarded and the first iron nail was held triumphantly aloft. Modern nails are made on machines and are very regular and round, but this was an old, hand-made example, its shaft and head formed square in section by well-aimed blows from the blacksmith's hammer. It was just what we had been looking for!

Metal-detecting gives instant results, and if not done properly can cause serious damage to the archaeology. Excavation, on the other hand, takes much more effort and patience – it's a bit like gardening, in that you only get out of it what you put in. The top of the bank was gradually revealed: the soil was lighter and more compact than the stuff that had been shovelled off. Then there were stones, half buried in steep scarp on the inside of the bank. They had been mixed in with the soil and packed in when the bank had been raised, to provide added strength. The front of the bank, which sloped downhill, was different: there were no stones and it was not as steep as the inside of the bank. It was making sense, coming together as a structure built to serve the specific function of protecting the Scottish guns from incoming English cannonballs. Had the English been less wily than they proved to be and tried to storm the hill, their first move would surely have been to use artillery to eliminate the Scottish guns.

Imagine the cannonballs arcing through the air towards their target. Well aware of what was coming, the Scottish gunners would have dragged their pieces back over the timber platforms, pulling the wide-mouthed barrels well away from the bank. When the heavy lead balls hit the outer scarp of the bank, instead of wreaking havoc they were harmlessly buried. The carefully gauged angle of the slope would have killed their momentum, while the soft earth soaked up the impact. This is why we found no stones in the front of the bank: in a bombardment they would have shattered and sent fragments, like deadly shrapnel, flying in all directions. Any remaining shock would have been absorbed by the body of the bank, and here the stones did their work, acting like a spine to keep the structure intact. At the right moment, the Scottish gunners would have loaded and pushed their carefully nurtured charges forward, putting match to touch-hole to fill the air with hot metal.

As it happened, the English did not launch an attack on Flodden Hill and the Scottish guns were never fired from this position. But none the less, for a few days this must have been a busy place. A good number of men

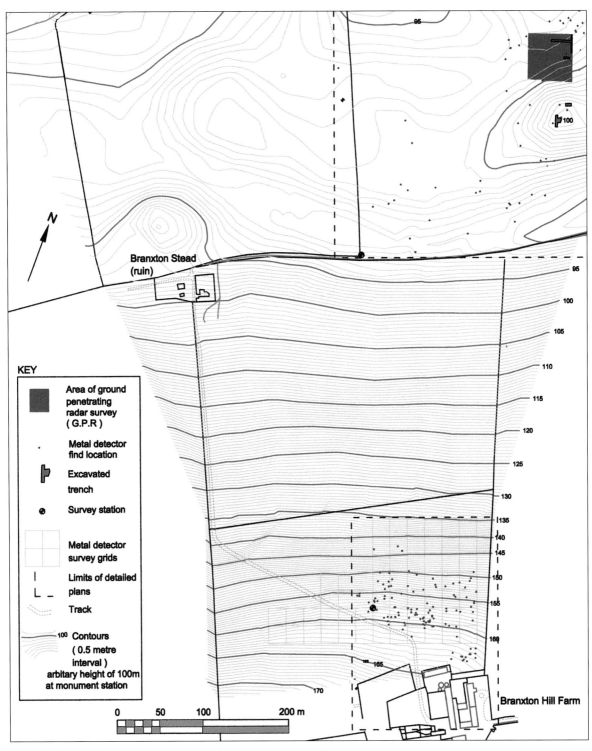

Survey map showing the trenches and the metal-detecting finds

were needed to throw up these impressive defences, and, indeed, James had a potential workforce of around 30,000 at his disposal. Then the platforms were knocked together inside and the hill-top echoed to the sound of heavy iron nails being driven into fresh timber. The guns, drawn by oxen and horses, were dragged in through a gap in the defences, and then the last part of the bank was thrown up behind them, sealing them in while they were manhandled into their final position.

For a day or two the gunners must have tended their charges closely, sighting them on potential targets, oiling and cleaning them and making final preparations for battle. They probably even slept near the guns in shelters erected within the emplacement, though they must surely have taken care to keep their cooking fires well away from their powder!

The second excavation trench provided some evidence for the gunners' domestic arrangements. A low gravel and earth bank may be all that is left of a small lean-to shelter built into the back slope of the scooped-out interior of the enclosure. One of the most important finds came from inside this structure. At first it seemed unassuming, just a small piece of red pottery. But this, we were told by our pottery expert, Bob Will, was a piece of redware. It wasn't fancy, not what you'd call Sunday-best china, just basic domestic pottery. This piece may have come from a beer jug, or a bowl for food preparation. But bog standard or not, for us it couldn't have been better, because this was vital dating evidence. Redware was in common usage at the time of the battle of Flodden, and may even have come from Scotland, although it was made on both sides of the border.

So there we were: hand-made nails, just as you would expect on an artillery platform; sturdy earthen banks to protect the guns; and then, to top it all, a piece of pottery of exactly the right period to tie the whole thing together. A good day by any archaeologist's standards!

But there was one question still to be answered: why was there a big gap in the bank at the front of the entrenchment? We think that, just as the guns were brought in through a gap in the bank which was then built up behind them, so the bank must have been torn down to get them back out. When it became obvious to James that the English had no intention of assaulting the hill and had moved further north, perhaps cutting off any retreat back to Scotland, the guns, along with the rest of the army, were rushed to Branxton Hill. To us, it seems almost a shame – all that hard work and attention to detail in preparation for an attack that never came. But in reality it seems unlikely that the gunners had any time to regret their wasted labours as they tore down the bank and harnessed their guns before racing to meet their fate on Branxton Hill.

We had found one gun emplacement, evidence enough that James had fortified the hill. But had there been more?

Although our site was large, it seems unlikely that it could have comfortably held many more than six big guns, and we know from historical accounts that the Scots had over twenty guns, so these must have been placed elsewhere on the hill. The investigated emplacement is positioned on the north- and east-facing slope of Flodden Hill. It seems highly likely that the south-facing slopes were defended in a similar fashion, as this is the direction from which the English army initially advanced towards the hill. But remains of

these south-facing defences have probably, over time, been destroyed by ploughing, as the fields here come closer to the top of the hill than on the north-facing slopes, where the trees have offered some protection.

The camp

On the eve of battle the Scottish army may have numbered between 25,000 and 30,000 men. They were accompanied by horses and livestock, with 400 oxen alone reputedly required to pull the cannons. In addition to the army itself, there were probably large numbers of camp-followers – soldiers' wives, craftsmen, traders and various shady characters hoping to profit from the suffering of others. Anyone who has

been to a rock festival or seen Glastonbury on the television does not need a vivid imagination to picture the impact that such numbers have on the landscape.

Many writers seem to assume that at this stage the Scottish camp was located on Flodden Hill. The army certainly appears to have positioned itself on that eminence in preparation for battle, but it seems just as likely that the Scottish camp was positioned at the foot of Flodden Hill, most probably at the base of its north-facing slopes. It is surely no coincidence that the farm which occupies this ground is known to this day as Encampment Farm. Here there is space to pitch tents and graze stock, and there are plentiful supplies of water from the streams running into the river Till.

The camp was abandoned rapidly on the morning of the battle and it appears to have been put to the torch by the departing army, perhaps preventing anything that could not be carried from falling into enemy hands. Although you may not expect a camp primarily made up of tents to leave much behind in the way of archaeologically identifiable remains, there must surely have been rubbish and latrine pits, and perhaps ditches to keep livestock penned in. The very act of burning the camp may also have left traces in the ground: burning alters the local magnetic field and these changes may be detectable using geophysical instruments such as the magnetometer.

In our tent, with the smelly canvas flapping and the kettle boiling, it did not take much to imagine ourselves there among hundreds of other tents as soldiers slept, ate, talked, laughed, drank, played dice and prepared their weapons for the coming battle. The name Encampment Farm carried with it some half-forgotten memory of that tent city and now, our geophysics done, we hoped to find some physical trace of it, despite the damage caused to the site by ploughs during the following centuries. Never a pair to step away from a challenge, we were determined to give it our best shot. We didn't expect to find the holes where the tent pegs had once been set but we did hope that some deep features might have survived. Surely 25,000 people congregated in the same place for a few days must have left something behind, but imagine looking for evidence of the Glastonbury festival 500 years after the last act has left the stage.

Iain Banks spent days in the fields, striding up and down in straight lines with his Heath Robinson contraptions. The resistivity probe – a pair of spikes which have to be pressed into the ground every time a reading is to be taken – looks like a zimmer-frame, but Iain needed to be fully fit to swing this thing forward with every step throughout the day. Once he'd finished with the resistivity probe, he went over the same ground with the magnetometer. This is less cumbersome – a simple metal tube attached to a trigger which is pressed every time the reading is taken – but because it detects changes in the magnetic field, it meant that Iain couldn't carry anything metallic in his pockets. So he is usually without money – one reason perhaps why he never has his hair cut; nor can he wear any clothes with metal zips or fasteners, so he is usually attired, not quite in the height of fashion, in wellies and tie-waisted jogging pants.

The geophysics had shown up some anomalies in the field next to the tent and so it was here that we directed our mechanical excavator. We had a big area to look at and the best way to get down to the archaeology was carefully to strip away the topsoil with a machine. Paul Duffy watched and guided as the bucket stripped layer after layer of plough soil away, until the change in the soil's colour and texture told him that the subsoil had been reached. This was where we would find any surviving archaeology, below the level disturbed by the blade of the plough. With the plough soil removed we shovelled and trowelled, skimming off more soil to create a clear surface where

any archaeology would reveal itself. We were looking for changes of colour and texture, splodges and shadows, subtle hints that the ground had been disturbed by human hand, hopefully some five centuries ago.

However, our labours appeared to be in vain, as Iain had suggested, cautious man that he is. Some of the anomalies proved to be mere variations in the natural geology, while others simply marked modern field drains. Nevertheless, there was archaeology here. As we worked away we started to come across very small pieces of coloured stone: chipped flakes and blades of banded agate and red chalcedony. These were old friends to us. Before we became seriously interested in battlefields, we had served our time as prehistoric archaeologists, looking at a human past several thousand years old. We knew instantly that these were stone tools, or microliths, from the Mesolithic period (meaning Middle Stone Age). They had been skilfully crafted in a world very different from our own, heavily forested but not long cleared of the great ice sheets that had covered northern Europe for hundreds of thousands of years during the Ice Age. There was no farming then; people lived by hunting animals and gathering wild plants and fruits, and the stone tools we now held may have been the tips of arrows or the blades of reaping knives. These people lived an almost nomadic existence, perhaps following herds of deer as the seasons changed, setting up camp and then moving on to pastures new. We may have been disappointed at not finding evidence of a camp 500 years old, but as archaeologists we could not help but be thrilled by this discovery of a camp around 9,000 years old!

Having drawn a blank on the lower fields, we

switched our attention to the hill-top, where most of the historical accounts told us the Scottish camp had been. On a grass-covered saddle on the edge of the forest Iain had swept and pricked the ground with his geophysical instruments. Once again, when the findings were processed through the computer, they showed up anomalies. Like a huge mechanical pet, the JCB faithfully trundled up the hill to the geophysical grids, where it would strip topsoil that wasn't as heavily ploughed as down below. Further down the slope towards Branxton Hill Farm was the ridge along which the pride of Scotland had arrayed itself before sweeping down to its destruction. It would not have taken the Scots long to reach the ridge from where the machine now worked, as the ground was pretty level and protected from the south by a gentle rise which would have sheltered tents from the wind and from the gaze of the English army as it made its way north from Wooler.

Sure enough, there was archaeology here – concentrations of stone and patches of darker soil. Paul and Iain worked away, cleaning and revealing, and things looked more promising: an arc of small stones appeared, running across the width of one of the trenches. The stones were set into a shallow slot scooped into the earth. Just possibly this is the sort of

trace a tent or temporary shelter may have left behind, the stones perhaps supporting thin stakes which would prop up a hide or oil-cloth roof, pretty much like the 'benders' that modern travellers live in. There were also a couple of post-holes elsewhere in the trenches, and these stone-lined holes may have once supported the central posts of other tents. The evidence was fragmented and thin on the ground, which came as no surprise – the amazing thing is that we managed to find any trace at all.

The last, and perhaps most dramatic, piece of evidence for the site of the camp actually came to light when we were surveying the gun emplacement, which was further along the hill to the east. Just behind the emplacement we came across a low bank, which ran as straight as a die along the crest of the hill. The ground among the trees on the other side of the bank, to the south, was pretty level and would have been an ideal place to have pitched tents. Although we did not have time to investigate

this feature thoroughly, we believe it may have been part of a defensive bank which was thrown up around the camp, again suggesting that the hill-top was heavily fortified. The gun emplacement lay just outside this bank and from here it covered the northern flank of the camp from attack. The bank may have encircled the entire hill-top, but beyond the protection provided by the trees all traces of it would probably have been removed by the farmer's plough. For the first time we had evidence of a heavily fortified camp – and right on top of the hill, where the historical accounts had said it was all along.

Metal-detecting the battlefield

Even broadminded archaeologists such as ourselves suffer pangs of guilt when we step on to a site armed with metal detectors – it's like being caught with a calculator during a mental arithmetic test. The relationship between detectorists and the archaeological community has not always been smooth, largely due to the activities of an irresponsible minority who have looted sites in the past. It was with some trepidation, therefore, that we built the practice of metal-detecting into the portfolio of techniques we have at our disposal. Luckily, the detectorists we've worked alongside have been imbued with the same respect for history and historical sites as archaeologists themselves, and both groups work together more and more now.

If proof were needed of the crucial role to be played by metal-detector survey, we got it at Flodden. Every day, at least one person on the team would remark on the sheer scale of the place and on how much ground we had to cover in the short time available. A large part of the solution to that problem was the enlistment – and tactical deployment – of a team of metal detectorists based in Tyneside. Given the chance of playing a part in a full-scale archaeological investigation of the battlefield, they jumped at it, and on the days we needed their services the car park near the Piper's Hill monument was crowded with enthusiastic volunteers. Detectorists are a fascinating breed. Each is equipped like an all-weather Batman, utility belts clanking with all manner of customized spades, trowels, knives and mini detecting probes; clad in combinations of ex-army camouflage gear and day-glo waterproofs, they work steadily and uncomplainingly through fair weather and foul.

Customary optimism notwithstanding, we had arrived at the battlefield with what we had convinced ourselves were realistic expectations. Central to that pragmatism was a belief that 500-odd years of ploughing – and all the rest of the disturbance and souvenir-hunting of times past – would have left behind little in the way of metal artefacts. So by the time we unleashed our detectorists on the battlefield proper – the opposing slopes of Piper's Hill and Branxton Hill – we had all but persuaded ourselves they would turn up an assortment of broken tractor parts and the ubiquitous aluminium ring-pulls.

Can you imagine what it was like for us, then, when Terry – one of the detectorists who would prove, in the days to come, to be our secret weapon – called us over to see 'something you might be interested in'? Terry and two of his colleagues had been deployed on the north-facing slope of Branxton Hill, just below the buildings of Branxton Farm. It was here, we knew from our maps, that the Scottish artillery and infantry would have been arrayed in the late afternoon of 9 September.

Though somewhat smaller in size than a cricket ball, the weight of the thing amazed us!

A lead cannonball, probably fired from a Serpentine; typical of the light artillery used by the English at Flodden

John Arthur, our topographic surveyor, had earlier laid a series of twenty metre square grids across the hillside. The brightly clad trio had been carefully criss-crossing until every centimetre of ground had been swept by their detectors, each signal from their machines marked with a pin-flag.

Having covered the allotted ground, the team had begun the process of excavating each find. The 'something' Terry had just unearthed was an English lead cannonball. Though somewhat smaller in size than a cricket ball, the weight of the thing amazed us! As we passed it eagerly from hand to hand, the sensation was genuinely frightening. Vivid though written descriptions of artillery duels may be – the deafening roar of each discharge, the clouds of smoke, the shot humming through the rain and wind before finding its target – the words are far removed from the reality. And it is

exhilarating to be the first people to touch that cannonball since it was fired (and on top of that, to know when it was fired). It was last handled as dusk fell on 9 September 1513, by an English gunner who had, moments earlier, plucked it from a basket of ammunition. It was loaded and fired, possibly in the direction of an opposing Scottish gun, possibly towards a mass of Scottish pikemen standing in the driving rain on Branxton Hill and awaiting the order to advance. The English gunners were firing uphill that day. As their weapons were lighter and of a smaller bore than those arrayed against them, they could take advantage of the gradient and direct their roundshot so as to set each one skipping over the ground in a series of murderous arcs before making contact around waist height. The ball that we were now passing between us would have been capable, at this range, of passing virtually unmarked through the bodies of many Scotsmen standing in ranks on that hillside. Lightly scratched and scored, it appeared as though it had indeed hit the ground during its flight. Whether or not it had met its intended target – or targets – we could only guess.

This was incredible! We had all but convinced ourselves that five centuries would have been more than enough time for the site to have been picked clean of finds. But here, to our amazement, was one of the artefacts at the top of our list, and with it the beginning of the archaeological proof of historians' claims. Now we could begin to say, tentatively of course but with the confidence that comes only from physical evidence, 'Here stood the Scottish army.'

Tempering our excitement with the thought that one cannonball doth not a battlefield make, we allowed Terry and his mates to get back to work. Sure enough, later the same day they ticked off two more of the items we'd hoped to find if we were to have any credible hope of pinning down the location of the Scottish host. Within metres of where Terry found the cannonball, the detectorists turned up a metal button, green with age and about the size of a 1p piece. The simple design on its face seemed to have been inspired by buttons carved from horn or bone, and typical of the type associated with the garb of a medieval Scottish soldier. Further down the slope of Branxton Hill, the team recovered a small rectangular piece of iron about 3in x 2in. Unprepossessing to the untrained eye, it might easily have been overlooked: closer examination, however, revealed it for what it was – armour plating for the medieval version of the flak jacket. Called a jack, this was a quilted smock worn by the common foot-

soldier to protect his trunk and arms. Pieces of iron were sewn into each quilt 'square', providing a useful combination of protection and flexibility. The piece recovered by our detectorists would have fitted perfectly into the modern jack we had tried on during a 'weapons drill' we were put through by Andrew Robertshaw, a National Army Museum historian and the man tasked with identifying our more obscure finds. These armour pieces, said Andrew, routinely wore through their stitching and fell to the ground – perhaps that was what had happened to this one.

Here, then, were tell-tale finds just where we had hoped for evidence for the deployment of the Scottish army. Like the Scottish soldiers looking down upon the Englishmen on that fateful day, the detectorists on Branxton Hill could easily make out their colleagues working on Piper's Hill. There we hoped to find evidence of the most savage fighting, for we believed it to be the location where at least one of the Scottish pike formations had encountered boggy ground on the day and, fatally, lost both its cohesion and its momentum. Seizing their chance, the English bill-men had advanced upon this beleaguered horde.

Again – and beyond our expectations – the lads came up trumps. Among the first treasures to be revealed, towards the foot of Piper's Hill, was a lead ball about the size and weight of a musket-ball. The Scots had brought an unspecified number of primitive muskets known as 'arquebuses' or 'hackbuts' to Flodden. These 'hook-barrelled' weapons – the new-fangled gadgets of the day – were capable of punching lead shot clean through even the best sixteenth-century armour at a range of up to eighty metres. For archaeologists, context and location are everything, and

to find the right size of lead shot in such a location was enough to pump the adrenalin again.

Elsewhere on Piper's Hill, some of the finds were of a more personal nature: a delicately fashioned copper-alloy buckle, part of the fastening for a leather belt or a piece of armour; half of another buckle, also copper alloy, clearly stamped with a Tudor rose; two medieval coins, one silver and one bronze. These are items that always give us pause. While cannon- and musket-balls are the very stuff of the mass-produced, business end of war, buckles and armour and coins represent individual human beings. The buckle with the Tudor rose emblem may have been commissioned by a wealthy man with both the money and the commitment to display his allegiance to his king and country. The armour plate was almost certainly part of the kit of a common man, equipping himself as best he could for the horror of hand-to-hand combat. The coins were perhaps part of individual soldiers' pay, or money scraped together by a man summoned to render his forty days' military service owed each year to the king. Each was last in the possession of a man fighting for his life. Perhaps some of them lived to fight another day; perhaps not. Whatever the case, these humble items unearthed by the metal detectorists are the physical remains of that day. They are not just *from* the battle of Flodden: in a very real sense, they *are* the battle of Flodden.

Mass graves and body counts

Men died at Flodden in horrendous circumstances which people today can scarcely begin to imagine, even with Hollywood's graphic portrayals of battle. Some battles are best remembered for the sheer number of dead, and Flodden is undoubtedly one of them. The history books tell us that the bloodiest battle on British soil was Towton, fought during the Wars of the Roses between the houses of Lancaster and York on 29 March

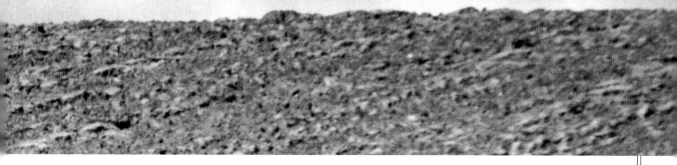

1461, and that between 22,000 and 28,000 men perished in vicious hand-to-hand fighting over the course of ten hours. Although the figures for Flodden are smaller, it is the scale of loss on the Scottish side for which the battle is best remembered.

The number of Scottish dead at Flodden quoted in English sources of the time varies between 10,000 and 17,000, while reported English losses are between 400 and 1,500. There is a case, though, for thinking that the losses on the Scottish side were exaggerated by contemporary English commentators – what better way to boost the importance of your victory than to play up the losses of your foe? A contemporary Scottish source, Buchanan, claims that 5,000 men never returned from the English campaign, a statement which implies that fewer than 5,000 Scots perished during the battle, as some of these fatalities would have occurred during other engagements, such as the various castle assaults. This is a considerable reduction, but if we accept that historical accounts can be biased, then what better way to play down a defeat than to minimize the losses suffered by your side?

The dead would have to have been buried somewhere. It is only in relatively recent times that soldiers killed in action have been afforded individual graves, the cemeteries of the First World War with their tens of thousands of headstones being the clearest example. In earlier times the usual method of burial was in mass graves, with the slain simply dropped into large pits without much in the way of pomp or ceremony. These graves were not usually marked with memorials, and so over time their locations have been lost.

Sometimes mass graves related to battles are unearthed by accident. The best-known in recent times was undoubtedly the discovery during building work of a pit containing the skeletons of around forty men killed at the battle of Towton. Studying these bones,

Armour fragment of Tudor rose

An arquebus ball

archaeologists came literally face to face with the brutal nature of medieval warfare, with many of the skulls and other parts of the body bearing the marks of terrible cutting and crushing injuries. Other than a single skull unearthed in a ploughed field, these are the only human remains known to have been uncovered from the battle of Towton, which does seem surprising given the supposed scale of loss.

Over the years Flodden has also given up some of its dead, even if only for fleeting moments. The first reported discovery was made in 1849, when St Paul's church at Branxton, just behind the English line, was largely rebuilt. The church was founded in the fourteenth century, and though local records suggest it was in a state of disrepair at the time of the battle, it is

not hard to imagine prayers being offered within its walls before and after the fighting. Being sacred ground, it would also have been an obvious burial place, and during the widening of the path through the churchyard a grave pit was uncovered. The then minister later wrote that the bones of both men and horses were observed, with several skulls 'heaped one on another'. The presence of horse bones has led historian Patrick Parsons to question whether these remains do indeed relate to the battle, as it would be highly unusual to bury horses in hallowed ground. The suggestion of disarticulated skulls stacked on top of one another is also interesting: does it mean that burial took place long after the battle when only skeletons were left to be buried, or are these the skulls of men decapitated during the course of the fighting? We may never know the answer to these questions through archaeological means, as the bones were covered over and rightly allowed to rest in peace.

A further discovery was made in 1918 when drains were being cut through fields near Piper's Hill. Andrew Rankin, the churchwarden at the time, stated that a grave pit was found in the fourth field west of the vicarage, at the foot of an eminence. It was said to have been several yards wide and contained the remains of men buried some three and a half feet below the surface. We have no idea how big this pit actually was, as we presume it was only disturbed along the line of the drain, and accordingly we have no idea how many skeletons it contained. Using modern geophysical techniques such as ground-penetrating radar, we hoped to relocate the site of this last grave in the vicinity of the memorial on Piper's Hill, which was built very soon after the discovery of the grave. Not only would the radar locate the grave, but it would also give us an idea of its overall size and, equipped with this information, we could estimate the number of men interred there. If casualties had been as great as suggested in some of the sources, a radar survey would help locate further graves in the area. Given the scale and unpleasant nature of the work of burial, especially several days after a battle, it seems unlikely that bodies would have been moved far from where the men fell.

The radar did its work, trundling across the ground with its wheels squeaking in protest. We looked at three areas, hoping that at least one of them would prove to be the site of a mass grave. Human bones were uncovered at two of these places when field drains were being cut in the nineteenth and early

Armour plate from inside a jack

twentieth centuries – these being the eastern edge of the field in which the monument stands, and a field further to the west. A third field, between the previous two, was also investigated, it being as likely a spot as any for a mass grave.

We were pleased when Jerry Hamer, our geophysicist, told us that the readings looked positive. The signals being bounced back to the receiver were showing underground disturbances not unlike those expected from a mass grave. We were pretty optimistic at this stage, having this state-of-the-art machine at our disposal and using it in places where we knew bones had been uncovered before. The computer print-outs lived up to Jerry's expectations and showed slices through the soil with distinct lines that looked like

through the soil with distinct lines that looked like the edges of large pits, which we thought might be graves.

There was only one thing to do: have a closer look and see if these radar anomalies really did add up to mass graves. We used a JCB over the areas which had produced the strongest radar signal. Its wide bucket was expertly wielded by the driver, Alan, and made short work of clearing back the soil in strips, with the spoil dumped at the sides of the trenches. Alan was a friendly chap who related that years ago, when he had been clearing drainage ditches not far from where we were, he had found an old sword. As he picked it up and realized what it was, it crumbled to dust in his hands. 'Oh, how we would love to find a sword,' we mused, as we watched another bucket of damp, sterile earth fall to the ground.

That was pretty much the way of it, really: bucket after bucket of soil scraped away, and no evidence of pits or graves – just clean, undisturbed subsoil. We were running out of time with nothing to show for it, while the trenches just got longer and longer. We wondered what the farmer, who had kindly given us permission to dig, would think if he looked out of his kitchen window to see his entire field piled up in one great mound of earth as we desperately searched for the graves of the Flodden dead.

There was one moment of relief, when we spotted a nicely shaped stone on the pile of excavated soil next to the trench. Once the dirt had been brushed off, it turned out to be a polished stone axe, a tool typical of the Neolithic period. It made up for an otherwise disappointing day. These tools were the equivalent of modern-day axes and are credited with clearing the great swathes of forests which covered Britain up until the beginning of the Neolithic period, around 5,500 years ago. This period saw a dramatic change in people's lifestyles: it was then that the wandering hunter-gatherers, such as those whose stone tools we discovered at Encampment Farm, settled down to grow crops and raise livestock.

Eventually we had to tell Alan to stop digging, because the trenches were far bigger than planned and there was still no sign of a mass grave. It was the same story in the other fields – nothing but gravel and sand, stones and field drains. At one point we narrowly missed breaking a water pipe with the JCB bucket. In frustration we started to question the accuracy of the radar survey, but after talking with Jerry it began to make sense after all.

Jerry explained that the radar sees differences in buried soil deposits. These may be caused by archaeological features such as pits or graves, but equally they may be caused by natural geological features. The point about the fields at the foot of Branxton Hill is that the soils are formed over geological layers deposited by water freed from the ice sheets at the end of the last Ice Age over 10,000 years ago. The ice melted to form streams and rivers, which carried with them sand and gravel that had been scraped up by the glaciers as they moved inexorably across the primeval landscape and, like giant bulldozers, reshaped valleys and carved mountains. The streams and rivers also scoured the earth, forming channels and gulleys, leaving behind the sand and gravel, which in time would fill up the stream beds and erosion channels until water could no longer flow through them. Geologists call such deposits fluvio-glacial – a succinct phrase for a mind-boggling process.

Our problem was that the radar, like an easily distracted sniffer dog, was picking up these channels and reading them pretty much like any other buried trench or hollow, including a mass grave. While this explained the radar readings, it didn't really dispel our surprise at not coming across a single grave – surely even chance was in our favour there? But the closest we got was a couple of sheep skeletons in the Piper's Hill field, where they had been buried by a farmer sometime over the past fifty years (the present farmer denied all knowledge when questioned about these deaths!).

'Oh, how we would love to find a sword,' we mused, as we watched another bucket of damp, sterile earth fall to the ground

battlefield area, but even so it raised the question of how many people were actually killed. Perhaps these negative results will add some weight to the arguments of historians who believe that the death toll, especially on the Scottish side, was much smaller than reported at the time.

Whatever the overall figures for Scottish losses, there can be no denying that one of the most striking features of the battle was the impact it had on Scotland's nobility. The roll-call of the dead resembles a gruesome version of 'The Twelve Days of Christmas' – not only was the Scottish king killed but also thirteen lords, twelve earls, two abbots, the Bishop of the Isles and the king's first son, the Archbishop of St Andrews. This scale of loss among the nobility is unsurpassed in medieval warfare. Patrick Parsons has recently suggested that this may have been because the battle was fought on foot. Traditionally, nobles and knights would have fought on horseback, and if things went badly for them they were often offered quarter and taken alive, thereby earning the captor a healthy profit when they were returned for a ransom. This process would be much more difficult if these men were on foot in the thick of the fighting, where, even when dressed in their finery, they would be much less visible and at greater risk than if they were on horseback.

The JCB had taken hours and hours and shifted tons of earth, but still there was nothing to show for it. If so many men had died during the battle and they had been buried close by, then surely we should have found at least some evidence of graves. It must take a lot of big holes to bury tens of thousands of bodies! Obviously, we may have missed the graves as we only had time to look at a relatively small proportion of the

WEAPONRY

HISTORIANS HAVE SPENT A GREAT DEAL OF TIME HOTLY DEBATING THE LIKELY SIZE OF THE TWO ARMIES THAT CLASHED AT FLODDEN. A SIMILAR, AND NO LESS HEATED, DISCUSSION HAS CENTRED ON THE SIZE AND NATURE OF THE HEAVY ARTILLERY DEPLOYED ON THAT FIELD – AND PARTICULARLY STRENUOUS EFFORTS HAVE BEEN MADE TO ESTABLISH EXACTLY WHAT HARDWARE THE SCOTTISH KING HAD TRAILED BEHIND HIM ON HIS MARCH SOUTH FROM EDINBURGH.

Mons Meg

These guns were an awesome assemblage – and it must have broken many a Scottish gunner's heart to abandon such treasure to enemy hands

THE SCOTTISH ARTILLERY

It's not difficult to see why the bulk of the available detail concerns the Scottish guns: contemporary and later accounts of the battle claim that, alongside thousands of their dead countrymen, the retreating Scots left behind all of their artillery. And what artillery! Thomas Ruthel, Bishop of Durham, described the Scottish artillery as 'the fairest and best that lately hath been seen', and he was well placed to judge, since his home at Norham Castle had fallen to James after a week of siege and bombardment in August 1513. Anyone reading the inventory of seventeen field pieces captured after the fighting can almost hear the satisfaction of the Englishmen detailed to compile the list of war booty!

They consisted of six 'culvering moyane' (serpentines); five 'great curtals' (cannons); four 'culverings pikmoyane' (sakers); and two 'gros culverings' (culverins).

These antiquated names all describe what the untrained modern eye would recognize as cannons of varying size and shape. The six culvering moyane, for instance, impressed the English Lord Admiral with their size and with the precision and skill of their makers. He noted that they were both larger and longer than anything Henry VIII had at his disposal. Any one of the curtals could hurl a cannonball weighing up to sixty pounds. Even the lesser culverins were loaded with twenty-pound balls. Taken together, these guns were an awesome assemblage – and it must have broken many a Scottish gunner's heart to abandon such treasure to enemy hands.

So far so clear, then? If the English salvaged seventeen Scottish guns from the bloodied field, where is the confusion and uncertainty? The problem is that some writers describe James leaving Edinburgh with rather more in the way of heavy guns than were recovered from Flodden – and also with different types and groups of hardware. Robert Lindsay of Pitscottie, writing more than fifty years after Flodden, credits James with as many as thirty pieces of heavy artillery. He also describes the now legendary set known as the 'Seven Sisters' – seven guns of equal size and shape – first mentioned in an inventory of the captured weapons written in London on 29 September.

ENGLISH ARTILLERY

The size and nature of the English guns at Flodden are not generally disputed. While historians speculate endlessly about the Scottish artillery, it is generally accepted that their opponents brought some twenty-three field guns. These are reliably described as consisting of eighteen 'fawcons' and five serpentines. It also seems clear that these guns were lighter – and perhaps more manoeuvrable – than those ranged against them.

In any event, taken together the Scottish and English artillery add up to more than forty pieces. Thus Flodden Field witnessed one of the greatest distributions of heavy guns of the period – a presence so notable, in fact, that its like was not to be seen again until the civil war in the middle of the seventeenth century.

HAND FIREARMS

Also available to the Scottish soldiers at Flodden were an uncertain number of 'arquebuses' or 'hackbuts', a primitive form of weapon fired from the waist or the shoulder like a musket. These weapons were extremely cumbersome, and the absence of any detailed reference to their use during the battle suggests that their impact on the field was relatively slight.

A FINAL BOW

Proof, if proof were needed, of the beautiful and deadly efficiency of the longbow lay for centuries in the silt and mud offshore from the port of

Southampton. Here amid the wreck of the *Mary Rose,* the pride of Henry VIII's fleet and a marvel of the age, lay a huge armoury of longbow shafts and arrows. What is remarkable here – perhaps even more remarkable than the state of preservation that marine archaeologists found when they raised the hulk in 1982 – is the evidence for the continued respect accorded to this most elegant of weapons. The *Mary Rose* sank in 1545 with the death of hundreds of seamen and the loss of one of the most fearsome war machines of its day. One of the first warships capable of firing a broadside, it was armed to the teeth with cannon of various sizes. And yet it is clear from the 137 bows and over 3,500 arrows salvaged from the wreck that the longbow was still a valued weapon more than thirty years after the last battle in which it was to play a significant part. In the hands of a skilled archer the bow was lethal at a range of 200 yards and capable of a rate of fire of ten shots a minute. By the time of Culloden, two centuries after the loss of the *Mary Rose*, a fully trained redcoat was doing well to lay down three rounds a minute from his Brown Bess musket – and with nothing like the same accuracy over the same distance.

In conjunction with the intermittent fire of roundshot from the guns, the English bowmen at Flodden had played no small part in harrying the Scottish centre to a standstill well before it could press home with its pikes. As the century progressed, however, greater emphasis would be placed on artillery and the development of hand-held firearms, and the days when the skies above a battlefield would darken with the deadly rain of thousands of arrows would become a thing of the past.

THE PIKE AND THE BILL

'The bills disappointed the Scots of their long spears, on which they relied . . . they could not resist the bills that lighted so thick and so sore upon them' – so wrote Thomas Ruthal, Bishop of Durham, on 20 September 1513. Despite all the complexities and uncertainties of Flodden, the big picture is clear enough: in the main, the matter was settled by the success of the English bill over the Scottish pike.

Money and heavy artillery were not the only things that James accepted from his 'auld ally' France as he prepared for war. Louis XII also dispatched forty captains and fifty men-at-arms from his own army – schooled, among other things, in the effective use of the iron-pointed pike. From the last quarter of the fifteenth century the law of the land in Scotland had demanded that all pikes imported or made there had to be at least eighteen feet long, after the fashion of the long pikes that had

In the hands of a skilled archer the bow was lethal at a range of 200 yards and capable of a rate of fire of ten shots a minute

Andy Robertshaw
shows us a replica of a
Scottish pike

been successfully in use in the Low Countries since the twelfth century. The Swiss and the Landsknechts (the 'country lads') of Germany had scored famous victories armed with such weapons, and it seems James was quite captivated by their potential.

The Swiss – a poor people often in conflict with their richer, horse-riding Austrian neighbours – turned their minds to ways in which a man could stand effectively before a galloping horse. They found it in history and in the stories of the Macedonian phalanx in ancient Greece – great squares of men armed with long spears held in front of them with both hands and running full tilt at their enemies. Provided that close formation and momentum were maintained, even cavalry were powerless in the face of such a charge. For the Scots, this tactic must have seemed like a natural progression from their own static schiltrons – formed in the same way by spearmen and used to devastating effect at Bannockburn in 1314.

But while the trick of the schiltron was to stand still and to hold . . . and hold . . . and hold in the face of hundreds of tons of horse-flesh bearing down at twenty-odd miles per hour, the crucial element of the phalanx was movement. And not just movement, but movement in choreographed perfection – shoulder to shoulder with your neighbours. If this integrity was maintained, all in the group might stay alive. But if it broke down and gaps began to appear in the line, then individual members of the phalanx might quickly find they were but single spines of that porcupine, alone on the field – and about as safe.

Our examination of the terrain has shown that Branxton Hill at its western end, down which the left flank of the Scottish army charged, is more gentle than the slope further to the east. This gentle slope breaks on to fairly level ground, thus allowing an ordered charge which maintained momentum – hence the success of Home's Borderers and Huntly's Gordon Highlanders in their charge against the English right. However, on the steeper slope to the east it would have been far more difficult to maintain a disciplined advance. To make things even worse, the ground at the foot of the hill was marshy here, and once across this mire the Scots did not face level ground but had to climb up Piper's Hill before they could close with the English. Not surprisingly, it is here in the Scottish centre that the phalanxes came apart. As men pushed forward, stumbling over comrades felled by arrows or roundshot, the vital cohesion of those formations began to break down. By the time they reached the English lines and sought to ram through the wall of waiting men, the crucial momentum had been lost.

Neil holding a replica of an English bill

Even where the phalanxes held together – and James's force is said to have driven Surrey's men backwards by some 300 yards – the Scots were to be punished for the second weakness of the pike. The English were armed with the bill, or halberd, an eight-foot-long shaft topped with a vicious combined axe and spear-head. Where those Englishmen held their nerve – and the line – all they had to do was wait until the enemy formation broke and then use their bills to disarm individual pikemen simply by cutting off the end of their pikes. Once a pikeman had been compelled to drop his useless remnant and draw his sword, he faced a sea of bill-wielding Englishmen. As soon as the advantage of the pike was lost – and here the phalanx is revealed as a one-trick pony – there was no fall-back position. James himself was armed with a pike and apparently impaled at least five men upon its point before he too succumbed to the almost inevitable efficiency of the bills arrayed in front of him.

In this regard, if no other, Flodden is a simple story. James employed a tactic perfected on the continent, and imported experts for the purpose, but failed to allow enough time for his men to practise the new technique. As if that wasn't enough, the massed ranks of his enemy were armed with one of the few potential antidotes to the pike – the bill. Combined with the sloping terrain and the pouring wet weather that so bedevilled the whole campaign, James's primary tactic almost appears doomed before the outset.

Once a pikeman had been compelled to drop his useless remnant and draw his sword, he faced a sea of bill-wielding Englishmen

1513

Neil as a Scottish pikeman
Tony as an English billman

THE AFTERMATH

LOSS ON SUCH A SCALE — COUPLED
WITH THE DEATH OF THE KING —
CAUSED PANDEMONIUM IN SCOTLAND.
THE IMPACT OF FLODDEN WAS FELT SO
KEENLY NORTH OF THE BORDER
BECAUSE THE DEATH TOLL WAS SO
GREAT AMONG THE GENTRY AND THE
ARISTOCRACY. THERE WAS HARDLY A
NOBLE FAMILY IN THE LAND THAT HAD
NOT LOST ONE OR MORE OF ITS SCIONS
AT FLODDEN. MORE THAN ONE LOST
ALL OF ITS MENFOLK. JAMES'S BODY
LAY UNBURIED IN SHEEN MONASTERY
FOR YEARS TO COME.

In Edinburgh, building work began on the Flodden Wall. Part of a panic-stricken defensive strategy, it was never actually needed, because England did not in fact invade Scotland during that period. Over twenty-three feet high and five feet wide, the wall was erected in a remarkably short space of time – albeit by highly motivated teams of volunteers. The now-famous Edinburgh Old Town Guard was formed at the same time – twenty-four good men tasked with keeping watch for invaders while the building work went on around the clock. When it was finished, the wall completely enclosed an area about one mile long by a quarter of a mile wide, and for the next two centuries hardly a building was erected outside it. The Castle, the High Street, the Grassmarket and the Cowgate, among others, were all within the confines of the barrier. Left with no room for outward expansion, the city architects turned their attention to exploiting the only direction open to them: upwards – up to thirteen storeys high. The site of the World's End Gate in the Flodden Wall – beyond which lay undefended territory and 'the end of the world' – is marked today by the World's End pub.

In the event, the English didn't attack, as Surrey's second-string army was worn out and had already achieved so much more than could have been expected of it. In Scotland, James IV's widow, 'English' Margaret Tudor, was appointed regent for their infant son. Crowned as James V, he would not be of an age to take up personal rule until 1528. Even without invasion, Scottish self-confidence had still taken severe punishment and would not properly recover for the rest of the sixteenth century. The loss of James IV was the loss of much of which the country had been proud. Easily the most popular and successful of all the Stuart monarchs, he keenly understood the importance of positioning Scotland as a part of Europe and not just England's poor northern relation. By the time of his death, aged forty, he had given the nation a sense of itself that would be a long time returning after such a disastrous defeat. Among much else, he had made the palaces of Holyroodhouse and Linlithgow into national treasures and had personally busied himself with the studies of the age. He can fairly be remembered as a Renaissance prince.

That bold gesture by Henry VII in 1502 – giving his daughter in marriage to the House of Stuart – had set in motion a train of events that would result in much more blood-letting in the future. It led to the accession to the English throne of the Stuart King James VI of Scotland as James I of England, and thereby laid the foundations for the Civil War in the seventeenth century, and for Jacobitism and its desperate intrigues, follies and bloody climax on Culloden Moor.

Edinburgh, showing North Bridge and the Castle

Archaeological Techniques: Field Survey

ONE of the most basic but no less important techniques used by the archaeologist is field survey. No archaeologist would dream of excavating a site before obtaining a detailed map or plan of the area in which he or she will be working. Ideally, this will show all the features, ancient and modern, visible on the ground, and allows the findings of the excavation to be tied into the landscape around the trenches. But not all archaeological fieldwork involves excavation, and survey can be a very useful tool in its own right, enabling us to understand the distribution of archaeological sites across the landscape.

Perhaps the simplest type of survey is the walkover, used to find sites that may previously have been unknown. We tend to think of archaeological sites being buried, with no visible trace left on the surface of the ground. But as the gun emplacement on Flodden Hill proved, archaeology can be visible, and in some cases it reveals quite dramatic remains. Think of standing stones, burial cairns, old field boundaries or, more up to date, abandoned railways. We found the gun emplacement simply by walking through the woods and looking for suspicious lumps and bumps in the ground, changes of topography which told us that the ground had been altered by human hand. In essence, this is what walkover survey is, just walking and looking. It is something that anybody with an eye for the land can do.

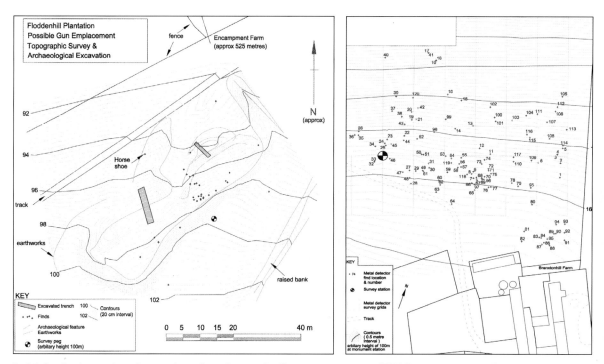

Left **John Arthur using the total station electronic distance measurer (EDM) to survey the site**

Above **Topographical survey maps generated by the EDM results**

Once a walkover has identified a site, we may then wish to carry out a more detailed survey. This is usually called a topographic survey, and is what we did at the gun emplacement: we created a detailed contour map of the banks and hollows in order to understand better the size and shape of the earthwork.

Not long ago the instrument most commonly used was a theodolite, which is essentially a telescope mounted on a protractor. Using the basic principles of measuring angle and distance, the theodolite can place any point in the landscape within a three-dimensional framework. Reading after reading is taken and marked using a staff like a very tall ruler, so a map is built up, and differences in height from one point to another allow the surveyor to add contours, just as you see on an Ordnance Survey map. These contours show changes in slope and gradient, as can be seen on the plan of the gun emplacement (above).

Technology has speeded things up though, and today the theodolite has been replaced by the electronic distance measurer. This clever device uses a laser fired at a prism to instantly measure angle and distance. Readings are logged in an onboard data-logger and then transferred to a computer. Software packages specially designed for the job convert these readings into a detailed plan which can be printed out to any scale. We used one of these instruments to survey our gun emplacement. ❀

Conclusion

IT is often the simple strategies – those that provide the simple answers – that are overlooked. Down the centuries, historians have wondered and debated about whether or not James fortified the natural defences of Flodden Hill. As part of their consideration of James's tactics, one historian after another has considered the possibility that he turned the hill into a fortress. Yet, amazingly, no one had taken the time to check the ground itself – to see what, if anything, survived. No one, that is, until us!

After all that speculation, we succeeded in settling this contentious issue just by taking a walk in the woods and using our eyes. Obviously, this initial discovery was followed up with the full suite of appropriate archaeological techniques – but the initial breakthrough was the work of the human eye. There is an old cliché that dismisses archaeology as the handmaiden of history. We would argue that questions like 'Did James make a fortress of Flodden Hill?' can be answered only by archaeology.

Fortress Flodden – for that is surely what it was – must have been quite a sight for the English soldiers who beheld it. Approached from any direction it would

have completely dominated the landscape – vast numbers of tents, banners flying, smoke from hundreds of cooking fires, and all of this surrounded and defended by freshly constructed ditches and banks bristling with some of the finest artillery of the age.

And so what does this tell us about James and his Flodden campaign? Clearly it was a campaign characterized by caution. Traditional historical accounts of the battle depict him as rash and impetuous. But while these adjectives may describe the last decisions he was ever to make, they hardly fit a man who took the time to build and defend his own fortress in a foreign land.

For all that the fortress was an impregnable stronghold, it must have become a millstone around his neck before the end. The very strength of his position made him steadfast in his refusal to meet the English on the Milfield Basin. Yet had James accepted Surrey's offer of a battle there, his pikemen would have deployed over precisely the terrain best suited to the phalanxes. It could all have been so different.

Instead, secure in his fort, he left the English with no realistic hope of fighting him there. So it was James's own actions that forced Surrey to make the greatest and most audacious tactical decision of his long career. The English had the initiative and James could do nothing but wait on the hill behind his defences and see if Surrey could out-think him. And out-think James is precisely what Surrey did: by outflanking James – and making him fear he was in danger of being cut off from his own country – he winkled him out of his protective shell. When James finally gave battle, it was in the wrong place and with the wrong weapons for the terrain.

Our simple strategies cast rather less light,

however, on the enduring myth of Flodden that thousands of Scots died on that field. To begin with, we must beware the hyperbole of contemporary chroniclers with political agendas. The only 'eyewitness' accounts of the slaughter were penned by Englishmen, and all bear testimony to vast numbers of dead Scotsmen. More intriguingly, much is also made of the kind of men who died – most notably the nobility and the clergy. Since their armour – the sort only rich men could afford – offered protection to the poorer-clad common men behind them, they were fated to fight at the front and so died in disproportionate numbers.

Even injecting a bit of reality into the higher estimates, the tenor of the historical accounts still conjures up a picture of carnage. Burying thousands of dead bodies was a massive task, requiring huge pits which common sense suggests would have been dug close to where the bodies lay. The thick of the fighting was contained in a relatively small area, in the low ground at the foot of Branxton Hill and Piper's Hill, and so logic dictates those mass graves must be in that vicinity. Farmers in the area have also reported finds of 'human' bone over the years, and these sites too conform to those parts of the field where graves would be expected.

What we did not expect – and what is almost inexplicable – is our failure to find so much as a single human bone. We happily admit that it would be easy to miss some of the graves – given the limited time available – but our strategy allowed for a thorough examination of three of the most likely spots. These areas were subjected to survey by sophisticated radar techniques and large areas of ground were stripped and checked. The absolute absence of remains, then, makes us begin to question the traditionally accepted scale of loss.

Could it be that the armies were smaller than has been widely reported and the death toll, therefore, lower? Could it also be that the large number of fatalities among the nobility and the clergy encouraged people to suppose that a proportionately high number of common soldiers must have died too? And in any event, it is surely to be expected that the accounts – written by victors conscious of their place in history – deliberately exaggerated the Scottish death toll to magnify the impact of the English success.

Absence of evidence, as the saying goes, is not evidence of absence. But the absolute absence of *any* human remains (or even of large pits dug to accommodate remains long since decayed) must force us to question whether it was the calibre of the dead, rather than the quantity, that led to a mythic death toll. It was, after all, the pride of a generation – the flowers of the forest – who were cut down at the battle of Flodden.

NEWARK 1642-6

NEWARK

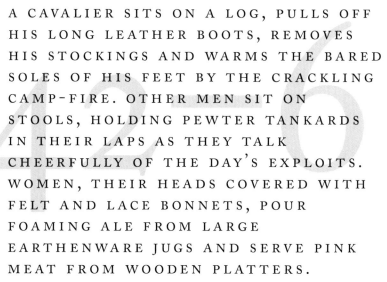

A CAVALIER SITS ON A LOG, PULLS OFF HIS LONG LEATHER BOOTS, REMOVES HIS STOCKINGS AND WARMS THE BARED SOLES OF HIS FEET BY THE CRACKLING CAMP-FIRE. OTHER MEN SIT ON STOOLS, HOLDING PEWTER TANKARDS IN THEIR LAPS AS THEY TALK CHEERFULLY OF THE DAY'S EXPLOITS. WOMEN, THEIR HEADS COVERED WITH FELT AND LACE BONNETS, POUR FOAMING ALE FROM LARGE EARTHENWARE JUGS AND SERVE PINK MEAT FROM WOODEN PLATTERS.

A musketeer

A musketeer lovingly oils and polishes the lock of his firearm and uses a ramrod to remove powder residue from inside the barrel. From close by comes the sound of a mandolin, its jaunty, paired-string notes prompting one or two children to dance. It is a peaceful scene, but earlier that day it had been very different.

The afternoon had started bright and blue, but the sun was quickly choked off by the clouds of black powder belched from muskets and cannon alike. Regiments of pikemen, Royalist and Roundhead, moved across the field, their weapons raised high. More musket shots clattered out, flames erupting first from the pan as the match was applied and then from the muzzle. Men fell in the face of this murderous fusillade but the tightly knotted masses of infantry continued to advance towards one another. The two armies closed, and the wooden shafts of the long pikes crashed together. Officers cried 'Push!' to urge on their men. Musketeers, their last shots fired, held their weapons by the barrel and, using them like clubs, swung them at the enemy. Swords flashed and the odd pistol shot rang out, but by then it was mostly down to the brute force of pike against pike. Feet were driven hard into the ground as push came to shove and the scrum developed into a desperate struggle for supremacy. Men staggered from the press, clutching wounds as they stumbled to the ground.

To the rear, banners and flags fluttered gently in the breeze, their brightly coloured fabrics adorned with regimental insignia. The Royalist commanders sat on horseback, their broad-brimmed hats trimmed with feathers and their chests striped with sashes of crimson silk. 'Well goes the day, sir!' exclaimed one bearded general to another, as they observed the forward progress of pikes doing good service for the king. 'Drive into them, men!' cried another. 'Show these rebel scum how a Royal army fights.'

But it was by no means a one-sided battle. With their chests covered in steel plate and their heads protected by lobster-tailed helmets the Roundhead cavalry harried the Royalist infantry. They hacked at foot-soldiers with their swords and used their pistols to shoot down pikemen they could not hope to get close to. Many fell and their bodies littered the field. Here and there women, their dresses spattered with blood, tended the wounded or wept over the dead while the battle raged on around them.

Let us return to the present, however. The battle has been won and lost. The Cavalier, his feet warmed, pulls his boots back on and cocks his ear to listen to the music. But now there is something else, a repetitive and insistent sound that jars with the melody. He reaches for a leather bag and pulls out a small black object. Holding it to his ear, he says, 'Hello, Jim here – sorry, had the phone switched off all day for the re-enactment. Wouldn't look too good if the thing rang half-way through the battle, would it!' he laughs.

This scene could have been played out at any number of events around the country during the summer months, where re-enactors stage mock battles for tourists. More than any other conflict, it is the English Civil War which draws people to participate and watch. These weekend

A Roundhead on horseback

With their chests covered in steel plate and their heads protected by lobster-tailed helmets the Roundhead cavalry harried the Royalist infantry

wars, with their colourfully costumed armies and casualties who pick themselves up to fight again, may give the impression that the war was a somewhat genteel affair, but in fact nothing could be further from the truth.

BACKGROUND

MORE THAN ANY OTHER TYPE OF CONFLICT, A CIVIL WAR STRIKES A DEEP CHORD WITHIN THE HEARTS OF A PEOPLE. THE WORDS CONJURE IMAGES OF BROTHER FIGHTING BROTHER AND FATHER FIGHTING SON. IT IS AN UNCOMFORTABLE CONCEPT THAT SUBVERTS HIGH-HANDED IDEAS OF A JUST WAR PROSECUTED BY ONE NATION AGAINST ANOTHER. IF THIS WERE NOT ENOUGH, THE ENGLISH CIVIL WAR ALSO BROUGHT THE EXECUTIONER'S AXE DOWN ON THE SACRED PERSON OF THE KING OF ENGLAND.

That said, why is the English Civil War different from any of the previous wars that raged over the British Isles, many of which were fought between the inhabitants of these islands? Certainly, the wars between the Scots and the English, and the English and the Welsh, are an exception, as all three countries were then distinct nations. But the Wars of the Roses were undoubtedly fought as a drawn-out civil war.

One reason why the English Civil War differs from these earlier conflicts is that it was not about one claim to the throne pitched against another. The struggle shook the very foundations of the monarchy and brought to an end the idea that the king or queen had a God-given right to rule as an autocrat. This was the first time on such a scale that the institution of Parliament, on behalf of the common man, stood up for its rights. Today, when the monarch is seen by most people as little more than a tourist attraction, it is hard to imagine a time when the head of state had absolute power over his people; a divine right inherited from his medieval predecessors. Parliament was there to express the views of a broader constituency, but the king had the final say on any decision and, furthermore, it only sat when he ordered it to – usually when he wanted to extract more money from his subjects. He also had the power to dissolve it whenever he saw fit.

The crisis that would lead to war began in 1641 when a rebellion broke out in Ireland and Charles I wanted to raise an army to put it down (there was no standing army in England at that time and indeed the first professional army was founded as a result of the Civil War). Parliament was unhappy about this as it felt that the king would use the army to enforce his will on his English subjects. As a result of the ensuing row, Charles dissolved Parliament and thereby set in train the bloody events that would bring about his own execution and the temporary abolition of the monarchy.

But as ever with history, nothing is simple. Even the term English Civil War is misleading as there were in fact three civil wars, and these involved Scotland as much as they did England. On top of all this, most people could be forgiven for thinking that the execution of King Charles I in January 1649 marked the end of the conflict. In fact the third civil war was fought after his death and 1650 saw a failed attempt by the future King Charles II to reinstate the monarchy through an army raised in Scotland.

Nor was it a simple case of the common man standing up for his rights against a power-crazed king. There was also a religious motivation, with Protestants fearing that a Stuart king might choose to

Opposite **Charles I**

The struggle shook the very foundations of the monarchy and brought to an end the idea that the king or queen had a God-given right to rule as an autocrat

**Charles I's failed coup against
Parliament in 1642**

promote Catholicism as the nation's faith of choice. And just like any war there was good, old-fashioned self-interest, with the rich and powerful on both sides seeking to ensure that any move they might make on the social scale was up rather than down. It should not be forgotten either that Members of Parliament represented the wealthier elements of society: they were not elected by common ballot as they are today. To an extent it could also be seen in terms of a regional conflict, with the north and west, initially at least, mostly supporting the king and the south and east backing Parliament.

The Parliament summoned by Charles to raise taxes for the 1641 Irish rebellion – the so-called Long Parliament – instead seized the opportunity to tackle the very notion of the monarch's rule. Enemies of the king were freed from prison. A death warrant for Thomas Wentworth, the Earl of Strafford, who had murmured to the king that an

Irish army willing to assert his Royal prerogative over Parliament awaited his orders, was prepared and, after great anguish, Charles signed the document. The Long Parliament pressed ahead, further shackling the king and, significantly, limiting his ability to raise cash. Painfully aware of the erosion of his position, in January 1642 Charles tried one last time to bend Parliament to his will with an outburst of bluff and bluster. Barging his way into the House of Commons with a troop of armed soldiers, he sought to arrest those MPs he considered to be the core of opposition to his Royal will. The stunt failed – his enemies had been tipped off and fled – and Charles had no option but to appeal to his subjects directly and urge them to ignore Parliament's rulings.

Parliament, however, held its nerve. Members of a more conservative bent – who retained a fundamental loyalty to the notion of monarchy if not necessarily to the monarch himself – distanced themselves from those pursuing a more radical stance opposed to Charles and all that he stood for, and sided with the king for the sake of maintaining the status quo. London was left firmly in the hands of a Parliament determined to take sovereign power into its own hands, and Charles and his supporters fled towards the north of the country. As far as Charles at least was concerned, this was intended merely as a temporary measure – with a view to regrouping and returning to crush what was shaping up into a full-blown rebellion. Initially he based himself at York but it was at Nottingham on 22 August that he raised his standard and called upon

his supporters – nobility and commoners alike – to rally to his side. Still there prevailed in the minds of many on both sides of the divide a desperate hope that none of this would lead to war. None the less, Charles set about raising an army in the time-honoured fashion, by issuing 'Commissions of array' demanding the military service of his subjects. Parliament too began drawing together an armed force ready to enforce its will.

However, years of peace on the British mainland meant the country was woefully lacking in men practised in the arts of war. Only the few who had offered themselves as mercenaries in the continental wars had any notion of how a modern conflict should be fought, and it was literally a handful of such men on either side who provided the slender backbones about which the hastily assembled armies were formed.

As for equipment, in the early stages of the war it was Parliament that controlled the principal sources of supplies, the main arsenals and the national fleet of ships. Charles, on the other hand, was beholden to the personal wealth of those nobles who backed his stance. Entire personal fortunes were offered up to equip and finance Royalist regiments, generating debts that Charles would never be in a position to repay.

1642–6

**William Cavendish, first Earl
of Newcastle**

Newark Castle

In every part of England, preparations were under way as each side assessed its position and dug in where it felt strong. There would be a war in the north, in the centre and in the west – and significant events would unfold simultaneously and independently in all three areas. In the north, the strategic significance of Nottinghamshire and, specifically, the town of Newark, was recognized by both sides from the very beginning. Newark sat at the junction of three crucially important lines of communication: the river Trent; the Roman road linking the east of the country to the west and known as the Fosse Way; and the Great North Road, connecting York and the capital. While Nottingham fell into Parliamentarian hands, Newark would remain stoutly Royalist for the entire war.

Charles's forces in the north were commanded by the first Earl of Newcastle, William Cavendish. With the importance of Newark in mind, he ordered the veteran soldier Sir John Henderson to make the town secure. As was the case with all of England's principal towns at the beginning of the war, Newark's defences were hopelessly outmoded. Its population had long since expanded beyond the confines of its medieval walls and its ancient castle – in which King John, unwilling signatory of

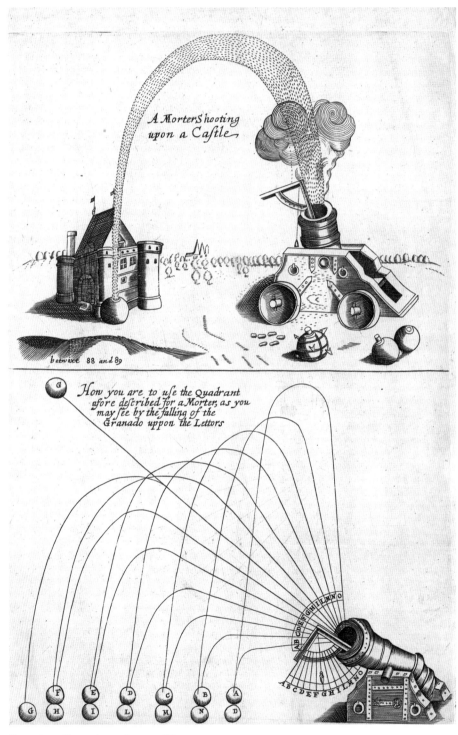

A Morter Shooting upon a Castle

betwixt 88 and 89

How you are to use the Quadrant afore described for a Morter, as you may see by the falling of the Granado uppon the Lettors

Seventeenth-century siege artillery

**Picture from a seventeenth-
century training manual showing
how to sight siege guns**

the Magna Carta, had breathed his last – offered scant protection from
the modern artillery likely to be brought to bear upon it. Henderson's
understanding of this prompted him to adopt a continental strategy. It is
believed he was helped by the Dutch engineer Bernard de Gomme (who
had come to England with Prince Rupert of the Rhine, Charles's
charismatic and influential nephew) and that together they set about the
business of modernizing the town's medieval defences. While stone
offered no real protection against modern guns, long, low and extremely
thick banks of earth certainly did – and a combined workforce of
garrison and townsfolk hastily constructed earthen banks and ditches
around Newark's perimeter.

Both the garrison and the defences were to be tested by three sieges:
the first siege of Newark hardly warrants the name, since it lasted barely
two days in Februrary 1643 before the Parliamentarians were driven off;
the second – from 29 February to 21 March 1644 – was more like the
real thing. The town was finally relieved when a Royalist force of more
than 6,000 mounted men and foot-soldiers led by Prince Rupert scored a
spectacular victory over a similar number of besiegers at the battle of
Newark. The defeated Parliamentarians were compelled to abandon
valuable muskets, ammunition and artillery, including the famous Sweet
Lips, a massive cannon sharing its name with a Hull prostitute, the
weapon's hometown.

Queen's Sconce from the air

The town was now commanded by Governor John Byron, a local man and an experienced and capable soldier. With Rupert and his forces gone to harry Parliamentarian forces elsewhere, Byron was all too aware that Newark remained vulnerable, and it was during this period that some of its most famous siegeworks were built, including the Queen's Sconce – a reference to Charles's wife, Henrietta Maria – that survives today as a truly awe-inspiring feat of engineering. More than three acres in area, the fort's banks still rear up to a height of some ten metres above its ditches, which are themselves up to twenty-five metres wide.

As the war wore on around the country, Newark held firm. Disastrous defeats for the Royalist cause at Marston Moor in 1644 and Naseby in 1645 might have been expected to weaken the town's resolve. Instead, it became a rallying point for those elements of the northern armies still able to mobilize themselves. In October 1645 Sir Richard Willys, who had replaced Byron as governor in the aftermath of the second siege, was himself removed from command after Charles had visited the town to bolster support there and found Willys living high on the hog and at odds with the local military commanders. Despite protests from Prince Rupert, a friend of Willys, the king replaced him with the hard-bitten veteran Lord John Belasyse, who had fought bravely at the battles of Edgehill and Naseby.

All too well aware that Newark was now but an island of Royalist resolve in a rising Parliamentarian tide, Belasyse dug in. He established a mint to counter the shortage of cash and galvanized the garrison and the townsfolk into one final, monumental round of defensive engineering. By the time the third and final siege of Newark began in November 1645, the defenders had created 'such deep graffs, bastions, horns, half-moons, counterscarps, redoubts and pitfalls and an impregnable line of sod and turf palisade and stockaded and every fort so furnished with great guns and cannons that this bulky bulwark of Newark represented to the besiegers but one entire sconce'.

It was not a moment too soon. In late November, a 7,000-strong army of Parliamentarian Scots under General Alexander Leslie, first Earl of Leven, moved to the town's northern and eastern fringes, while 9,000 more under General Sydenham Poyntz, commander of the northern Parliamentarian forces, occupied the south and east. The stage was set for a classic confrontation of an unstoppable force against an immovable object.

General Sydenham Poyntz

THE BATTLE

NEWARK'S DOUGHTY POPULACE –
TOWNSFOLK AND GARRISON TOGETHER
– WAS LIKE A STAG AT BAY. TRUE,
THERE WAS NOWHERE TO RUN – NO
HOPE OF ESCAPE OR RESCUE – BUT
STILL ITS HEAD WAS DOWN AND ITS
DEADLY ANTLERS HELD POISED TO
SPEAR ANY OF THE WOLVES THAT
MIGHT MAKE A LUNGE FOR ITS THROAT.
NOW TIME BECAME ITS ENEMY TOO:
HOW LONG COULD IT REMAIN ON ITS
FEET? HOW LONG COULD IT STAY
ALERT?

The first wound to cause real distress was the bloody lunge at the small Royalist garrison of Shelford Manor, which made clear the murderous intent of the predators. The soldiers at Shelford were commanded by Philip Stanhope, whose father, the Earl of Chesterfield, owned the pile. Poyntz had earlier offered Stanhope terms for surrender, but the gesture was flung back in his face. Far from surrendering, Stanhope and his men had promised to lay the Parliamentarian-held Nottingham Castle 'as flat as a pancake'. And so it was that on the morning of 3 November Poyntz's mighty force approached Shelford village itself, where they encountered a handful of Royalist soldiers secure in the church tower and suffered the indignity of being fired upon by the few muskets there. The defenders had pulled up the ladder and the bell ropes and refused all demands to come down, even when threatened with death. Bales of straw were piled at the base of the tower and set alight, and the smoke finally forced them down. Among their number were a woman corporal and a small boy, and under threats from his captors the lad declared that he knew a weak spot in the defences of the manor itself and that he would show the attackers the way.

Armed with this crucial intelligence, the Parliamentarians turned their attentions towards the garrison itself – fewer than 200 men – but found there was still much to be done to break the defenders' resolve. A massive bulwark faced the attackers, and as they battled grimly to fill the ditch in front of it with bundles of timber they came under bitter musket fire from the soldiers manning the palisade. Struggling forward to climb it, they found their ladders were too short – and the Royalist soldiers galled them further by throwing down logs that cracked bones and swept the assailants back into the ditch. A brutal fire-fight ensued until finally the defenders were driven back and the Parliamentarian soldiers broke through into the interior of the compound and attacked the manor house and its outbuildings. The fighting was hand to hand now and the Royalists defended grimly, but the attackers pushed in for the kill. Stanhope, according to the victors' account, was found cowering in an upstairs bedroom of the manor house and dragged downstairs. Beaten to within an inch of his life, he was flung naked on to a dunghill within the compound. Just how bloody the final moments were remains uncertain, for while Parliamentarian sources would later claim that quarter was given and around 140 prisoners taken alive, Royalist reports of the aftermath spoke darkly of far fewer survivors.

That night, the sky above Shelford was lit up by the burning manor house. Some would later say that the local folk, tired of the excesses of

A massive bulwark faced the attackers, and as they battled grimly to fill the ditch in front of it with bundles of timber they came under bitter musket fire from the soldiers manning the palisade

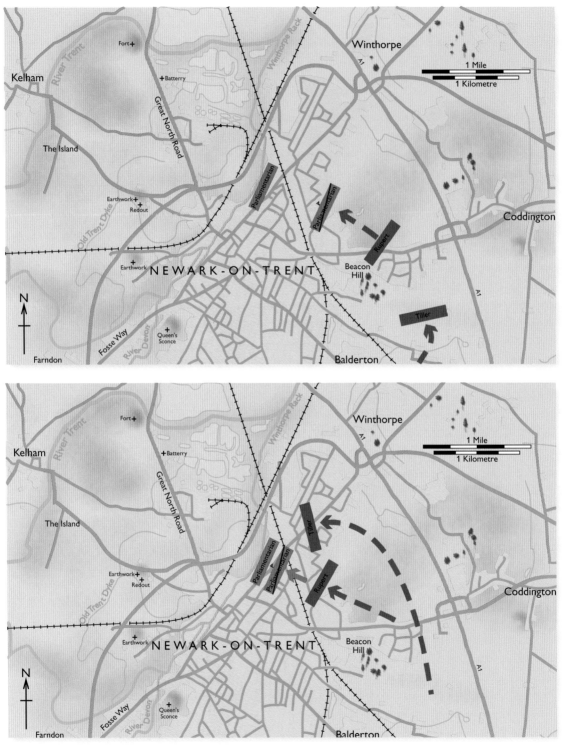

Movement of troops during the battle of Newark superimposed on a modern map

the garrison that had manned the place for so long, put it to the torch themselves to ensure that no occupying army would trouble them further. The burning of Shelford lit a fire under King Charles too. Having been in Newark since October, the sharp treatment dealt out to his garrison at the manor persuaded him that the place was now, quite literally, too hot for him. Taking a bodyguard of mounted men, he abandoned the town that had been the proudest symbol of his defiance of Parliament and made for his headquarters at Oxford. The following day, the Parliamentarians advanced upon the nearby Royalist garrison at Wiverton Hall, but the soldiers there backed down without a fight. First blood to the Parliamentarians then, but the campaign was far from over.

Safe behind their bastions and banks and ditches, their palisades and stockades – and with their artillery trained upon every possible line of attack – the town of Newark was enduring a bitter winter as best it could. Sweet Lips may have been in her element among the soldiers barracked there, but the living was certainly hard. Though the autumn's harvest had been stored away, the good folk of Newark would be eating their horses before the end. Still, they had fire enough in their bellies to gall their tormentors.

General Poyntz must have grown heartily sick of the place as 1645 gave way to 1646 and still it refused to yield. The Scots held the northern and western approaches, while Poyntz himself had the south and east, but he was not sufficiently in control to make the siege really bite. In January a Royalist force of 800 mounted men and 300 infantry swept out of the town for a raid so daring and audacious that it almost defied belief. In a classic guerrilla movement, they advanced on Poyntz's own base at the nearby village of East Stoke. Having taken scores of prisoners, apparently with little effort or cost to themselves, the cocky Royalist band made straight for Poyntz's own living quarters – and failed to take him prisoner by no more than a whisker.

Perhaps this was the last straw for the Parliamentarian commander. In any case, he now set to with a will and steadily erected a cordon around the town: a massive 'line of circumvallation' – banks and ditches – had cut off the south and east of the town by March, and to the north and west the Scots were reinforcing their hold with a massive encampment they called Edinburgh. But still the defenders took the fight to the besiegers: while the Scots were still at work a Royalist force attacked them and narrowly failed to drive them away from the town altogether.

This was among the last of the offensive manoeuvres, however, and

In January a Royalist force of 800 mounted men and 300 infantry swept out of the town for a raid so daring and audacious that it almost defied belief

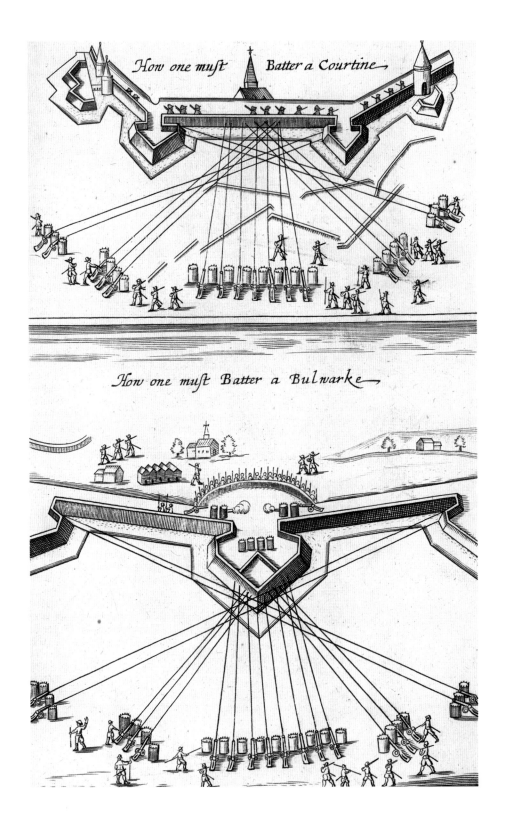

as winter gave way to spring, Newark was struck by plague. How long could it hold on? With his line of circumvallation in place, Poyntz ordered his sappers to tunnel towards the Royalist lines. At the end of March, with the sappers within a pistol shot of the defenders, Poyntz called upon Belasyse to surrender the town. The governor asked that he be permitted to find out the king's response to the command, but this request was turned down flat. In fact, information was still passing into and out of the town by means of spies moving between the lines. One vital nugget of information came to Belasyse via the belly of a Royalist, encased in a lump of lead!

Newark was now a stinking, pestilential place – its plight made all the more insanitary by Poyntz's order that the river Trent be dammed and diverted. On 27 April Belasyse sent men to Poyntz's headquarters to discuss terms of surrender, and on the same day Charles left Oxford and travelled to the outskirts of the town. The king was not quite ready to give up his crown, however, and he initially hoped to exploit divisions between the Scots and English forces. Offering himself to the Scots, he hoped to persuade them to turn against his English foes. But it was not to be. They quickly disabused him of the belief that he was anything more than a prisoner and told him that he must order the surrender of Newark.

On receiving word of the king's order, Belasyse is said to have wept, believing that the town could yet hold out. The mayor too has gone down in local legend as having urged Belasyse to 'trust in God and sally forth'. But there was no last, noble charge. The surrender of Newark, which had held out for so long against all that war and pestilence could bring to bear, was formalized by a signature at midnight on 6 May 1646.

Newark was now a stinking, pestilential place

WHO FOUGHT HERE

MANY AND VARIED ARE THE WARS THAT
FIRE THE IMAGINATIONS OF MODERN
MEN AND WOMEN. AT VARIOUS TIMES
THROUGHOUT THE YEAR, THE HILLS –
AND MOST CERTAINLY THE FLATLANDS
– ARE QUITE LITERALLY ALIVE WITH
THE SIGHT AND SOUND OF BATTLE:
GLEAMING, ARMOURED ROMANS;
HORDES OF BEARDED, MARAUDING
VIKINGS; PLAID-WEARING, HOWLING
HIGHLANDERS; SERRIED RANKS OF
REDCOATS – ALL CONTINUE TO COLOUR
OUR LANDSCAPE WITH FAITHFUL RE-
CREATIONS OF THEIR HEROES' BEST
AND WORST ENDEAVOURS.

CAVALIERS AND ROUNDHEADS

Where the warriors of old left off, the re-enactors gamely continue in their clubs and societies, accurately re-creating the weapons, kit, tactics and lifestyles of our military past.

Kings of all such clubs – in terms of member numbers, at least – are those that re-enact the battles of the English Civil War. It is the practices of these men and women (and even their children) that have informed our generation's ideas about foppish, dashing, Cavaliers and aggressive, humourless Roundheads (their distinctive bowl-shaped hairstyles comically predating the Beatle-cut by more than 300 years). The story goes that when the king's soldiers first appeared before the London mob they were ridiculed for their similarity to the Spanish king's *caballeros*. This became in time 'Cavaliers', and the Royalists hit back by laughing at the short hairstyles of their Puritan foes – hence 'Roundheads'.

But in fact there were more visual similarities than differences between the opposing factions. The bulk of the fighting men depended upon clothing supplied to them – increasingly as the war dragged on and individuals' own gear simply wore out. Reds and blues would have been common on both sides, given that it's simpler and cheaper to dye

Oliver Cromwell

with primary colours; buff and undyed woollens would have been widespread too, for the same reasons of ease and economy.

Re-enactors are naturally drawn to the more eye-catching elements of historical garb. This as much as anything else has fixed our image of the Cavalier with his signature plumed and wide-brimmed hat. In truth, however, these were expensive items and would have been worn in the field only by officers and wealthy men – but on both sides.

THE NEW MODEL ARMY

The English Civil War wrought huge changes upon the whole ethos of soldiery in the British Isles. The first battle – at Edgehill, in October 1642 – was fought, in the main, by armies hastily assembled from among the civilian population. Such had always been the way of things on this side of the Channel, with monarchs and lords with war on their minds having first to recruit the bulk of their forces from the largely untrained and barely armed common men. Gathered together only in times of need – often by opponents of the monarch rather than the monarch himself – these ad hoc armies were of dubious quality and usually composed of men more interested in going home than into battle. Furthermore, there have always been men and women who are driven to fight by passion, politics or belief. The English Civil War was certainly no exception and there were many whose personal convictions drove them willingly to one or the other.

By the time of the decisive battle of Naseby, in June 1645, however, the Parliamentarian cause was being fought by a full-time army of soldiers paid for by taxation. This was the so-called New Model Army, raised at the insistence of Oliver Cromwell, who understood that part-time warriors were often unreliable and rarely well-motivated.

The notion of a standing army was one thing, its creation quite another. Existing Parliamentarian regiments formed the foundations of the new force, but all had been depleted to a greater or a lesser extent by the prosecution of the war so far. Topping up the numbers meant recruiting in a manner little different to that practised by monarchs and their lords through the centuries. Each county under Parliamentarian control was ordered to provide a quota of men – pressed into service if necessary – and desertions and plain no-shows were considerable as a result, so the fledgling New Model Army that took the field in 1645 was a little light in numbers and, we can be sure, contained several disgruntled and unwilling recruits. Not the most glorious of beginnings perhaps, but from these foundations was to grow the first professional army the country had ever produced.

Neil wearing armour of the period

A standing army needs standardized equipment as part of the glue that holds it together as a unified force, and this requirement swiftly generated a whole industry. The truth that there's money to be made from manufacturing the tools of war was understood just as clearly in the seventeenth century as today. The clothing, weapons and the rest of the kit required by a professional army – made to order to the exacting standards of military uniformity – were being commissioned and consumed on a grand scale. Talking of uniformity, it was in the development of the New Model Army that the genesis of our modern idea of different sides identifying themselves in 'team colours' is to be found.

Armour and weapons of the period

We must not overlook how revolutionary the creation of this first standing army was. It is in Cromwell's desire for a professional and fully trained force that we find the seeds of war as a full-time job. Whereas armies in the past had lasted only as long as the war of the moment before melting back into the fields and villages and towns, the New Model Army was here to stay. This was a machine that would never again be turned off and would, as a result, steadily consume men and materials. It would occupy its recruits, furthermore, with a lifetime of (mostly poorly) paid employment. It was the foundation of the red-coated army that would in time make indelible marks around the world.

WEAPONRY

The main weapons of the English Civil War were the musket and the pike. At the start of the conflict muskets were largely of the matchlock variety: muzzle-loading, they depended for ignition upon a length of slow-burning matchcord soaked in saltpetre. Herein lay the main handicap for the musketeer: having first poured powder into the barrel from one of the containers strung around his shoulder on a bandolier, popped in the ball, then the wadding – pushing each item home with a

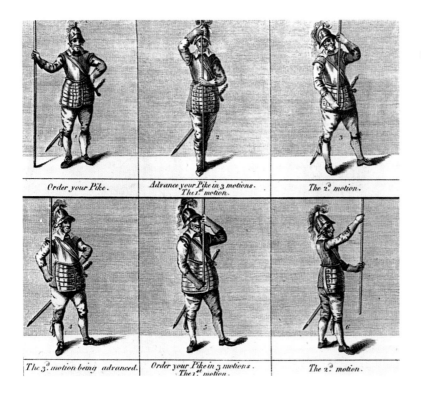

Order your Pike. | Advance your Pike in 3 motions. The 1st motion. | The 2d motion.

The 3d motion being advanced. | Order your Pike in 3 motions. The 1st motion. | The 2d motion.

Old English pike exercises

ramrod – and primed the pan with powder, he was dependent upon the matchcord for the firing. This was used in two-foot lengths cut from a coil and had to be kept alight at both ends in wind and rain. Even if it stayed lit, it might sputter and spark, igniting the powder in the pan and setting off the weapon prematurely. To make matters worse, the constantly burning cord was an early warning for enemies waiting in the dark – and night-time surprise raids were somewhat handicapped by the presence of hundreds of little orange lights bobbing among the otherwise invisible host!

Oliver Cromwell was among those commanders who recognized the advantages of a newer type, the so-called firelock musket, which employed a simple trigger mechanism to make a flint spark against a steel plate in order to ignite the powder in the firing pan. More familiarly known to us as a flintlock, it had clear advantages over the matchlock: no more worries about the cord going out and no more fear of a smouldering end igniting the powder in the bandolier or in the barrels that were often close by. Preferable though it may have been, however, the majority of musketeers in the English Civil War relied not on the flintlock, but on the matchlock.

The main weapons of the English Civil War were the musket and the pike

A pair of flintlock pistols

Simplicity is often the reason for the extremely long life of a weapons system, and this was never truer than in the case of the pike. The pike formation used by infantry in the medieval and later periods was the natural descendant of the phalanx of the ancient Macedonians, and often just as effective. The weapon of the mid-seventeenth-century pikeman ranged in length from twelve to eighteen feet. He fought in formation, supported by musketeers, and was heavily armoured with a ridged helmet, breast- and back-plates, a steel gorget to protect the throat, and tassets to cover the thighs. In order to carry the weight of all that armour, the pikeman was usually selected from among the brawniest stock available. As well as the pike, with its steel head and extending languets reinforcing the shaft to prevent its head being lopped off, he carried a short sword. As if his trials weren't great enough – encumbered by more metalwork than the average ironmonger's shop – bright sparks among the contemporary military intelligence conspired to make his lot even harder. For a time, some pikemen were additionally equipped with longbows or even muskets.

CAVALRY

The mounted horsemen must surely have been the glamour boys of both sides in the Civil War. Elevated above the workmanlike toils of the infantrymen, cavalry produced the kind of shock tactics that only tons of galloping horseflesh can provide.

The flintlock was more common among the mounted men as the matchlock was all but unusable from the unstable platform of a

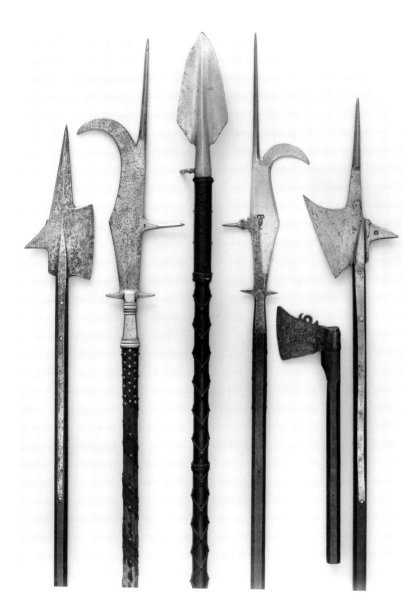

Left **Various steel pikes**
Above **An Ironside**

galloping horse. Fully armed, a Civil War cavalryman was equipped with a carbine (short-barrel) musket, a pair of pistols and a sword. Lancers were still in use among the Scottish regiments – they were used to great effect by Scottish Parliamentarians at the battle of Marston Moor – but were generally out of favour. Armour too was on the wane – or at least under review – for mounted men. Famously, Cromwell's Ironsides wore breast- and back-plates on horseback and there are mocking references

in the sources to Lobsters – the cuirassiers, a minority who wore full (and, by this time, largely obsolete) armour.

As the war progressed, cavalrymen increasingly dispensed with metal armour in favour of a sleeveless jacket with a skirt made of toughened ox hide (the description 'buff' comes not from the dull yellow colour of such leather but from its original source of supply – buffalo hide). Such a garment was some defence against sword and missile and had the virtue of offering much greater mobility in the saddle.

Horse-riding and horse-owning are now – and were then – more associated with the moneyed classes than the mass of the population. Since large sections of the former group sided with Charles, cavalry was more strongly represented in the Royalist camp, particularly in the early stages of the war. Mounted men were deployed by both sides, however, and with varying effectiveness. Animals trained for the noise of battle were by no means the only beasts on the field, and a cavalry charge propelled in part by horses more familiar with the farm than the fight would often go on for miles – long after the initial shock of the thrust had passed. While they galloped on – perhaps in pursuit of those they had routed, perhaps not – the infantrymen they had left behind would often have time to re-form and rejoin the fighting.

Glamorous and impressive they may have appeared, but the cavalry of the English Civil War were most assuredly a mixed bunch, their effectiveness often watered down by lack of discipline. But as Cromwell demonstrated at Marston Moor, well-deployed and well-organized cavalry could change the course of a battle.

A cavalryman

King Charles I of England in Cavalier dress

THE AFTERMATH

NEWARK WAS NOT PUT TO THE TORCH
FOLLOWING ITS SURRENDER, NEITHER
WERE ITS PEOPLE PUNISHED NOR THEIR
HOMES AND GOODS CONFISCATED. THE
SOLDIERS WHO HAD OCCUPIED THE
TOWN DURING THE LONG MONTHS OF
SIEGE WERE PERMITTED TO LEAVE
WITH THEIR MUSKETS, AMMUNITION
AND HORSES. THEIR HEAVY GUNS,
HOWEVER, WERE SURRENDERED, SWEET
LIPS PASSING FROM ROYALIST HANDS
TO PARLIAMENTARIAN. THOSE WHO
WISHED TO STAY IN NEWARK WERE
PERMITTED TO DO SO ON THE STRICT
UNDERSTANDING THAT THEY WOULD DO
NOTHING MORE IN SUPPORT OF THE
KING'S CAUSE.

On 8 May 1646 Governor Belasyse led out his army for the last time, and they were replaced by local people summoned by a Parliamentarian order that they should swiftly set about dismantling the town's defences. The Parliamentarian force, however, did not stay long enough to ensure that the job was completed – and who could blame them for wanting to quit that plague-stricken place? The result was that they left the most spectacularly well-preserved set of siege works to be found anywhere in the country.

The end of the siege of Newark did not quite bring the end of the war. Charles's erstwhile headquarters at Oxford held on without him until the end of June, and the king spent the rest of 1646 and the first months of 1647 being passed around the country like an unwanted birthday present before finally being dropped from the peace negotiations altogether.

Oliver Cromwell continued his rise to dominance, but with the defeat of the king came an increasing perception, even by Parliamentarians, that he regarded the New Model Army as his own private bodyguard. By now regarded by many as a dictator, Cromwell went to war again in 1648 when the king escaped and formed an alliance with the Scots. The second Civil War came to an end on 19 August 1648, when the New Model Army defeated the Scots at the battle of Preston. The king was recaptured and, fearful that there would be no peace while he lived, Cromwell's Parliament sentenced him to death. The execution took place at Whitehall on 30 January 1649. The unbelievable had happened: the king put to death, the monarchy abolished and a republic declared.

Charles's head had barely been severed from his body when his son returned from exile in France to be proclaimed King Charles II, in Edinburgh in February 1649, though Cromwell was too busy conducting a brutal campaign against Catholics in Ireland to take much notice. In June 1650 the third and final English Civil War broke out, and on 4 September Charles and his Scottish allies were defeated by Cromwell and his New Model Army at Dunbar. Charles crossed the border and moved south. But as Charles Edward Stuart was to find in 1745, support in name does not necessarily result in large numbers of English recruits, and his advance to London was stemmed at Worcester, where the final battle of the war was fought on 3 September 1651. Charles fled to France and Cromwell was pronounced Lord Protector – some would say king by any other name.

Cromwell died at Whitehall on 3 September 1658 and the pomp and circumstance surrounding his funeral was almost regal. His life-size

Cromwell was pronounced Lord Protector – some would say king by any other name

At the High Cort of Justice for the tryinge and iudginge of Charles Steuart Kinge of England January xxix Anno Dm 1648./

Whereas Charles Steuart Kinge of England is and standeth convicted attaynted and condemned of high Treason and other high Crymes And sentence uppon Saturday last was pronounced against him by this Cort to be putt to death by the severinge of his head from his body Of which sentence execution yet remayneth to be done. These are therefore to will and require you to see the said sentence executed In the open Streete before Whitehall uppon the morrow being the Thirtieth Day of this instant moneth of January Betweene the houres of Tenn in the morninge and fyve in the afternoone of the same day with full effect And for soe doing this shall be yor sufficient warrant And these are to require All Officers and Souldiers and other the good people of this Nation of England to be assistinge unto you in this service Given under our hands and Seales.

To Collonell Francis Hacker Colonell Symonds and Lievtenant Colonell Phayre and to every of them.

Jo: Bradshawe
Tho: Grey
O Cromwell
Edw: Whalley

M. Livesey
John Okey
J Danvers
Jo. Bourchier
H Ireton
Tho. Mauleverer

John Blakiston
J Hutchinson
Willi Goffe
Tho: Pride
Pe: Temple
T Harrison
J Hewson

Hen: Smyth
Per: Pelham
Ri: Deane
Robert Tichborne
H Edwardes
Daniel Blagrave
Owen Rowe
Willm Purefoy
Ad: Scrope
James Temple

Henry Marten
Vint: Potter
Wm: Constable
Rich Ingoldesby
Will: Cawley
Jo Barkstead
Isaa Ewer
John Dixwell
Valentine Wauton

Sir Hardres Waller
Edm: Ludlowe

Tho: Horton
J Jones
John Browne
Gilbt Millington
G Fleetwood
J Alured
Robt Lilburne
Will Say
Anth Stapley
Gre: Norton
Tho: Challoner

Symon Mayne
Tho: Wogan
John Venn
Gregory Clement
Jo: Downes
Tho Wayte
Tho. Scot
Jo: Carew
Miles Corbet

effigy was displayed in Somerset House, and his body was laid to rest in Westminster Abbey. But not for long.

The monarchy, under Charles II, was restored in 1660 and the king wanted revenge for the death of his father. In a bizarre act supported by Parliament, the bodies of Cromwell and several other prominent Parliamentarians were exhumed and taken to Tyburn, where the corpses were hung and then beheaded. Thus Cromwell met a similar fate to that doled out under his supervision to the unfortunate Charles I. The last resting-place of Cromwell's headless body is unknown, although some believe that it was buried on the battlefield at Naseby, the site of his final victory over the forces of Charles I. For several years his head was to be seen adorning the roof of Westminster Hall till one day it was blown down in a storm, and from there it passed through various owners over the years, sharing a fate not too dissimilar to the head of James IV of Scotland after the battle of Flodden, and was only finally laid to rest in 1960, when it was buried near the chapel of his *alma mater*, Sidney Sussex College, Cambridge.

Execution of King Charles I at Whitehall, 30 January 1649

Above Charles I's death warrant
Below A mortuary sword decorated with a pikeman holding a pike

the dig

AN obvious difference between a siege and a battle is time. In a battle two armies meet face to face and do their best to destroy one another, all of which may take just a couple of hours – that's certainly the case for most of the battles discussed in this book. But in a siege one army settles down behind the walls of a castle, town or city while the other sets up camp outside and waits for the defenders to come out and fight, starve to death or surrender – a wait that may take weeks, months, even years. The first siege of Newark lasted just a couple of days and is barely worthy of the name; the second siege was a bit more like it, at three weeks; and the third siege lasted a very respectable six months.

A siege is essentially a war of attrition, and as such may lack the obvious dynamism and drama of a battle, although the siege itself may involve numerous skirmishes and even full-scale battles (as with Newark). However, for the archaeologist the siege has one great advantage: this more sedentary type of conflict means that a much broader spectrum of activities are taking place and hence more evidence should be left behind. The attackers build siege works and, denied the luxury of fixed accommodation, have to build their own camps, which themselves may be surrounded by fortifications. The besieged have to construct defences to keep the attackers out. All these activities should leave physical traces behind. Well, that's the theory!

Newark, one of many towns besieged during the English Civil War, has a particularly fine collection of monuments related to the conflict, most of which are protected as scheduled ancient monuments. The most famous of these is the star-shaped fort known as the Queen's Sconce, a Royalist defensive work built outside the town. This impressive structure, with its deep outer ditch, high banks and artillery bastions, is recognized as the best-preserved Civil War earthwork in Britain. Not

all of Newark's earthworks have borne the test of time so well: to the north was a fort very similar to the Queen's Sconce, known as the King's Sconce, but this was later buried under a boiler-works as the town expanded in the late nineteenth and early twentieth centuries. Many other sites have also fallen victim to later development, including Colonel Gray's Sconce, which was built by the Parliamentarian besiegers as protection for a bridge over the Trent but was unfortunately destroyed by the construction of a sewage treatment plan in the 1960s. But it hasn't all been the fault of modern development: many of the defences were dismantled after the town's surrender.

It is largely thanks to two maps (see overleaf), drawn up at the time of the siege, that we have any idea of the scale and appearance of many earthworks that have long since disappeared. The best-known of the maps was drawn up by the Parliamentarian surveyor, Clampe; the Royalist map is less detailed, probably because the map-maker was largely confined to the town. Both maps show the main defensive work was a bank and ditch thrown up around the town, which by this time had outgrown its medieval walls. The besiegers' response to this was to encircle the entire town and its defensive works with a barrier of their own, known as the circumvallation, designed not only to prevent the Royalists from getting out but just as importantly to prevent a relieving force from getting in. Most of these earthworks were dismantled by the local population, although small fragments do survive today,

Clampe's map

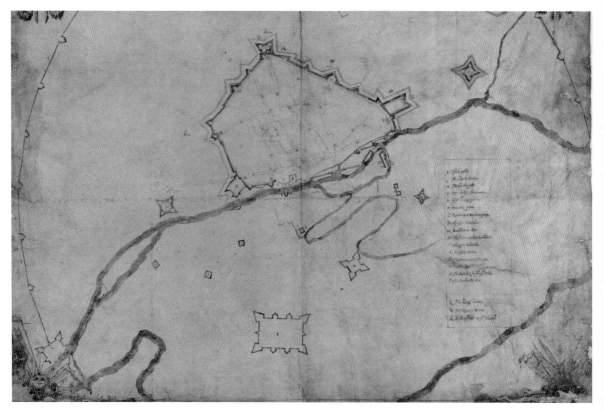

Royalist siege map

and it was here that we hoped our archaeological survey techniques would help us rediscover them. But first we paid a visit to Shelford Manor, the Royalist stronghold and scene of a vicious fight as the Parliamentarians advanced on Newark in preparation for the third and final siege.

Beneath the barricades: digging the defences of Shelford Manor

Shelford Manor, lying some ten miles to the south-west of Newark, grew up out of the ruins of a priory and was the family seat of the Earl of Chesterfield, a Royalist supporter. Occupying a tactically important position next to the river Trent, together with Wiverton Hall and other sites it provided a strong outpost to Newark. The manor house itself remained reasonably unmolested during the first and second sieges, but as the Parliamentarians advanced on the town to commence the third siege they were determined to eradicate this nest of Royalists for once and for all.

Shelford was garrisoned by just under 200 men, under the command of Colonel Philip Stanhope, the fifth son of the earl, and the manor itself had been heavily fortified in 1643, with ramparts and palisades thrown up behind the moat. Despite the barricades and the bravery of the soldiers behind them, there was little they could do in the face of the overwhelming force of Poyntz and his army. After two days' fierce fighting the defences were stormed and the entire garrison was put to the sword. Not surprisingly, Wiverton Hall, on hearing the news of Shelford's fate, surrendered soon after without putting up a fight. But if the slaughter at

Shelford was also meant to put the frighteners on the population of Newark, it didn't work, and Poyntz had to wait another six months before he could consider his job done.

Shelford Manor has had a colourful history and is no stranger to archaeologists. The house was once the home of Lord Carnarvon, who became famous not only for his discovery of the tomb of Tutankhamun in Egypt, but also, so the story goes, for the curse which his disturbance of the tomb unleashed. We had never given much thought to the story of King Tut's curse. Not, that is, until the van carrying our surveying team to Newark was hit by another car, killing our good friend and project geophysicist Jerry Hamer. We all miss him. But we still don't believe in the curse, nor does Jerry's girlfriend, Lorna, who very bravely went on to do the work that Jerry never got the chance to do.

Both topographic and geophysical surveys were carried out at Shelford. The topographic survey, which examined the shape of the ground itself, revealed a number of striking features. In a field just to the north of the house we came across a long, wide, grass-covered bank, parallel to the road that runs past the western side of the house. The bank went on to join a low knoll, which we could tell from the survey plan had a definite curve to it. The knoll itself sat behind a shallow ditch, which ran across the next field from east to west. Following the ditch across the road and into the woods next to the river, we found better-preserved sections of what must have been the moat which had surrounded the Manor. We followed the moat through the woods, where in places it still had water in it, back across the road and along the front of the house to the south. The moat disappeared under modern farm buildings on the east side of the house and could not be traced through the field beyond the farm buildings, although a pond in that field may be a medieval fish pond once fed by the moat.

After we had traced the course of the moat around three sides of the house, we realized that the long bank which ran parallel to, but quite a distance behind, the moat on the west side of the house could be part of the rampart which had been constructed by the Royalist garrison in 1643. This made the curving knoll at the northern end of the bank a good candidate for a half-moon battery, behind which cannons would have been positioned.

Now we knew what the surface of the ground looked like, we started the geophysical survey, which would allow us to see under the ground. Lorna concentrated on the field with the bank running through it, using both the gradiometer and resistivity rig to cover every inch. Geophysics results are usually fairly abstract affairs, with a splodge here and a faint line there, and need to be deciphered by an expert like Lorna or Iain. But even to duffers like us, the results from Shelford were clear to see. The plotted data showed straight lines with right angles – rectangles and squares. There were buildings under the ground!

We could make out several buildings, scattered across the field. As we studied the data we wondered whether these were part of the priory or later buildings related to the manor at the time of the battle. One of the structures ran beneath the bank and so was more likely to be an earlier building, as its remains had been buried under the rampart. Another building was visible to the east, on the other side of the field.

We used the geophysics results to locate our

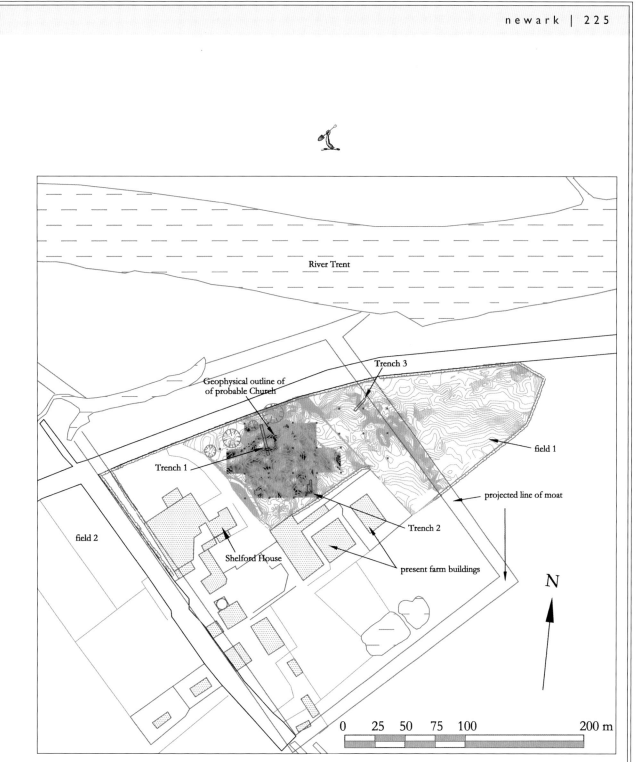

River Trent

Trench 3

Geophysical outline of
of probable Church

Trench 1

field 1

projected line of moat

field 2

Trench 2

Shelford House

present farm buildings

N

0   25   50   75   100   200 m

Map showing the geophysical plots and trench locations at Shelford Manor

Recording a trench at Shelford Manor

trenches carefully. We placed one excavation trench over the bank, cutting through its entire width from east to west, and also passing over the building as it ran under the eastern edge of the bank. The second trench was placed over the other building, again running from one side to the other. We scraped off the turf and topsoil from both trenches using a JCB, as usual inspecting the bucket for archaeology underneath its steel lip.

Our first surprise came with the trench over the bank. We had expected the bank to be formed from soil, but beneath the grass and topsoil we came across a tightly packed layer of bricks and stone. They were old bricks, hand-made, quite thin, and lacking the stamps that mark out more modern types. It looked as though the rampart was largely made from brick, probably collected from ruined or demolished buildings, which had been heaped up with stone and earth. Today, the rampart survives only as a low, wide bank, but at the

time of the battle it must have been much higher. The account by Lucy Hutchinson, the wife of Colonel Hutchinson, the commander of the Parliamentarian troops who stormed the manor, tells us that the ramparts were so high that the attackers had to use dumped bails of sticks and ladders to get over the rampart wall. This task was made all the harder by the defenders who swept the enemy from their ladders by throwing logs down on top of them. The present condition of the rampart is no doubt a result of the deliberate levelling of the defences after the battle.

Before we could more fully understand the construction of the rampart, we first had to extend the excavation down through part of it. We did this at the eastern end of the trench, where the geophysics had shown a buried building. We cut down through the bricks, which was pretty hard work, and underneath we came across a thin, sterile layer of soil, below which we hit something quite different. There was a hard surface beneath the soil, in places formed by flat, carved stone and in others by poured mortar. On this surface, which at first looked like a floor, we found pieces of dark, almost black, glass. But this was no ordinary glass: it had been decorated with curved lines applied in red paint, and the edge of one shard had been shaped into a curve by a skilled craftsman with a special tool – these were pieces of a stained-glass window. We found more evidence of these windows, in the form of lead strips, which held the pieces of glass together, and stone mullions, the upright columns from multi-arched windows. Stained-glass windows were not just for decoration in churches, they served an educational function too. Few people in medieval society were literate, and so the Church realized that stained-glass

The tiled floor of the priory church at Shelford Manor

windows were an ideal vehicle for instilling the basics of Christian belief and illustrating the scriptures.

But did the stained glass mean we had found a church? The priory would certainly have had a church at its centre, but stained glass may have been used in other types of building, such as the refectory, where the monks would have taken their meals. We needed more evidence, and indeed the surface we had first thought to be a floor was shaping up into something quite different. The feature was now looking more like a buttress, a heavy rib protruding from the outside face of the wall. Buttresses had two functions: they strengthened high walls such as those in a church, and they also gave buildings an air of grandeur. We re-examined the geophysics plot, and now we could identify what looked like buttresses protruding from the corners and faces of the building, which itself now appeared to have a cruciform shape.

There was more to come. As we worked back from the buttress, carefully trowelling away the earth which covered the remains of the building, we came across the line of a former wall which had been

Trench running through the defensive rampart at Shelford Manor

deliberately removed, and beyond this what was definitely a floor. How could we be sure it was a floor? Because it was covered by the most beautiful set of glazed tiles! The ceramic squares were orange, red and yellow. Some were plain, others were highly patterned with designs of rampant lions and flowers, for example. We consulted an expert about the tiles and discovered that they were probably of local manufacture and of a type found on a number of religious sites in the Midlands. We were most excited to discover that they were probably made in the early thirteenth century, which might link them to the foundation of the priory. Surely, this was yet further proof that we had indeed found the site of the church.

We were all excited by the church, and agreed that

here was some of the best archaeology we had ever worked on. So carried away were we that it took some discipline to return to the much scrappier pile of rubble that lay over the spectacular ruins of the church. We joked that most archaeologists would have dug straight through the rubble just to get to the church. But it was really the pile of old bricks that we were after – this was our rampart.

Our topographic survey had shown us that the moat on the west side of the house ran north to south through the woods. Although the moat ran parallel to the rampart, it was quite a distance away and so would not make sense as part of the defences. With this in mind we set out to find a ditch closer to the outside of the rampart, possibly running along its base. As the rampart had been dismantled and its remains spread over a wide area, we thought the best place to look would be under the rubble. Our excavation through this part of the rampart was interrupted by the discovery of bones, but our initial excitement subsided when we realized that we were dealing with the skeleton of a dog which had been buried in the top of the rampart remains. Unfortunately we ran out of time before we could prove whether or not there was a ditch underneath the rubble. We think what may have happened is that the medieval priory moat was integrated into the defences as much as possible, but the area it encompassed would have been too large for the small garrison to defend and would have required the construction of great lengths of rampart. Hence the defences were pulled back some distance behind the western side of the moat and a new ditch was cut.

But where did all the brick come from? It certainly didn't come from the church. The layer of soil separating the rampart from the church underneath it indicated that the remains of the church were at least partially buried by the time the rampart was built, and anyway the church was built of stone, not brick. We thought we might find answers in our other trench.

From priory to manor – the second trench

Removal of the turf and topsoil in the second trench exposed two parallel stone walls belonging to what looked like a long building. The outer face of the eastern wall was angled at the base, like the buttress had been in the other trench. But the inner part of the wall was filled with rubble and was a lot rougher, possibly part of a later modification to the building. We also found part

of a doorway and to one side of it the base of a column, which would have supported an arch. The other side of the doorway lay under the edge of the trench, so we had little idea about its width. The outside edge of this wall had been partially buried beneath a layer of hard-packed gravel and sand, which again pointed to a later phase of building use, perhaps as part of the farmyard connected to the manor house.

The inside of the building was mostly covered with earth, but along the inside of the eastern wall was a small paved area composed of flat stones and a broken roof tile. Again, we thought this could be evidence of later use of an earlier building. Digging down through the earth inside the building, we found broken tiles, much plainer than those from the first trench, which might have formed part of the floor. We also came across crumbled fragments of red-painted plaster that had covered the original walls.

All the evidence from the second trench pointed to quite an elaborate building that had fallen on hard times and been reused for more basic purposes later on. The original building had well-made stone walls, painted

The skeleton of a dog buried in the remains of the rampart

Helen composes her memoirs!

plaster walls on the inside and an ornate doorway. We also found fragments of glass, window mullions and lead, but the glass was plainer than that from the first trench, as were the fragments of floor tiles. This was undoubtedly part of the priory – maybe the chapter house or even the refectory, as oyster shells and animal bones were recovered from the deposits. After the dissolution of religious houses by Henry VIII in the mid sixteenth century the priory was abandoned and some buildings may have been demolished to provide building material for the manor house – this seems likely in the case of the church. Other parts of the priory may have been reused as outbuildings for the manor house, such as a stable or animal byre.

We found very little brick from the second trench, so the building we unearthed there did not appear to have been the source of the bricks used for the rampart. On the other hand, we should not overlook the fact that all we really encountered were the foundations. Later walls may indeed have been constructed of brick, and all trace of these may have been removed when the bricks were taken away to build the rampart.

Out in the fields – the metal-detector survey

The excavation at Shelford had surpassed all our expectations. We had uncovered evidence of the rampart and also well-preserved remains of the priory, including the church. What we had not found in our trenches was direct evidence of fighting, in the form of battlefield artefacts. This was where we hoped our metal-detector survey would come up trumps. Not wanting to disturb the important archaeological deposits in the field we had excavated, we confined our metal detectors to the field to the north, which was cut through by the silted remains of the moat, and a small field immediately to the south of the house. As usual we had set out surveying grids to make it easier to record the position of the finds. Our group of hardy volunteers set to work and soon we had a healthy crop of flags springing up in both fields.

When it came to excavating the metal-detector signals, we had our usual share of tractor parts and other modern bits and pieces. But there was also something very old: we found our first-ever Roman coin, but, interesting as it was, it had nothing to tell us about the battle of Shelford Manor. In fact we found relatively little related to the battle. We came across several musket-balls from both fields, some of which had been mashed as though they had hit something hard. But at the end of the day we had covered only a small area and more battle debris may await future discovery.

The search for 'Edinburgh', the Scottish camp

After the fall of Shelford and Wiverton, the Parliamentarians and their Scottish allies could invest Newark itself. They tightened their stranglehold by digging the circumvallation, the bank and ditch barrier that encircled the town, and constructed forts and gun batteries. The troops also needed somewhere to live, and for the vast majority this meant large communal camps. The Scots set up theirs to the west of the town on the area known as the island, as it was cut off from the surrounding land by a split in the course of the river Trent and could be reached only by bridges. The Scots numbered about 7,000 and so required a large area to accommodate them. Clampe's map shows a small town of tents laid out in rows surrounded by quite a complex earthwork: the camp is defended by a four-sided bank and ditch with diamond-shaped bastions on each corner of this square; midway along each of the sides protruded a smaller demi-bastion.

The camp sat astride the road from the villages of Kelham and Muskham. The bridge at Muskham was defended by a fort built by the Royalists but captured by the Parliamentarians in March 1644 during the second siege. This fort survives to this day, and during the summer it is covered by tall grass and nettles because the farmer cannot take his mower on to this scheduled ancient monument.

The Scots, no doubt yearning for their homeland, christened their camp Edinburgh, and were to spend the next six months there. Unlike the fort at Muskham, there is little or nothing left of the Scottish camp. The banks were pushed back into the ditches and over the centuries the plough has obliterated all trace of what must have been quite an impressive fortification, so the huge fields on the island cannot really be described as remaining for ever a piece of Scotland! However, having come down from north of the border we could not resist trying to relocate the site of the camp.

We had certainly arrived at the right time as the barley had just been harvested, which meant that we could get in and do a geophysical survey. As the area would have taken weeks to survey in its entirety, we had little choice but to pick a spot and hope that we would find some trace of the camp there. We did not choose at random, though: one possible portion of

Edinburgh's bank and ditch has been identified and archaeologists have used this, in conjunction with Clampe's map, to plot the entire camp on a modern map. In fact this fragment was in an area still to be cropped and therefore out of bounds to us, so we concentrated on an area where we hoped to find the western bastion.

Lorna produced some promising results with her geophysics survey and we targeted a couple of spots for trial trenching. However, when we removed the topsoil we found no trace of the camp, which was a bit of a let-down after the great results we'd had at Shelford. But we still had one card up our sleeve – the metal-detector survey. Even though we had failed to find any structural remains, we still hoped to find metal artefacts related to the six-month occupation of this site by the Scottish troops.

We did as much metal-detecting as time allowed, and our expectations were met: apart from the usual amount of modern rubbish, there was also a good

selection of material clearly of Civil War origin. We found musket-balls scattered across the area, including one example that still had the sprue on it. (When molten lead is poured into a musket-ball mould the channel through which it passes is called a sprue or nipple. After the lead has hardened, the nipple is snipped off with a pair of pliers before the ball can be loaded.)

As we walked across the fields through the stubble, we also encountered large quantities of iron slag. Slag is the waste product from the smelting process, and the army would have included smiths and metalworkers, whose job would have entailed processing the iron for all manner of objects, such as horseshoes, wagon fittings, swords and even armour. Here was evidence for the wide variety of activities essential to keep an army in the field.

The survey also gave us a number of non-ferrous, copper-alloy objects. Andy Robertshaw told us that one of these, a flat disc with hinge brackets, was the lid from a large powder flask – its size suggested it was for use with a cannon rather than a musket. Although Clampe's map doesn't show any guns in the Edinburgh camp, there were a number of gun emplacements on the island and big siege guns played a central role in bombarding the town and making life unpleasant for its inhabitants. We haven't yet worked out what all the copper-alloy objects are: one piece looks like a fancy

strap or hinge from a wooden box – probably a box belonging to an officer rather than a lowly foot-soldier.

The variety of both military and non-military metal artefacts is just the sort of thing we would have hoped to recover from a long-term army camp. We failed to find any evidence of the defences but we did find plenty of debris. This may indicate that we were actually inside the camp and had therefore missed the ditches that once surrounded it. Once again, the metal-detector survey had proved its worth. We would love to go back and take another shot at finding the camp defences – we know they're in there somewhere!

Playing the field – digging for Poyntz

Putting the search for the Scottish camp behind us, we moved to the south of Newark. The flat ground beside the river is covered by football pitches, and changing rooms stand where the Parliamentarian commander, General Poyntz, had his headquarters. This was the site of his main camp, which Clampe's map shows to have been heavily defended by ramparts and bastions. Close by was the Royalist Queen's Sconce, and in between the opposing strongholds Clampe's map shows a small rectangular redoubt with several guns blasting away at the Queen's Sconce, which is depicted returning fire with its own guns.

We wanted to see if we could find any trace of the HQ, the camp and the redoubt. Lorna carried out a

Opposite left **Musket-ball with nipple left from casting**
Opposite right **Raw material of lead musket-balls**
Left **The lid from a powder flask**

geophysical survey across a corridor which stretched all the way from the foot of the Queen's Sconce to the north, to the back of the playing fields to the south. The ground is divided into three areas: next to the Sconce there is a football pitch; to the south of this is a smaller area with trees and the changing rooms; and beyond this is another football pitch.

Using excavation, we tested geophysical anomalies in the southern field and the area of the sports pavilion. The readings from the field revealed a wide, linear feature, which we thought might be a buried ditch, so we opened a trench at this point. The bucket cut through a really deep deposit of topsoil and subsoil, which after a metre or so brought us down on to natural gravel. We had seen this before in Scotland: we were on sands and gravels which had been laid down by rivers and streams that flowed from melting glaciers around 12,000 years ago. Our linear feature was not a ditch, but a natural river bed that had become choked with sand.

Abandoning the south field, we turned our attention to the area behind the changing room. Here we had not only a geophysical anomaly but also the slightest trace of a grass-covered bank, which ran from east to west. We manoeuvred the JCB through the trees and set it to work. The soil was much shallower here, and very soon we reached a sandy subsoil, which very promisingly had a band of darker soil running through

it. We jumped in with our trowels and began to clean back, hoping to get a better look at what was going on. Almost immediately we found a piece of pottery, possibly a rim sherd from a seventeenth-century stoneware jug. This was a really good start.

At first we thought the dark soil was the fill of a ditch, but it was on the wrong side of the bank, which we could see gently rising up at the end of the trench closest to the Queen's Sconce. This didn't make sense. The ditch should have been outside the area enclosed by the bank, not inside. But slowly, with more digging and head-scratching, we realized that the darker soil was not the fill of a ditch at all, but old plough soil. There was a gap between this and the bank, and this may have been where the old horse-drawn plough had been turned when it came to the end of its furrow. There was an interesting little story here. Although the townsfolk had been ordered to dismantle the earthworks after their surrender, we know that this was not necessarily done – you only have to look at the Queen's Sconce. If a long stretch of bank was left intact, it may have been used as a means of dividing fields, rather like a hedge, once the area returned to agriculture. Over time the bank may have subsided and even been passed over by the plough, thus smoothing it out and leaving nothing but the faint bump we can see today. It's swords into ploughshares all over again! ❖

Archaeological Techniques:
Seeing Underground with Geophysical Survey

THE classic image of an archaeologist at work is of a figure kneeling in a trench, painstakingly revealing buried objects with trowel and brush. This picture is not inaccurate – far from it – and we still rely on precisely these tools to investigate the remains of the past.

Excavation, however, is both time-consuming and expensive (assuming the diggers are being paid rather than volunteering their services for free!). Furthermore, digging is destructive: no matter how much care is taken, the very act of digging causes irreversible damage to the remains that are being investigated. For these reasons, archaeologists try to minimize the amount of excavation required, and since the 1950s, they have been borrowing and customizing techniques and equipment developed by geologists – another group who want to know what is going on beneath their feet. Almost like the X-ray specs advertised in the back of science-fiction comics, the equipment they use lets them 'see' through the topsoil to whatever is buried beneath. These are the techniques of geophysical survey and they enable archaeologists to pinpoint buried 'anomalies' – features such as wall foundations, trenches, rubbish pits, latrines and other items that may relate to past human activity.

The geophysical techniques employed by archaeologists fall into the following three distinct categories.

Magnetometry: Certain human activities cause small disturbances to the earth's local magnetic field and can be detected by machines called magnetometers. Building a fire and digging a hole are two examples that cause permanent, localized disturbances to the natural magnetic field of a ground surface. They will show up on maps produced by processing the information collected by the magnetometer through a computer.

Resistivity: An electrical current passes more quickly through wet material than dry. Buried wall foundations composed of stone will tend to drain and dry out more efficiently than the soil around them, and such features will therefore be more resistant to the current passed through them by a resistivity meter than the soil on either side. When the information gathered by the meter is processed, walls will be revealed as lines of 'high resistance'. Conversely, the soil that gradually fills up an ancient ditch will probably be looser – less densely compacted – than the soil into which that ditch was originally dug. The looser 'fill' will tend to retain more moisture than the surrounding, densely packed soil, and so will show up on the map as a line of 'low resistance'.

Ground-penetrating radar: The same radio waves that enable air traffic controllers to locate aircraft which they cannot see can be used to reveal the positions of buried structures and features. When a GPR unit is passed over a ground surface, radio waves are emitted that penetrate the ground surface and then bounce back from any buried objects they hit. A computer analyses the returned signals and builds up a picture of whatever is directly underneath the unit.

Opposite **Excavating the trench at Poyntz's headquarters**
Above **Tony in his temporary home**

All three of these techniques can be used, separately or in tandem, to construct a picture of what is buried under our feet. This information enables archaeologists both to maximize the chances of finding remains of human activity and to minimize the area that needs to be disturbed by digging. It is also true, however, that these machines cannot be 'tuned' to look for archaeological remains. They will all faithfully detect the location of any buried 'anomalies', but they cannot explain what those anomalies actually are. And so while geophysical survey is an aid, it is not the answer. Each anomaly must still be excavated in the traditional way so that it can be examined by the most efficient piece of equipment available to archaeologists – the human eye.

Conclusion

Of all the projects we have undertaken, our work around Newark was perhaps the most ambitious in scope. Each of our three main areas of investigation was separated from its nearest neighbour by several miles. Although it was a logistical nightmare at times, piling the whole team into the van and hitting the road every time our focus of operations shifted, this was an inevitable consequence of tackling the events of a siege rather than a battle. The actions we were interested in had been geographically wide-ranging and spread out over a period of months, rather than concentrated over a few fields and lasting just a matter of hours.

The events at Shelford Manor came closest to the norms of a battle, with fierce fighting confined to a small area. That said, the results of our metal-detector survey were somewhat surprising in that it failed to uncover much evidence of a life-and-death struggle. This may, however, be partly the product of our strategy, which deliberately avoided coverage of the area occupied by the medieval priory. Our spectacular geophysical survey results made it obvious that the buried remains of the priory and later structures were relatively well preserved: as such, they represented an important part of the archaeological resource perhaps not best served by metal-detecting. Metal-detecting is a suitable technique in certain circumstances – indeed, for most of our battlefields – but here we felt that the excavation of small, carefully placed trenches was a much more appropriate strategy. The result of this work speaks for itself, our efforts being rewarded with a unique insight into the history of the priory and dramatic evidence of the remains of a very substantial defensive rampart at the time of the battle of Shelford Manor.

If a siege can be described as a waiting game, then there must be places where the opposing sides congregated during the quiet periods. The besieged were obviously confined within the town, although defences like the Queen's Sconce were located some distance outside the main defensive ditch. The besiegers, on the other hand, would have to make their own domestic arrangements, and we know from contemporary accounts and maps that the attacking forces constructed well-defended camps around the outside of the town. We had mixed fortunes in our search for two of these main centres of military population, Poyntz's headquarters and the Scottish camp known as Edinburgh.

Our investigations to the south of the Queen's Sconce confirmed that years of agriculture and horticulture in an area now covered by football pitches had removed most traces of Parliamentarian activity. What we did find were slight traces of a defensive bank, which may relate to Poyntz's headquarters and camp or the forward gun redoubt. If nothing else, even this partial survival, along with the Queen's Sconce, is evidence that not all military structures were deliberately dismantled after the siege.

There have been several attempts by historians and

Opposite **Bronze fitting from a horse's harness**
Above **A coin**

archaeologists to locate the remains of the Edinburgh camp, but ours has probably been the most intensive. In contrast to our efforts at Shelford Manor, the metal-detecting survey here proved to be quite informative. We found relatively high concentrations of camp-related metalwork, including musket- and pistol-balls and what may well prove to be personal effects such as coins and metal fittings from wooden chests. Additional finds such as iron slag and lead waste tell us that general metalworking and the production of ammunition took place here, activities clearly related to the general upkeep of an army at a site occupied for several months.

One intriguing aspect of this work were the finds of old bricks which were scattered across the fields: did the camp include not just tents but also more substantial buildings? If so, this would tie in with the portrayal of what look like houses among the tents on Clampe's contemporary map of the siege of Newark.

CULLODEN 1746

CULLODEN

THE TOWN OF INVERNESS SITS ASTRIDE THE RIVER AFTER WHICH IT IS NAMED. THE BANKS OF THE NESS ARE JOINED BY A NUMBER OF BRIDGES. TO THE NORTH IS AN ELEGANT PEDESTRIAN SUSPENSION BRIDGE WHICH HAS A DISCONCERTING WOBBLE AS WE WALK ACROSS IT. FURTHER UPSTREAM, BENEATH THE CASTLE, THE ROAD CROSSES A MODERN CONCRETE SPAN, AND MOST DRIVERS WHO PASS OVER IT MUST SURELY BE UNAWARE OF THE DARK SECRET OF ITS PREDECESSOR. BUT IT'S ALWAYS THE SAME – ONCE YOU SCRATCH THE SURFACE THE STORIES TUMBLE OUT.

Opposite **Inverness Castle and Bridge, c. 1900**
Left **Bonnie Prince Charlie**

After the battle of Culloden came the retribution, and for a while Inverness took on the role of prison and execution ground

After the battle of Culloden came the retribution, and for a while Inverness took on the role of prison and execution ground. With the tollbooth quickly filled to brimming, the heavy doors of the churches were bolted shut, and God's house became a jail to hundreds of wretched Jacobites, with prayers perhaps the only comfort against the mounting filth and numbing hunger. Wounded soldiers lay alongside those who had come through unscathed, and surgeons were forbidden to tend the dying.

It was the flags which first caught our eye . . . The space between the two is where, on that awful day, most of the deaths occurred

Today it is hard to imagine the pain and fear as we walk along the riverbank past Castle Street and over the new bridge. A drawing of the town in 1750, shortly after the rebellion, shows an elegant stone bridge, built in 1685, supported by multiple arches. Beneath the cobbled surface of this much older structure – which was swept away by a flood in 1849 – was a chamber, a tube-like hollow set deep into the bridge. While the flood may have swept away the stone and mortar, the memory remains, an echo of a much darker time – and a much darker place.

Into this nightmare scene they dropped Anne MacKay. It was her punishment for helping a Jacobite officer escape from the cellar in which he was held, but his conditions could hardly have been worse than those in which Anne now found herself. Her cell was so narrow that she was forced to stand for days in agony. Despite this horrific treatment, all efforts to make her betray her comrades were in vain, and eventually the authorities let her go. Meanwhile, the sentry whom she had distracted while the Jacobite made good his escape was sentenced to 500 lashes.

Judging by old pictures, Inverness was a pretty place, the level ground on both sides of the river providing an ideal spot for a town to develop. The Moray Firth, a wide, ragged inlet, was an excellent shelter for ships, which brought both riches and ruin to a place that even when small was perhaps a little too big for its own good. A sense of the historic town can still be seen in the narrow wynds and churches. Things have changed now, of course: the castle has been rebuilt in the Victorian style, and the hills are covered with pebble-dashed bungalows. The main road south is now known as the Golden Mile after the industrial parks and car show-rooms which continue to spring up alongside it.

The turn-off to Culloden is jointly signposted to the airport, today's equivalent of the old harbour, linking the town with the outside world. The brown tourist signs show crossed swords, and the name Drumossie appears here and there. The road follows a high terrace and fields roll down to the shores of the Firth, where the dark water stretches out to the hills of the Black Isle on the far shore. But for the most part the view is obstructed by trees and houses.

It was the flags which first caught our eye. The red pennants flapping high above the moor mark the line of the Jacobite positions as they are thought to have been on the day of battle; almost immediately the yellow flags of the government line come into view some 500 yards further up the road. The space between the two is where, on that awful day, most of the deaths occurred. Even if we hadn't already been aware that this ground was special, we would soon have been enlightened:

there are books – and scones – a-plenty to be had in the visitors' centre, and there can be little doubt the National Trust for Scotland have put a lot of effort into showing off this site, which is certainly the most emotive of all their properties. There is no castle here, or fancy manorial pile with ornate garden attached, just a stretch of scraggy moor. After we'd watched the stirring audio-visual display and seen the impressive collection of glass-encased weapons, we left the comfort of the building and the ready understanding it provides. Away from the facts and artefacts, we were on our own, left to walk over the battlefield. Now our imagination had to take over and like a time machine carry us back to that cold and miserable day on which the fight took place.

BACKGROUND

ON CULLODEN MOOR ON 16 APRIL 1746 THE KING'S ARMY IN SCOTLAND GOT DOWN TO MESSY, BLOODY BUSINESS WITH THE SOLDIERS OF THE JACOBITE REBELLION IN THE LAST PITCHED BATTLE FOUGHT ON BRITISH SOIL. IT WAS ON THIS MISERABLE PATCH OF MOORLAND THAT CHARLES EDWARD STUART — BONNIE PRINCE CHARLIE — LOST HIS DREAM — IN AMONG THE BODIES OF MEN AND ANIMALS, THE DISCARDED AND BROKEN WEAPONS, THE MUSKET-BALLS, THE PERSONAL BELONGINGS AND EVERYTHING ELSE THAT AS ARCHAEOLOGISTS WE COME IN SEARCH OF.

CHARLES PRINCE REGENT,

His SPEECH to His ARMY,

When He began His March to meet General *Cope* at the Field near *Dudiston, September* 20th, 1745 ;

THe PRINCE being clothed in a plain *Highland* Habit, Cocked His Blue Bonnet, Drew His Sword, Threw away the Scabord, and Said,

GENTLEMEN, Follow ME, By the Affistance of GOD, I will, this Day, make you a Free and Happy People.

The SPEECH of Sir JOHN COPE General of the USURPER'S Army, a little before the Engagement, on *Saturday* the 21ft *September*, 1745, at *Prefton-Grange*, Six Miles Eaft from *Edinburgh* ;

GENTLEMEN, You are juft now to Engage with a parcel of *Rable*; a parcel of *Brutes*: Being a fmall Number of *Scots Highlanders*. You can expeft no Booty from fuch a poor defpicable Pack. I have Authority to Declare, That you fhall have Eight full Hours Liberty to Plunder and Pillage the City of *Edinburgh*, *Leith*, and *Suburbs*, at your Difcretion, with Impunity.

Opposite **King George II**
Above left **James Francis Edward Stuart, father of Bonnie Prince Charlie**
Above right **Broadsheet published by the Jacobites after the battle of Prestonpans**

Charles Edward Stuart had crossed to Scotland in July 1745, eventually raising his standard at Glenfinnan, at the head of Loch Shiel, on 19 August. It was from here that he set out for London and the throne of the Hanoverian King George II. Charles's father was James Francis Edward Stuart, son of King James II of England and himself a pretender to the crown. His supporters called themselves Jacobites (derived from Jacobus, the Latin for James) and had made previous ill-starred attempts to put him on the British throne during the first quarter of the eighteenth century. Nevertheless, little fanfare greeted Charles's arrival on the Hebridean island of Eriskay, and without the charisma and dogged determination of the man himself, the whole affair would have ended there and then, without the loss of life – and of a way of life – that followed.

Word of the latest Jacobite venture spread, however, and the die was well and truly cast after the 'gentle' Lochiel, acting chief of the Camerons, threw in his lot with the prince. The MacDonalds of Keppoch stepped up as well, and 1,200 men moved east and south, side-stepping the British garrisons at Fort William and Fort Augustus but gathering momentum and recruits all the while.

Bonnie Prince Charlie entering Edinburgh

1746

King George and the British government, well aware of the rising tide, quickly mobilized an army under Lieutenant-General Sir John Cope. Cope chose to avoid a head-on clash and marched north to Inverness. With the road now clear to the south, Charles took advantage and by early September he was in Perth. Here the prince was joined by his most able recruit, Lord George Murray, a veteran of the earlier Jacobite campaigns of 1715–16 and 1719 and a fine soldier and leader of men.

Growing in strength, confidence and tactical know-how all the time, Charles pressed southwards. Edinburgh offered little resistance – apart from the British garrison in the castle, which was effectively placed under siege – and the prince happily took up residence in the palace of Holyroodhouse, home of his Stuart ancestors.

Sir John Cope embarked his men at Aberdeen and sailed to Dunbar, where he learned of the Jacobite occupation of the capital. Intent upon delivering it from rebel hands, he made it as far as Prestonpans, just east of the city. There, on 21 September, he was out-thought and outmanoeuvred by the Jacobites. Having approached the British camp across a marsh in the half-light before dawn, the Highlanders unleashed their charge. This tactic, which was so hopelessly deployed on Culloden Moor the following April, fully achieved its intended effect on the field at Prestonpans. The government line broke and Cope's troops were chased from the field in a little over ten minutes.

The Jacobite army continued its march south, hoping to collect support from the north of England before advancing on London. But while there was some vocal enthusiasm for the cause south of the border, it never brought about any worthwhile swelling of the ranks. None the less, the Jacobites' southward advance continued, gaining control of Carlisle on 16 November and Manchester on 28 November. Then to Derby – but here the story enters the territory haunted to this day by 'what ifs' and 'if onlys'.

Some of the primary sources seem to suggest that the advance into England was already considered futile by some of the prince's advisers. Certainly, several bodies of government troops were now ready to tackle Charles's Jacobites, most notably a force led by the Duke of Cumberland, son of George II and therefore a young man with the greatest motivation for protecting the crown. There was little real support from English Jacobites, and the Highlanders, strangers in a strange land, were increasingly turning their gaze to the north and to home. Before the year was out around 1,000 of them had slipped quietly away and headed back to the familiar surroundings of their glens. Most ominously of all, perhaps, the prince and Lord George Murray, lieutenant-general of his army and his most able soldier, had already argued bitterly.

Whatever happened, whatever was said, whatever counsel was given and whatever taken, the Jacobite army turned round at Derby and headed for home, perhaps with a view to facing the growing threat of a government counterattack on their native soil. Following a successful holding engagement at Clifton, in Cumbria, they crossed back into Scotland on 20 December. It had been a miserable march north. Spirits were low and tempers frayed. But a return to familiar surroundings restored some of the old confidence. New recruits – Mackintoshes raised by Lady Mackintosh while her husband, the clan chief, fought on the side of the government, and regulars from France – brought fresh blood, fresh impetus to the cause.

It was just as well that there was still fight in Jacobite hearts, because General Hawley – later to be known as 'Hanging Hawley' – had marched out of Edinburgh with 8,000 government troops. But at Falkirk

Lord George Murray

The Duke of Cumberland

on 17 January 1746, the terrain, disciplined volley-fire and that devastating Highland charge brought another resounding victory for the prince. And it is surely worth noting that, despite the withdrawal from England, this Jacobite army had yet to taste defeat. London and the crown were no longer under immediate threat, but the Jacobite reputation was intact. Still intact, too, was the reputation of the Highlanders' charge.

Whether it was failure of command, confusion in the half-light of the dismal winter's evening that followed the battle at Falkirk, plain fatigue, or some other bitter mix of factors, the Jacobites failed to follow through. Perhaps if they had pursued Hawley and harried his troops in their withdrawal from the field, they might have found their former momentum. But the opportunity passed by unheeded, or slipped through weary fingers and was lost. Hawley returned to Edinburgh and to his nickname, hanging his own deserters on gallows raised in expectation of rebel necks to stretch.

The Jacobite army turned north in February, towards Inverness. Abandoned by the government garrison just days before, the town was open to the rebels and Charles made it his home on the 21st. While he settled in, wining and dining Inverness society, his army broke into small units and began a successful campaign of assaults upon Highland garrisons at Fort Augustus, Fort William, Blair Castle and Fort George.

The tide, though, was already turning. The initiative lost by the prince post-Falkirk fell into government hands and was not surrendered again. The Duke of Cumberland had taken command of the greater part of the army in Edinburgh, marched them north via Perth and reached Aberdeen on 27 February. He crossed the Spey on 12 April. His force – 9,000-strong, even without the 5,000 German regulars he had left behind in Dunkeld under Prince Frederick of Hesse to guard the road south – closed rapidly on Inverness. Warships and transports under the command of Rear-Admiral Byng shadowed the duke's advance from the Moray Firth and kept the army amply provisioned. By 14 April he was in Nairn.

Aware of this impending threat, but far too slowly, Charles sought to reunite his scattered army for battle. Debate rages to this day about the wisdom of the choice of battlefield. Whatever the truth of the matter, on 15 April Charles led his men out on to Drumossie Moor, east of Inverness, and into the lands close by Culloden House, owned by Duncan Forbes, Lord President of the Court of Session. Taking the recently vacated house for his headquarters – for Forbes was a government supporter – the prince ordered his army to be drawn up in two lines. This was a grim rehearsal of the order in which they would be drawn up the following day.

The Jacobite army was in no state for battle. On 15 April a notable proportion of the force was still scattered to the four winds, foraging, and those who did muster on the field that day were poorly provisioned and demoralized. The prince's commissariat in Inverness was a shambles, and food that should have been sent out never arrived. Many of the men were complaining bitterly, even within earshot of their commanders, about their unhappy circumstances.

Although he was eager to demonstrate his own abilities on the battlefield, in the past Charles had mostly left strategic decisions in the hands of his commanders, and so he again accepted Murray's suggestion that a surprise night attack should be launched on the government camp. Those soldiers, Murray reminded the prince, would be spending the night toasting the duke's twenty-fifth birthday, and he suggested the Highlanders should fall upon them just before dawn while they were still befuddled with drink. So it was that around 4,500 Jacobite men set out that night to march the eight miles to the enemy camp outside Nairn. Progress over the rough ground in the dark was hard, and the need to move without making any noise made it harder still. And in the event it was all in vain, for with two miles still to go dawn began to break. The sound of a drum beating in the distance made it clear that surprise was lost.

The Jacobites were ordered to about-turn and march back to Culloden and the moor. A force that had been tired, hungry and in poor sprits before the march was all but desolate now. Muscles ached, empty bellies growled. Officers and men lay down to sleep where they could. The prince managed a few hours in bed in Culloden House, his boots still on his feet. On the morning of 16 April the well-drilled lines of the government troops came into view. For the Jacobites, pipes and drums sounded the alarm and the wakened soldiers pulled themselves together as best they could and formed up in the same lines as the previous day. There was no time for fresh orders.

Muscles ached, empty bellies growled. Officers and men lay down to sleep where they could

WHO FOUGHT HERE

A RED-COATED SOLDIER MARCHING ALONG
THE ROAD FROM NAIRN TO CULLODEN MOOR
IN APRIL 1746 WAS A WRETCHED CREATURE.
LOATHED AND FEARED BY CIVILIANS, ILL-
TREATED AND BRUTALIZED BY HIS LEADERS,
HE WAS A TOY TO BE DRESSED UP, USED AND
THROWN AWAY. YET DESPITE THE DAY-TO-
DAY MISERIES, LIFE IN THE KING'S ARMY
WAS OFTEN A STEP UP FOR A POOR MAN
WHO MIGHT OTHERWISE HAVE FACED
UNEMPLOYMENT AND ITS ATTENDANT
HORRORS.

From his meagre pay, a percentage was stopped to go towards the cost of his uniforms, his daily bread and his kit. Bread, water and cheese formed his staple diet, and if he wanted to supplement this humble fare with meat or beer or whatever, then it would cost him again.

Beneath the scarlet-red, skirted, black-buttoned coat he wore a long waistcoat over scarlet breeches. Round the breeches went white gaiters that covered the leg to the middle of the thigh. His hat was a black tricorn and his neck was supported by a stiff leather collar. He slung his cartridge bag from a white, pipeclay-stiffened belt over his left shoulder. Round his waist hung a short sword and a bayonet. The rest of his kit – spare clothes, food rations and the like – he carried in a back-pack. His main weapon was the Brown Bess musket, borne over the right shoulder.

Discipline was instilled through fear – fear of the lash, fear of hanging and the rest of the casual brutality meted out by officers – and when normal recruitment tactics failed to keep the numbers up, a man might be pressed into service against his will and with no hope of reprieve. In contrast to the Jacobites, the force led on to the field at Culloden by the Duke of Cumberland was a professional army. Alongside the ranks of Englishmen were regiments of Lowland Scots and Highlanders; within the cosmopolitan mix were Germans and a fair share of Irishmen and Welshmen – full-time soldiers all.

Accurate figures for the government forces at Culloden are as hard to come by as those for the Jacobites. The duke's force outnumbered the prince's men – that much is certain – but estimates for the total range between 7,000 and 9,000. The bulk of this force was made up of fifteen regiments of regular infantry, supported by the Argyll militia and a company of Loudon's Highlanders. In addition, the duke had in the region of 800 cavalry.

The details of the duke's artillery are well recorded: his artillery train consisted of ten three-pounder guns and six cohorn mortars. While the Jacobite guns were in the hands of what might be described as unenthusiastic amateurs, the duke's were controlled by Brevet-Colonel William Belford, an experienced officer who demanded the highest standards of professionalism from the men in his command.

Discipline was instilled through fear – fear of the lash, fear of hanging and the rest of the casual brutality meted out by officers

THE LIFE OF A CLANSMAN

It was not just the Highland soldiers but also their centuries-old culture that faced destruction that April morning. The clansman was dependent upon his chief like an infant upon his father, but by 1746 this ancient way of life was already in decline. Roads built by General Wade twenty years before in the aftermath of earlier Jacobite rebellions had done more than open up the mountains to the king's soldiers. They had also exposed the Highland chiefs to the economic practices of southern landowners – and what had been a trickle of new ideas since the latter half of the seventeenth century was now a flood. Where once they had believed themselves to be fathers to those who shared their names, they now increasingly saw their role as that of a landlord with tenants.

Despite this climate of change, enough of the old ways persisted in the hearts and minds of the men from the mountains. By tradition, a clan chief measured his wealth by the number of fighting men he could summon to his side. In return for this duty of service, a clansman had the right to keep animals and grow crops upon land owned by the chief – though the concept of ownership here was vague and based as much on word of mouth and precedent as on any written title. A refusal to answer the call to arms would not be tolerated. If the chief's tacksman, or agent, announced it was time to go into battle, any man resisting would see the roof of his family's home burned.

The battle of Culloden

Living was hard. The herds of black cattle were a mainstay, and therefore the target of endless thieving raids by clan against clan. Oats and barley were grown in the thin soil. For those with land on the coast, seaweed was the traditional fertilizer to boost the nourishment in the earth. From this subsistence, a Highlander also provided food for his chief's table and money for his purse.

Visitors to the Highlands today are struck by the emptiness, the absence of people, for mile after mile, glen after glen. Nothing but sheep picking their way across hillsides dotted with the foundations of long-abandoned settlements. But it wasn't always like this. A man who left his Highland home in 1745 to march south behind his chief would have crossed a well-populated landscape, peppered with buildings for people and animals.

If he was poor, the clansman would be dressed in a plaid, a six-yard-long, six-foot-wide woollen shawl folded to make a skirt around the waist and thighs, with the rest wrapped over one shoulder. He might be armed in the classic style, with broadsword and dirk, pistols and musket; if his circumstances didn't allow this and yet he was still summoned to fight, he would bring what he could – axe, scythe, anything that came to hand for a man as used to farming as to fighting.

The prince's army was primarily Catholic and certainly dominated by Highlanders. But this was not a battle of Scot against Englishman, or between Highlander and Lowlander, or Catholic and Protestant. There were Englishmen and Lowlanders in the Jacobite ranks. And while the majority of the Presbyterian Campbells fought for the duke, those from Glen Lyon fought for the prince. Also among the 5,000 or so Jacobites facing the duke's army that day were regulars from the French army – men of the Scots Royals and Irish Picquets (Irish Picquets being French-speakers of Irish descent serving in distinct Irish regiments). For the men of the prince's army, then, there were as many reasons for fighting as there were tartans on the field.

The Jacobite army also had a force of cavalry, of uncertain size but probably numbering no more than 300. These men were on lighter animals than the mounted force protecting the flanks of the duke's army. A reading of the history books reveals further uncertainty surrounding the nature of the Jacobite artillery. It is generally accepted, however, that the prince was able to deploy three pairs of guns, lighter than those of the duke and manned by less experienced and poorly trained gunners.

If the chief's tacksman ... announced it was time to go into battle, any man resisting would see the roof of his home burned

A major of the Clan Chattan regiment

THE BATTLE

ACCORDING TO THE TRADITIONAL VERSION OF EVENTS, AT ABOUT ELEVEN O'CLOCK IN THE MORNING THE ARMIES FACED ONE ANOTHER ACROSS A FEW HUNDRED YARDS OF MOORLAND. IT WAS RAINING – IN FACT, THE RAIN WAS MORE LIKE SLEET, AND THE WIND DROVE IT INTO THE HIGHLANDERS' FACES. THE GOVERNMENT ARMY HAD FORMED ITS LINES IN A MATTER OF MINUTES WITH THE PRECISION OF WELL-ORDERED MILITARY DRILL: TWO LINES OF INFANTRY, THE FRONT INTERSPERSED WITH PAIRS OF THREE-POUND GUNS; CAVALRY ON THE FLANKS; RESERVES TO THE REAR.

Watching this set-piece unfold were the prince's Jacobites, who were also formed in two lines. The front line, which included the artillery, was a little longer than, and placed at an angle to, the government's: the Atholl Highlanders, the Camerons and the Stewarts on the right faced the red tunics across 500 yards of heather and mire; the MacDonalds of Keppoch and Clanranald and Glengarry on the left had a further 300 yards to run. In the second line were the Angus regiment, the Duke of Perth's contingent peppered with the scarlet of government deserters, and Scots Royals and Irish Picquets from the French army. A motley collection of mounted troops at the rear formed a bodyguard for the prince.

A Jacobite gun fired over the heads of the government infantry, provoking a swift and sure response from the opposing three-pounders. According to tradition, most of the Jacobite casualties were sustained in the next half-hour while they stood there in the sleet awaiting the cry of 'Claymore' and the freedom to charge. Meanwhile, government dragoons and cavalry under the command of Kerr and Cobham, with Campbells on foot in support, moved swiftly across the dead ground sloping steeply towards the river Nairn, out of sight of the rebel right, to try to outflank the Jacobites round the walls of Culchuinag Farm.

Suffering badly from the effects of withering roundshot, furious and horrified beyond endurance, Clan Chattan burst forward from the centre of the Jacobite front. Witnessing this charge, Murray's Atholl men, the Camerons and the Stewarts of Appin did likewise. Somewhere near the middle of the field, still well short of the government front line, roundshot and then grapeshot forced Clan Chattan to veer right. They collided with their right-hand neighbours, who themselves had been pushed towards the left.

The charge faltered – slowed by collision and artillery fire – then came on again. The clansmen on the right wing managed to break through Barrell's regiment in the front line before encountering more grapeshot and murderous volleys of musket fire from the troops in the second line. Desperate remains of the Chattan men finally reached the left of the government line too, driving through it only to die upon the bayonets of the regiments stepping forward into the breach.

Out on the Jacobite left, a third of the MacDonalds never managed to come within a hundred yards of their foes opposite. At first seeking to draw on the government infantry – by dashing forward and then feinting back – they were cut to pieces long before they could mount any vestige of a charge.

A Jacobite gun fired over the heads of the government infantry, provoking a swift and sure response from the opposing three-pounders

The Duke of Cumberland at Culloden

In the centre and on the Jacobite right, the fighting was man to man – so close that government soldiers were dying from wounds inflicted by the dirk as well as the sword. But the government troops did hold the second line here, and furthermore the men under Wolfe, positioned at right angles to the rest of the line, were pouring a withering fire into the flanks of the rebels, who realized they had no choice but to turn back.

Murray, having seen enough of the carnage to know what must be done, galloped back to the Jacobite line and summoned the reserves. They came on, but too late. Advance was impossible through the retreating Camerons and Stewarts, who were being harried by Cobham's and Kerr's horse. The prince's adjutant and quartermaster-general, John William O'Sullivan, himself falling back in the face of the slaughter, declared, 'All is gone to pot.' While the duke began to revel in success, the prince left the field.

Swords of (left to right) the Marquis of Tullibardine, Bonnie Prince Charlie and the Earl of Cromarty. 'Claymore', (from the Gaelic for the great sword), is often taken to refer to the older type of two-handed sword but it more properly refers to the basket-hilted sword as shown above

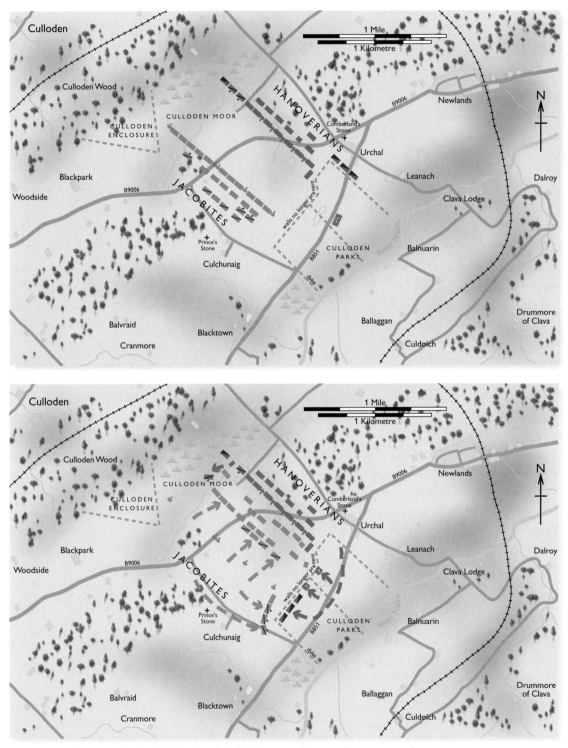

Movement of troops during the battle of Culloden superimposed on to a modern map

TACTICS

In the weeks leading up to the battle of Culloden, the government soldiers in the field received two pieces of tactical advice that were to prove crucial. Separately they provided new ways of facing up to the legendary ferocity of the Highlanders' charge. Applied together, as they were at Culloden, they served to inflict a devastating refutation of their opponents' military traditions.

The first, issued to the soldiers of the government army in Edinburgh on 12 January by General Hawley, commanded the infantrymen to hold firm – and hold their fire – until the last few yards of the Highlanders' frenzied advance:

'...they give no quarters... they are the most despicable enemy that are'

> *The sure way to demolish them is, at three deep, to fire by ranks diagonally to the centre, where they come, the rear rank first, and even that rank not to fire till they are within ten or twelve paces; but if the fire is given at a distance, you probably will be broke, for you never get time to load a second cartridge, and, if you give way, you may give your foot for dead, for they being without a firelock, or any load, no man with his arms, accoutrements, etc., can escape them, and they give no quarters, but if you will but observe the above directions, they are the most despicable enemy that are.*

The second tactic, famously employed at Culloden, was as simple as it was lethal. Each infantryman in the government line was ordered to attack not the howling Highlander directly in front of him, broadsword upraised for a devastating downward slash, but the man on his attacker's left. This way, rather than snagging his bayonet in his attacker's targe and laying himself open to the broadsword or the dirk, he was able to thrust into the unprotected right side of a Highlander preparing to fell the comrade to his right. He had, of course, to trust that the comrade on his left would deal with the enemy bearing down upon him in the same manner. It also helped if the Highlander was left-handed!

Silver-mounted targe

THE AFTERMATH

CULLODEN IS REMEMBERED FOR MANY THINGS: FOR THE BRAVE BUT FUTILE HIGHLANDERS' CHARGE, FOR THE FINAL DEFEAT OF THE JACOBITE CAUSE, AND FOR BEING THE LAST BATTLE FOUGHT ON BRITISH SOIL. BUT PERHAPS MORE THAN ANYTHING ELSE IT IS THE BRUTALITY METED OUT BY THE GOVERNMENT ARMY AFTER THE BATTLE THAT HAS CAPTURED THE POPULAR IMAGINATION, ESPECIALLY IN SCOTLAND. IT INCLUDED THE KILLING OF JACOBITE WOUNDED AND CIVILIAN BYSTANDERS, AND EARNED THE DUKE OF CUMBERLAND THE LASTING EPITHET OF 'BUTCHER'.

There are a number of eyewitness accounts describing the actions of Cumberland's troops after the battle, many in the form of letters. Today such actions would be described as war crimes, in breach of the Geneva Convention, which among other things insists that enemy wounded and prisoners be treated in a reasonable manner. Indeed, the supposed burning of wounded soldiers in the barn at Old Leanach at Culloden (see page 282) has a direct parallel in conflicts as recent as Kosovo, where several cases of buildings being set on fire with people inside have been reported and are being investigated.

There seems little reason to doubt the many eyewitness accounts of brutality after the battle of Culloden, but can we in hindsight really call these war crimes? There is a long history, even within the British army, of severe treatment being doled out to captured enemy soldiers or wounded. Perhaps the best-known example is Henry V's order that the French prisoners at Agincourt be executed. According to Shakespeare, this was in revenge for a French assault on the young boys attending the baggage train, but military historians such as John Keegan suggest the slaughter was carried out to pre-empt a possible assault on the English rear by what was fast becoming uncontrollable numbers of French prisoners. Another celebrated victory in British military history occurred during the Anglo-Zulu war of 1879 when the small garrison of the mission station at Rorke's Drift fought off around 4,000 Zulu warriors, an action which earned an unprecedented eleven Victoria Crosses. An aspect of this engagement that is not usually dwelt upon is the killing of the Zulu wounded who littered the ground after the battle – a cruel act no doubt, but even wounded warriors who were beyond available medical treatment still posed a threat.

Warfare, then, is obviously a brutal business despite the existence of rules of engagement. Nowhere has this been better demonstrated by archaeologists than at the Wars of the Roses battle site of Towton, where the examination of skeletons from a mass grave discovered some distance from the scene of the fighting has revealed horrific injuries from cutting and thrusting weapons, many of them to the face and head. Such carnage has done much to dispel any lingering belief that medieval warfare was a chivalrous affair tinged with romance.

Looking at the battle of Culloden through the eyes of the government soldiers, therefore, it should not be forgotten that the Jacobites had given them savagely short shrift at Prestonpans, some six months earlier. There, once the Jacobite charge had successfully broken the government line, the routed troops were mercilessly run down by the triumphant

There seems little reason to doubt the many eyewitness accounts of brutality after the battle of Culloden, but can we in hindsight really call these war crimes?

rebels and little mercy was shown to those not fast enough on their feet. Even taking all the above into account, however, there is still the issue of the faked order.

THE FAKED ORDER

It is his Royal Highness's positive orders, that every person attach himself to some Corps of the army, and remain with that Corps night and day, until the Battle and pursuit be finally over; and to give no quarter to the elector's troops on any account whatsoever, this regards the foot as well as the Horse. The Order of Battle is to be given to every General officer, and every Commander of a Regiment or Squadron. It is required and expected of each individual in the Army, as well officer as soldier, that he keep the post that shall be allotted to him; and if any man turn his back to run away, the next behind is to shoot him. No body, upon pain of Death, is to strip slain, or plunder, till the Battle be over. The Highlanders to be in their kilts, and no body to throw away their guns.

By HRH Command George Murray

Historians have expended much ink in their consideration of what archaeologists could fairly describe as a partial artefact. The written orders that Murray issued to his troops the day before the battle remained unchanged when the two armies finally faced one another. They were not intended to detail the strategy and tactics of the forthcoming action, for these would change by the moment once the fighting started. Rather, the orders were meant to provide an overall framework within which the army was to operate, and they essentially told every man what was expected of him. They provide some interesting insights into the character of warfare and the Jacobite army itself.

'*and if any man turn his back to run away, the next behind is to shoot him.*' Cowardice was not viewed kindly, and each man was given the liberty to shoot any of his comrades who turned to flee the field. In more recent times, however, the task of execution became the responsibility of the officers, and not any soldier who happened to be close by.

'*The Highlanders to be in their kilts, and no body to throw away their guns.*' The throwing away of guns has, for obvious reasons, remained a major military offence, and during the First World War was deemed an act of cowardice equivalent to desertion. However, in the context of the Jacobite army, whose weapon of choice was the broadsword, we must read another meaning entirely into this order. For some of the soldiers, the temptation would have been to drop the musket and unsheathe the sword. Despite the battle order forbidding them to throw away their guns, however, the Highlanders would have had to drop their muskets when in close combat, as reloading and firing would no longer be possible and Scottish muskets did not carry bayonets.

'No body, upon pain of Death, is to strip slain, or plunder, till the Battle be over.' Looting of the slain after a battle had been a common practice throughout history, and for poorly paid soldiers (the Jacobite army hadn't received any wages for weeks or even months) the promise of money or valuables taken from the enemy was an important motivation. The pillaging of battlefields by victorious soldiers and camp-followers would later be followed by farmers picking up objects from their ploughed fields – and nowadays by collectors using metal detectors. All of which obviously makes the archaeologist's job more difficult as the amount of available evidence is reduced. The order in this case, however, alludes to looting while the battle is on-going, with no commander wishing to see his troops emptying the pockets of the dead while there was still fighting to be done.

'and to give no quarter to the elector's troops on any account whatsoever.' It is this section of the orders that has attracted most attention. It is widely believed that following the battle a set of Murray's orders fell into government hands and were rewritten to include this phrase, thus providing justification for the killing frenzy which resulted in the subsequent slaughter of civilians and wounded soldiers. ❧

Cowardice was not viewed kindly, and each man was given the liberty to shoot any of his comrades who turned to flee the field

the dig

THE most obvious aim of the archaeological investigation of a battlefield must surely be to locate the site of the fighting. Only rarely will this be marked by preserved archaeological remains, an obvious example being the surviving First World War trench lines on the Western Front. Battles on the British mainland were usually mobile, open engagements that have left little, if anything, in the way of archaeological features. What we do find, however, is the debris of war, the missiles fired and the objects dropped in the heat of battle.

At Culloden today the battle lines of the opposing armies are marked out by two lines of flags, the Jacobites red and the government yellow, some 500 yards apart and at a slight angle to one another. They are thought to represent the final positions of the armies at the start of the battle, just before the Jacobites charged towards the government troops. During our investigation we wanted to check whether these flags really do mark the exact lines of 16 April 1746. In order to do this we carried out a metal-detector survey on the right wing of the Jacobite position and the left wing of the government's, where there was ferocious fighting during the battle, with the Jacobite charge reaching the government line on its extreme left, and the outflanked Jacobite right coming under attack from government troops who had broken their way through the walled enclosure of Culchuinag Farm.

As ever, we found no difficulty in recruiting enthusiastic volunteers from the local metal-detector club, and some of them had worked with archaeologists before. Prior to their arrival, that part of the paddock-like field marked by a visitor orientation sign as Barrell's position, and so presumably the point at which the Jacobite charge struck home, had been pegged out. Today it is covered with closely cropped grass and

Clockwise from top left **A kilt pin; a piece of grapeshot; a close-up of a piece of grapeshot**

crossed by a number of paths which lead to other parts of the battlefield. Because of the large numbers of visitors who pass through this area, it came as no surprise when many of the metal finds turned out to be things like modern coins and ring-pulls from drinks cans. Though one or two interesting items did emerge, including the back plate from a brass button which probably came from a soldier's tunic, there didn't appear to be the quantity of artefacts we would expect from the place that had witnessed the heaviest fighting. But rather than jump to the conclusion that all the dropped artefacts from this battle had long since been collected, we extended our survey into the Field of the English, some considerable distance beyond the point at

which the supposed end of the left wing of the government line was signposted. It was here, in the longer grass, that we began to make our most striking metal-detector discoveries. Some distance forward of the marked government line, we found lead balls. Some of these were musket-balls from a Brown Bess, and several of them had been distorted after hitting either their targets or the ground. Holding them, you cannot but help imagine the horrific injuries they must have caused as they smashed through flesh and bone. The misshapen nature of the balls, which in some cases were squashed flat, means that they were fired at close range, perhaps into the Jacobite charge just before it hit the front of the government line. A pistol-ball was also

recovered here; a pistol, having a much shorter range than a musket, would only be used up close, possibly by an officer.

Without doubt, what brought home to us the ferocity of the close-quarter fighting was a brass strap. As we wiped the dirt from it, we were pretty sure it had, until sometime before midday on 16 April 1746, fixed the trigger guard into the wooden stock of a Brown Bess musket. Our weapons expert, Andrew Robertshaw, from the National Army Museum in London, later confirmed this impression. The piece was twisted and bent with a tell-tale half-moon hollow on one edge, created in an instant when a musket-ball smashed into the weapon and tore the strap away from it. Again, only a weapon fired at close range could have caused such damage – perhaps it was the last shot of a Jacobite before he dropped his musket and went in with the sword. This find may suggest that the Jacobites

were not as quick to abandon their muskets during the charge as many accounts would suggest, and indeed that they had followed Murray's order not to do so. But the most hair-raising aspect of this find was the realization that this part of the musket was where it was held, and so it seems highly likely that the projectile pierced not only the metal and wood of the gun but also the hand of the soldier holding it, perhaps even killing him. Imagine, this was just one incident among many, one small ripple in that raging sea of pain.

Further evidence of the brutality of the battle emerged from the ground in the form of heavily misshapen lead balls, some of which looked more like cubes. Slightly smaller than musket-balls, they were in fact case shot or grapeshot which had been fired, dozens at a time, from a cannon. We know from historical accounts that grapeshot was fired into the charging mass of the Jacobite line, where its shotgun-like scatter would have cut horrific gaps through the oncoming clansmen. A number of these balls were found not very far forward from the debris dropped during hand-to-hand fighting, where they appear to have been fired at almost point-blank range into the Jacobites.

The role of the artillery during the battle has been the cause of some debate, especially with regard to the amount of time that the Jacobite ranks endured the government barrage before they charged forward. Some historians say the barrage lasted upwards of half an hour and was responsible for massive losses on the Jacobite side, while others claim it lasted only ten or fifteen minutes. Searching for new sources of information in the special collections department of Glasgow University Library, we were really excited to find a previously unpublished letter from a government officer the day after the battle, in which he states:

> When our cannon had fired about two rounds, I could plainly perceive that the rebels fluctuated extremely and would not remain long in the position they were in without running away, or coming down upon us, and according as I thought in two or three minutes they broke from the centre in three large bodies, like wedges and moved forward.

If we can place any reliance on this description – and it was written the day after the battle – then the Jacobites do not appear to have waited very long at all before rushing forward. And as the government cannon therefore did not have time to fire many rounds, the Jacobite losses suffered at this stage might well have been fewer than is usually thought. This conclusion may also be supported by the lack of Jacobite graves on the line itself – if large numbers of men had fallen here, they would surely have been buried on the spot rather than carried several hundred yards to the clan cemetery.

Not all the finds from the government left related to weaponry. An important discovery was a brass button which, unlike the button previously mentioned, had an insignia on it. The raised design is very faint, but if you look carefully you can see a crown and a scroll beneath it which would have carried an inscription. The crown would have appeared only on the badges of line regiments such as Barrell's and Munro's, and so this button is further evidence that this was the location of the government left. The button may have been pulled or even cut off a soldier's tunic as he struggled with a Jacobite, each tearing at the other in a desperate fight to the death. These are the moments we had set out to find.

The back of a brass button

Missing in action

The most moving monuments on the battlefield today are undoubtedly the low grass-covered mounds of the mass graves of the clans, each of which is marked by its own rough headstone bearing the clan name. It is estimated that around 1,200 Jacobites were killed or wounded as opposed to just 350 government troops.

Judging by the shape of the mounds, the grave pits beneath appear to have been rectangular trenches, possibly cut by spades normally used to tend the fields or dig for peat – a bleak task for tools intended to help provide nourishment and warmth. Of course, new jobs for old tools were also found during the battle itself, where the more poorly equipped units of the Jacobite army turned agricultural implements into weapons: the battlefield museum contains several examples of scythe blades mounted on the end of poles to create a sort of billhook or pike – a modification which turns the biblical phrase 'swords into ploughshares' on its head.

Burial did not take place immediately after the fighting was over. According to eyewitness accounts, the government soldiers kept relatives and friends at bay for a day or so, cordoning off the battlefield while they systematically dispatched the wounded and looted their bodies of valuables. Eventually, though, the dead were collected from the field wrapped in their plaids, which

served as shroud and container in which the already decaying corpses could be taken to the grave site. Wherever possible, bodies would be buried near to where they lay, so it is no coincidence that the graves are to be found close to where many of the Jacobites died in the assault on the government left wing. Likewise, if you look carefully among the scrub to the north of the cemetery, there is a partially hidden stone which marks the graves of the MacDonald clan near where they fell in their desperate charge on the right wing.

As people sympathetic to the dead and their cause performed most of the burials, it could be argued that they would have done so with care and consideration, rather than simply bundling the bodies into the ground. On the other hand, the sheer scale of the operation would not have allowed much in the way of pomp and ceremony. When the pits could accommodate no more corpses, the newly dug earth was replaced, the reduced space available for it producing the hummocks and mounds that can be seen today.

Today the clan graves are enclosed within a small copse, the trees separating them from the rest of the battlefield and giving the place a feeling of tranquillity reminiscent of a pretty church graveyard. It was not always thus. Until the 1980s the road actually ran through the middle of the cemetery, with cairns positioned on either side of it. If you stand on the grass between the cairns, you can still make out the bump in the ground caused by the camber of the road. The road was built in the 1830s, some eighty years after the battle. To this day there are stories of graves being disturbed during its construction, and these bones must have been moved elsewhere.

The battlefield memorial

Using ground-penetrating radar, a survey was conducted across the cemetery. Both the cairns and the space between them, previously the road, were scanned. The results clearly showed that there were graves under the ground where the road had been, which are obviously no longer marked by cairns. We also confirmed that each of the cairns has a pit beneath it, which would argue against the suggestion that they may be mere monuments or cenotaphs rather than real graves.

It may seem strange that the graves of the government troops, who after all won the battle, are not memorialized in the same way as the Jacobites. Not far from the Jacobite cemetery is a solitary boulder, its flattened surface bearing the inscription 'Field of the English – they were buried here'. As the stone was probably not erected until the mid nineteenth century, when Duncan Forbes of Culloden House set the headstones on the clan graves, we cannot be certain that this spot corresponds exactly to the English graves.

The stone stands near an area known as the Field of the English, and this suggests that their grave could in fact be anywhere within the field.

A local story, which may have a grain of truth in it but has probably been embellished, tells of a small shepherd boy who, on hearing scraping noises, climbed over a wall into the field. Here he saw government soldiers digging a trench and burying their dead. It is said that one of the soldiers discouraged the lad's inquisitiveness by slapping his face with a severed hand. This may have been an attempt to keep the burials – and the extent of their losses – a secret, or it may reflect nothing more than a cruel sense of humour and dislike of the local inhabitants.

As has been suggested, the mounds that overlie the clan graves are probably the result of excess soil caused by placing so many corpses into the trench, although this also had the effect of creating a visible marker. There seems little reason to doubt that a similar mound or mounds were created during the burial of the government dead – but what happened to the mounds?

It seems likely that the government dead were buried on arable land quite close to the Leanach farmstead. In April, when the battle was fought, the field would have been free of crops and may even have been freshly ploughed, creating an ideal place to dig graves with minimal effort. However, as the agricultural cycle continued over the generations, any mounds thus created would have disappeared entirely as they were slowly worn away under the blade of the plough. Eventually the plough cut deep enough to disturb the remains of the dead, and there are several accounts of human bones being picked up from the surface of the field.

Once we had finished the survey of the clan cemetery, the radar machine was moved into the Field of the English to try to find the missing graves of the government troops. Very quickly, a large anomaly appeared on the computer screen; after the data had been processed we were presented with a large rectangular hole. Only with excavation will we know for certain whether this is a mass grave. But if it is, its size would indicate that the government dead should be numbered in hundreds, as opposed to some contemporary figures which were as low as forty.

If we look at the possible government grave and its position in relation to the clan cemetery and to the metal-detector finds which pinpoint the left wing of the

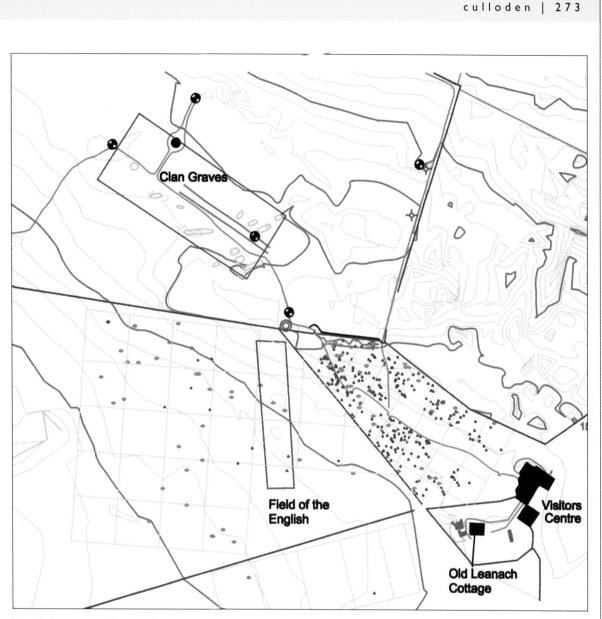

Metal-detector and ground-penetrating radar surveys

government line, the pattern is quite striking. The clan graves are located directly in front of the government line, while the government graves are located immediately behind it. We can imagine individual bodies, both Jacobite and government, lifted from the tangle of corpses. The government troops would have been buried first, pulled from where they had fallen in the line and placed in the ground close by, behind the line. When permission was given to bury the Jacobites several days later, their corpses were carried back over the ground they charged across on that awful day, and buried in freshly dug pits.

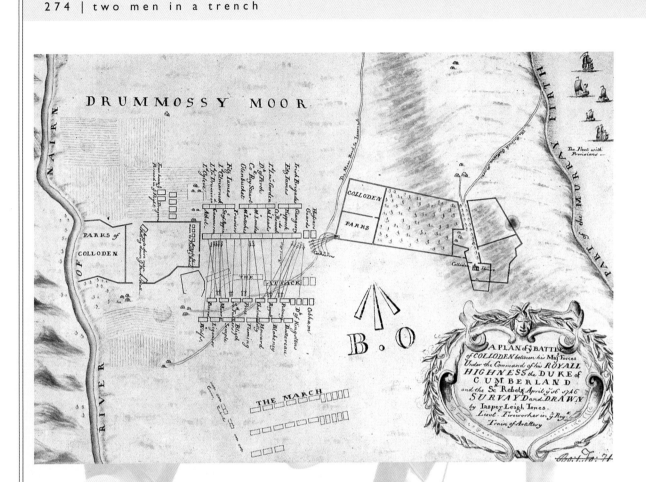

Archaeological Techniques: Using documents

MOST people imagine the archaeologist is concerned exclusively with digging holes or cleaning artefacts, whereas documents – be they maps, diaries, official records or books – are the province of the historian. While it is fair to say the archaeologist deals mostly with the landscape and the things people have left in it, no archaeologist can begin to understand the human past without using documents of some sort. Even students of prehistory, for which of course there are no written records, will at least consult maps, excavation reports and other relevant publications.

Documents take on a whole different meaning to the archaeologist interested in the historical period (in

Britain, that's everything after the Romans, who introduced writing to this country). This obviously applies to anyone interested in historic battlefields: battles are important events which give rise to numerous documents, as officers make reports to their commanders, combatants and eyewitnesses write their diaries, poets and song-writers compose odes and ballads, while broadsheets and newspapers provide their own accounts. Useful as these are, it is important to realize that some of the authors may not have been at the battle, while other accounts may wish to give a spin to certain events, perhaps glorifying a particular commander or regiment. There is an old saying that

Left The Jasper Leigh Jones map

'history is written by the victor', and this should warn us to be cautious and not believe everything we read.

In researching the battle of Culloden we came across a very rich collection of documents, some of which have never been published. To give an idea of the insights that this sort of research can provide, we have included short extracts from two letters. The first is from a government officer and was written from his camp at Inverness two days after the battle. He describes the advance on the Jacobite lines just before the battle began:

> ... as we drew nearer Culloden, two or three honest persons, who had been sent for that purpose, returned and informed the Duke, that the Rebels were formed with their Right to the Water of Nairn and their Left to the sea, leaving the Parks [i.e. the grounds enclosed with stone walls] of Culloden in the Rear of their Left intending as the English Army marched along the High Road to Inverness to take it in the flank, or fall upon the Head of its March; and the better to conceal their purpose and lull us if they Could into a fatal Security they, contrary to their usual custom sent out no Hussars nor people to reconnoitre us, in hopes that we, deceived by the quiet that reigned all about us, might at once fall into the snare they designed us ...

Now a Jacobite officer describes the same event in a letter to a friend in London. He begins with the return of the bedraggled Jacobite army from the aborted night march:

> They killed what cattle and sheep they could find; but few of them had time to make Any Thing ready, before the Alarm came of the enemy being on their march, and approaching. The horse of the Prince's Army had been all on so hard Duty for several Days and Nights before, that none of them were fit for patrolling at that Time.

These two accounts are clearly at odds with one another: the government officer believed the absence of Jacobite scouts was a deliberate ruse aimed at drawing Cumberland's troops into a trap; the Jacobite claims this was due to there not being any mounted scouts available. In this case the Jacobite account would appear to be the simpler and more reliable explanation, with the claims of the government officer merely serving to enhance the scale of Cumberland's victory and to portray the Jacobites as sneaky and underhand.

Early maps and documents relating to historical events can be found in most libraries, but the most important collections are to be found in places such as the National Map Library of Scotland and the Scottish Records Office, both of which are in Edinburgh. Two of the most important sources in England are the National Records Office and the British Library, both in London. The latter boasts a map collection numbering some 4.2 million sheets.

The most common and influential documentary sources for any battle are undoubtedly the maps produced in its aftermath. These may have been drawn up under the orders of commanding officers to provide an official record, or scribbled in letters by combatants wishing to explain to their families or friends where things happened and where they themselves were on that fateful day, rather like obtaining a postcard with your hotel on it and drawing an arrow to 'my room'. Some are composed the day after the battle while others appear months or even years later. The ones that appear in today's history books and battlefield guides rely on the earlier maps as their source, but it becomes difficult to tell one recent map from the next as they become more and more standardized; like a fossil, the truth becomes cast in stone. What may be quirks or simple inaccuracies in one early map seem, in later maps, to be ironed out in favour of a consensual mean.

Most of the maps, old and new, show the various regiments as neat rectangles drawn out in straight lines, which is what a regular army is all about – order and discipline. This would undoubtedly have been more appropriate to the government army, which was drilled and trained to move according to strict rules. The Jacobite army, on the other hand – at least its clan-based regiments – would have been less symmetrical in their disposition: they were not professional soldiers but farmers and herders, come to do their chiefs' bidding. The traditional way of fighting in the Highlands was based not on a drill-book, but on the need to move quickly over rough terrain and engage the enemy as soon as possible. During the initial artillery bombardment of the Jacobite positions, clansmen ran forward from their lines, banging their shields with their swords, shouting at their foe and goading them to come and 'have a go'. Obviously, such behaviour cannot be captured on a map, but these incidents serve to remind us that the battle was an animated, fast-moving, ragged affair.

Some maps try to show action by using arrows and lines to portray movement. A map drawn very soon after the battle by Lieutenant Jasper Leigh Jones, a 'fireworker', or artillery officer, on the government side, not surprisingly goes to some lengths to demonstrate the part played by the artillery. The government cannon are depicted in five pairs just to the front of the infantry, while the Jacobite guns are arranged in a set of five on each flank and a pair in the centre. From the muzzle of each gun is drawn a line that cuts straight across the space between the two armies and terminates on an enemy gun or a body of men. One such line joins a government gun with Keppoch's rectangle and has the inscription 'round shot' – it was these heavy balls which shattered the Jacobite ranks. Most intriguing, though, is what appears to be a duel raging in the corner of the Culloden Enclosure, near the King's Stables, behind the Jacobites' left wing.

The map shows a lone Jacobite gun set defiantly behind the Enclosure wall. Very close by are four government cannon and three cohorn mortars blasting away at the solitary gun with their inky lines. The cannon lines are straight, while the mortars send out graceful curves as they lob their balls high up into the air and drop them down on top of the target – could it be that the mortars were needed to get shots up over the Enclosure wall? The records tell us the government army had ten three-pound guns and six cohorn mortars, and the map clearly shows all ten guns in action on the front line, which means that the four guns engaging the single Jacobite gun must originally have been among the ten on the front line, but were redeployed later in the battle. What we are seeing on Jones's map appears to be a desperate last stand on the part of the Jacobite gunners, many of whom had been killed by the initial government barrage.

But did this duel actually take place? There are no clear written accounts of this action, although the lead-up to the duel may be referred to in an account by a government soldier which appeared in the *London Gazette* on 26 April 1746:

> . . . and his Royal Highness having sent Lord Bury forward, within one Hundred Yards of the Rebels, to reconnoitre something that appeared like a Battery to us, they thereupon began firing their Cannon which was extremely ill pointed: Ours immediately answered them, which began their Confusion. They then came running in their wild manner.

Even though this memoir describes the main exchange of fire between the government and Jacobite artillery, it is not unreasonable to think that the 'something that appeared like a Battery' may well have been the single gun that was spotted by Bury's men as they tried to move round the Jacobite left. A single Jacobite gun does appear in the corner of the Enclosure on at least one other map, drawn by Finlayson in 1746, but there is no reference to government guns being brought forward to engage it. When all is said and done,

Paul and Iain discuss the geophysics results

Jones's map seems to be our only specific source, but how much faith can we put in it? The fact that it was drawn by an artillery officer who would have paid very close attention to the guns certainly works in its favour, but does his pictorial rendition accurately portray the facts? Is there any way that archaeology can help us to verify this story?

The most obvious physical remains of the duel would be the ordnance – the balls and bombs fired by the guns and the mortars. The drawing shows seven pieces of artillery in action against the Jacobite gun; even if each of these pieces was fired only once, that would be seven huge chunks of metal flying through the air. Some of these may have smashed into the wall, knocking out stones and blowing holes in it before falling to the ground. Others may have missed their target altogether and simply thumped into the soft earth. While the cannon would have thrown solid balls at the enemy, the mortars lobbed a powder-packed bomb with a burning fuse timed to ignite the charge as, or just before, it landed, the explosion turning the outer casing into murderous shards of flying metal. Such intensive bombardment may well have left a detectable collection of cannonballs and shrapnel concentrated within a fairly small area of ground. In addition, we could expect to find splintered rock from the wall, equipment and possessions dropped by gunners, and even metal fittings from the Jacobite gun, for there seems little reason to doubt that eventually it would have been hit by the government artillery.

But soon after arriving at Culloden, we received some important – and depressing – news about the area where we had hoped to unearth traces of that desperate last stand. Though battles may draw brief and bloody attention to a particular location, for the rest of the time people must go about their normal business there. And so it was that in recent times the area we had pinpointed from our sources as the site of that fascinating gun battle had attracted the attention of a group of metal detectorists. Given permission by the then landowner, they used their equipment to scour the entire area related to that long-ago duel, though it is doubtful that the ground had any great significance to them: it seems clear the only logic to their targeting of that crucial area was that it was as close as they could legally get to what they understood to be the battlefield.

In any event, they were thorough. The present landowner, who acquired the land some time after the metal detectorists had completed their work, told us the team had successfully collected 'bucket-loads' of musket-balls, cannonballs and other relics of the battle. Left behind at the end of their unofficial 'excavations', the haul remained above ground and in those same

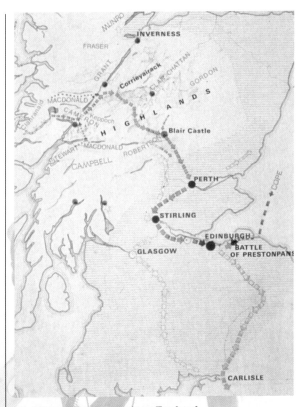

The Jacobite advance into England

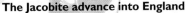

buckets until the previous landowner grew tired of the clutter and put it all out with her rubbish. Thus the fascinating remains of our duel – the material evidence that would have allowed us to colour in the vague outlines we had of the last moments in the lives of those Jacobite gunners – have gone for ever.

In the light of this information, and with time pressing, we had to abandon our plans to pursue that duel. Perhaps some vague traces do exist, but not enough to claim our time on this particular project.

Battlefield archaeology is a new and developing discipline. Part of the rationale for studying these places is to enable battlefields to be more accurately identified and documented. This in turn will make it easier to protect these sites and ensure that the unregulated activities of a minority do not destroy vital, fragile

evidence of these moments from our past. Much valuable work has already been done by metal detectorists working hand in glove with the archaeological community. The sheer scale of many battlefields, and the fact that much of the physical evidence comes in the form of metal, mean that battlefield archaeology depends on the expertise of properly supervised and responsible metal detectorists. Our experience in pursuit of the duel at Culloden amply illustrates the need to develop and deepen this potentially symbiotic relationship. ❦

Conclusion

MOVING forward to the left of the Jacobite line, we passed through a corridor where very few finds were made, a gap corresponding to the space over which the Jacobites charged. Then around 300 metres away from the government position we started to find more musket-balls. These could not have been fired at the Jacobites from the government line, as the maximum range of a musket was only about 100 metres, and some of the balls were distorted after being fired at close range. This scatter of finds therefore marks the point at which government troops successfully outflanked the Jacobite right.

A gap of only 300 metres between the government left and the Jacobite right is much less than the 500 metres traditionally referred to and reflected in the present-day display of the battlefield. Our evidence points to the lines being much closer together, each side being further forward than the flags on the ground indicate. This conclusion matches the previously quoted government officer's letter, which goes on to say:

> When we were within three hundred yards of the rebels, they fired from the battery of four pieces – which they had in the centre but with little or no effect.

This means the Jacobites had less ground to cover during their charge. It is also possible that the government left and the Jacobite right were closer together than other points of the line, if the lines were drawn up obliquely to one another, as is actually suggested by most of the battle maps. The charge itself is also described in our letter:

> ... they broke from the centre in three large bodies, like wedges and moved forward. At first they made a feint as if they would come down upon our right, but seeing that wing so well covered, and imagining that they might surround the left because they saw no cavalry to cover it, two of these wedges bore down immediately upon Barrell's and Munro's Regiments, which formed the left of the first line and after firing very irregularly at considerable distance, they rushed furiously upon 'em, thinking to carry all before them, as they had unfortunately done on former occasions, however they soon found themselves grossly mistaken, for tho' by the violence of the shock Barrell's regiment was a little staggered ...

This description matches all the other accounts, with the Jacobite line breaking from the centre and right towards the government left. The shorter distance between the opposing lines here may be one reason why the government left suffered the brunt of the charge – the Jacobites on the other wing had much more ground to cover under heavy cannon and musket fire. However, our topographic survey has revealed another possible cause for the splitting of the Jacobite charge.

Most books on the battle refer to Culloden Moor as an open space, almost like a flat playing-field, and certainly the maps show little in the way of slopes or gradients. However, detailed survey has shown that the battlefield in fact consists of a series of depressions and ridges, many of which you cannot really see today because of the high vegetation and trees, the most significant being a hollow which is now occupied by the clan cemetery and a slight spur which runs up the centre of the battlefield from the Jacobite line to the government line.

These features would have had two effects. First, the hollow may have obscured at least some of the government left from the view of the Jacobites as they waited to charge; the government right, however, was positioned on more level ground and would have been clearly visible. It is therefore not surprising that the Jacobites favoured an approach towards the government left, as they would be better shielded from enemy fire. This may also explain the stories about the Jacobite left being rather slower to charge than their centre and right, as they would have been running into much heavier fire. The second effect brought about by the terrain was the splitting of the charge by the spur in the centre, funnelling the Jacobite right towards the extreme left of the government line.

The evil that men do

All the maps drawn in the immediate aftermath of the battle show a cluster of buildings, usually three, just behind the left of the government line. Though the exact location differs on many of these maps, there is little reason to doubt that these buildings relate to the farmstead of Old Leanach, one of which supposedly survives on the site today, albeit much modified. As for the other buildings, if you look carefully at the ground next to the surviving house, there are grassy lumps and bumps, with a stone sticking out here and there. These remains, at first uninspiring, are tell-tale signs to the archaeologist that something, possibly a building, once stood here.

According to the National Trust's guidebook, they are all that is left of the Red Barn, the name given to the building which was reputedly put to the torch by government troops while it housed dozens of Jacobite wounded. But how do they know this and where does the story come from? Here the major source is a collection of eyewitness accounts, many in the form of letters, collected by the Reverend Robert Forbes, a Jacobite sympathizer from Leith, near Edinburgh.

> there were a great many wounded in houses on the field of battle, the orders given were that the houses should be burnt and all within them, and if they offered to come out they should be shot. It is impossible to know what number suffered. There were three tenants' houses and all their office houses. The first that ventured to go near that place saw most shocking sights, some of their bodies boiling and others lying with the marks of their ruffels, which when they touched they went into ashes.

Not liking to travel too far to work, we pitched our tent next to Old Leanach cottage and the remains we were going to investigate. The only way to find out whether these unassuming lumps really were the remains of the Red Barn, and whether they had anything to tell us about this horrible act of cruelty, was to excavate them. So after some discussion over tea, we marked out an excavation trench inside the area enclosed by the banks, which logic suggested was the inside of the building, while we placed other trenches over the banks, which we thought were the outside walls. Then the team, overseen by our old mucker Paul Duffy, began the hard work of carefully removing the turf with spades.

Sure enough, there was a wall under the turf, although it had crumbled and been robbed for stones to be used elsewhere. Before we started excavation, we had been quite excited by the fact that the bank looked as though it ran under the gable end of the cottage at an angle, suggesting that the cottage sat on the remains of an earlier building. So we thought the remains we could see on the ground may indeed have come from a

Our tent with Old Leanach cottage behind

building which stood at the time of the battle and could even have been burned down. As it happened, though, once we had removed the turf and trowelled away enough soil to take a look at the buried wall, it became obvious it did not in fact run at an angle to the gable end but instead went straight towards the corner of the building, creating a rectangle with the cottage. It now looked as though our buried wall did not run under the cottage but had simply been erected against the gable wall, probably after the cottage had been built rather than before.

Excavation of the interior trench also produced disappointing results. If we were excavating the site of a building, we would have expected a floor of some sort – paved or cobbled or just trampled clay. But the soil, carefully removed in layers, went deeper and deeper without any sign of a floor appearing. Some artefacts

were recovered, including shards of broken pottery, some of it nicely decorated and perhaps from somebody's best dinner service.

In one part of the trench a hole full of stones was uncovered, and between the stones we found an old leather boot with its rusted hobnails still in place, but it was obviously not much older than the late nineteenth or early twentieth century. The stone-filled hole looked like a rubble drain which had been constructed after the enclosing wall to remove water, perhaps heavy rainfall, from the structure. The presence of the drain and the rich, organic nature of the soil cast further doubt on the existence of a building: the soil was of a type commonly found in places where crops have been grown and is sometimes called garden soil, and the drain would have prevented it becoming waterlogged.

Not only could we find no floor, but there was also

no trace of burning. Timber is present in most buildings, and traditional post-medieval Scottish Highland structures would have included curved beams to support the roof. If a building had caught fire or been put to the torch, the timber would have been turned to charcoal, which survives very well on most archaeological sites, sometimes for tens of thousands of years. Small traces of charcoal were found in the upper soil levels, but these appeared to represent either ashes from a fire which had been dumped there or the burning of scrub vegetation; there was no evidence of a large-scale fire engulfing heavy timbers as would be expected in the case of a burning barn. On a more gruesome note, we may also have expected to find traces of burned human bone, as this also survives well in its carbonized state.

All the evidence from the excavation pointed away from the site being the remains of a burned barn and towards it being a walled, unroofed enclosure inside which crops had been grown. In short, what we probably had was the site of the kitchen garden related to the cottage which stands today. A pottery expert examined the shards and none of them dates back before the early to mid nineteenth century. This evidence, along with a photograph of the cottage taken in the 1890s, in which it looks very similar to the building as it appears today, implies that the remains on the site relate to a period much later than the battle, with no evidence for buildings which stood on the site in 1746.

This conclusion was reinforced by a second excavation on the other side of the cottage. Again, the evidence pointed to activity related to a nineteenth-century smallholding, with nothing to suggest anything on the site as early as the battle. Even with modern development, including the car park and the visitors' centre, we would expect some evidence of eighteenth-century activity, even a scrap of pottery, if the original Leanach settlement had been in the immediate area of the cottage.

Excavation has proved that the remains traditionally thought to represent a barn burned after the battle are in fact much later in date and belong not to a building but to a garden wall. But does this mean we can discount the story of the burning barn and the atrocity committed inside it? Certainly not. Rather, the total lack of evidence for eighteenth-century activity on the site strongly suggests that the original settlement of Leanach is to be found elsewhere. Early maps suggest a degree of uncertainty about its exact position, though most of them show the farmstead somewhere near the left of the government line. As the metal-detector survey has pushed this point further to the south, then we may have to move the position of the barn along with it. It is our belief, after considering all of the evidence, that we should move closer to the river Nairn, into the field next to the Field of the English, if we want to find remains contemporary with the battle and to prove or disprove the story of the burning of the Red Barn.

FIRTH OF FORTH 1939

FIRTH OF FORTH

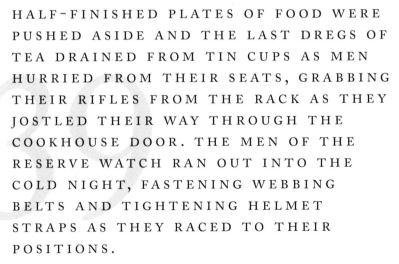

HALF-FINISHED PLATES OF FOOD WERE PUSHED ASIDE AND THE LAST DREGS OF TEA DRAINED FROM TIN CUPS AS MEN HURRIED FROM THEIR SEATS, GRABBING THEIR RIFLES FROM THE RACK AS THEY JOSTLED THEIR WAY THROUGH THE COOKHOUSE DOOR. THE MEN OF THE RESERVE WATCH RAN OUT INTO THE COLD NIGHT, FASTENING WEBBING BELTS AND TIGHTENING HELMET STRAPS AS THEY RACED TO THEIR POSITIONS.

Opposite Inchkeith island

LAND DEFENCE SCHEME 255 COAST BATTERY RA

GEOGRAPHY
The southern end of INCHKEITH, for the defence of which
255 Coast battery RA is responsible, is characterized
by the fact that landing facilities from shallow craft
exist practically speaking all round. It is less
probable that such landings would be made from the
western side owing to the minefield in the south
channel.

INFORMATION
(a) ENEMY. An attack on the island may be in the form
of a 'Nuisance Raid' by a small force with the object
of doing as much damage to equipment as possible,
followed by a retirement or sacrifice of the force
concerned, or a landing in force with the capture of
the island as its objective.

(Extract from standing orders for the defence of Inchkeith island during the
Second World War)

The siren which had so rudely interrupted their supper wailed like an
injured animal, as it had on many previous nights, but whether this was
simply another exercise or the real thing no one could tell.

No one that is, apart from the men posted in Electric Light
Emplacement number one, which overlooked the southern tip of the
island. Their beat was the southern channel, from where the Firth of
Forth stretches out towards Edinburgh, which as usual showed not a
single light, as a precaution against air-raids. In contrast, the searchlight
cut through the dark and threw pin-sharp shadows off Long Craig,
which at low tide marked the extreme southern point of the great spine
of rock known as Inchkeith. Suddenly the piercing beam caught a small
boat. The dozen or so men on board shielded their eyes from the stark
white light and hunched forward in a futile effort to hide from the
halogen eye. As the beam swept over the surface of the water, more
boats were picked out. The searchlight battery's duty sergeant cranked
the dynamo on his telephone and yelled into the mouthpiece: 'Light
number one here. Boats approaching from the south-east, range 200
yards! Sound Action Stations!'

*The searchlight
cut through the
dark ... As the
beam swept over
the surface
of the water,
more boats were
picked out*

(b) OWN TROOPS. Forces available in Southern Sector will be:

PERSONNEL	WEAPONS			
	RIFLES	BOFORS	BRENS	STENS
20	20	1	4	4

INTENTION
(i) 255 Coast Battery RA will destroy all enemy forces attempting to land in the southern sector.

(ii) There will be no withdrawal.

The defence of the island is based mainly on fire power with automatic weapons covering all likely approaches. Each locality is responsible for its own defence with as far as possible localities supporting each other.

It is anticipated that the forces and weapons available on 'ACTION STATIONS' will be as follows:

	Troops	Weapons		
		Rifles	Brens	Stens
NORTH SECTOR	100	100	4	4
SOUTH SECTOR	20	20	4	4
WEST SECTOR	25	20	4	4
MIDDLE SECTOR	20	20	3	1

One of the guns on Inchkeith being fired at night

Some of the small inflatable boats were spotted before they had the chance to come ashore, but others managed to avoid exposure from the searchlight. German troops made their way over the shingle spit which connected Long Craig to the island. They ran at a crouch, holding their weapons low as they removed the waterproof covers from the muzzles and pulled back their cocking levers in readiness for action. Two men dropped to the ground in unison and quickly brought their machine-gun to bear against the searchlight, which was still a threat to the boats that had yet to reach the shore. The staccato bark of the heavy gun was followed by the lighter rattle of the machine-pistols as the force deployed across the beach and began its assault in earnest.

Operation Sealion, the German invasion of the British mainland, was scheduled to begin in seven hours' time and a specially trained force of commandos from the German navy had been given the task of neutralizing Inchkeith's guns and other coastal defences, thus clearing the way for the northern invasion fleet to sail unmolested up the Firth of Forth. Disembarking from two U-boats which had surfaced in the mouth of the Firth, the commandos had rowed to the island, one group heading for the southern end, where the beaches provided the most suitable location for an amphibious landing, while another landed at the northern end, where they faced the daunting task of scaling the cliffs. All had gone well until, at the last minute, the wind drove one of the lightweight vessels into the beam of the searchlight and instantly deprived them of the element of surprise.

They ran at a crouch, holding their weapons low as they removed the waterproof covers from the muzzles and pulled back their cocking levers in readiness for action

```
AMMUNITION
The allotment of ammunition per rifle, Bren, Sten and
the number of Grenades (M36) held is as follows:

                    Rifles    Bren      Sten    Grenades

'A' Sector (NORTH)  200       2,600T    384     250
                              5,400B

'B' Sector (SOUTH)  200       2,600T    384     100
                              5,400B
```

```
50 rounds are issued to each rifleman; the balance is
held in reserve in each sector.

Each Bren post is allotted 5,000 rounds ball [B] and
1,500 rounds tracer [T]; the balance is held in reserve
in each sector.
```

Even as the men of the Reserve Watch jumped on to the firing step in the concrete trench, the men of the Duty Watch were shooting at the figures on the beach. But their rifle fire was ragged and stilted at first. All the training in the world could do only so much to prepare them for the reality of combat. Sensing that his men were rattled, a sergeant, hardened to trench warfare in an earlier generation, offered words of encouragement. 'Calm down, lads, fire at the muzzle flashes. Find your targets!' But as the Reserve Watch joined battle and the Bren gun opened up from its pit, it was hard to hear anything above the ear-splitting din.

Even so, the corporal on the Bren gun muttered to himself, 'Johnny, get your gun, Johnny, get your gun'. This was no half-whispered order to his subordinates but a chant he'd learned in training, each utterance serving to time the depression of his finger on the trigger, as longer bursts would overheat the barrel and jam the weapon. His fire was directed into the beam of the searchlight, which thanks to its heavy concrete bunker had thus far escaped all German attempts at destruction. Bullets riffled through the water and then, as they found their mark, tore into the rubber sides of the flimsy craft and the dreadfully exposed bodies of the men on board.

Just when it seemed the noise had reached a deafening peak, the Germans on the beach threw high-explosive charges into the barbed-wire entanglements in front of the trench. Earth and stones rained down on the troops and ragged gaps appeared in the firing line as casualties mounted. Then, to the rear, a star-shell flare exploded high above the island, the phosphorous charge burning a dazzling white, as it descended in a gentle spiral on its small parachute. There was a crackle of distant gunfire as the second German assault force reached the top of the north cliff. The hundred men stationed in 'A' Sector were engaged.

1939

During the early part of the Second World War there was a real fear in Britain that Germany would invade, and the extracts from standing orders quoted above give some idea of how seriously this threat was taken. Although the orders are real, the battle scene described above is obviously a figment of our imagination. As we all know, the Germans, after failing to take control of the air during the battle of Britain, never got the opportunity to put their invasion plans into practice. Today, thanks to books, films and television programmes, we all have some idea of the scale and horror of the conflict. Knowing the outcome of the war, it is

Tony with a Lee Enfield .303 rifle and Neil with a Bren gun

perhaps more difficult to imagine just how frightening life must have been on the British home front during those dark days. We hope that our investigation of the military archaeology of Inchkeith island, and a consideration of the other defences in and around the Firth of Forth, will provide some food for thought.

BACKGROUND

IF THE EVENTS OF THE SECOND WORLD WAR COULD BE PORTRAYED AS A HUGE FAMILY TREE, OUR EYES WOULD BE DRAWN TO THE BIG NAMES SCATTERED AMONG THE BRANCHES: POLAND, DUNKIRK, PEARL HARBOR, EL ALAMEIN, STALINGRAD, NORMANDY. HERE ARE THE PIVOTAL POINTS UPON WHICH SO MUCH HISTORY TURNED AS THE LARGEST AND BLOODIEST CONFLICT IN THE HISTORY OF THE WORLD RAN ITS COURSE. PLACING THE DEFENCE OF THE FIRTH OF FORTH AGAINST THE BACKGROUND OF THAT CONFLICT SEEMS SIMPLE ENOUGH NOW: THE AREA WAS FORTIFIED AGAINST AN INVASION THAT NEVER CAME.

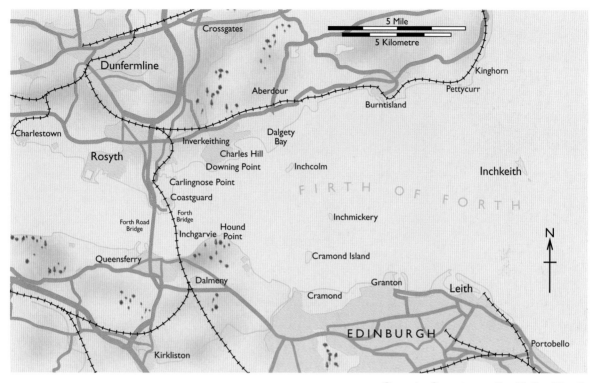

Opposite **Sunset over the Firth of Forth**
Above **A modern map of the area**

On our family tree, what happened here would appear as a distant
relation to the main events – the almost indecipherable name of a third
or fourth cousin, several times removed. History would allow little space
for events in the Firth of Forth, such as they were.

But in those first days and months of the war, who knew where the
pivotal points would be? Who could have predicted, in the anxious days
that followed Britain and France's joint declaration of war on Germany
on 3 September 1939, where the fate of the world would be decided? The
men and women who were serving on the Forth had every reason to
believe they might at any moment find themselves in the front line. They
were stationed on one of the most heavily defended estuaries in the
British Isles, facing east towards the aggressor. Since the First World
War, the Forth had been a crucial spot in the minds of those tasked with
defending Britain against seaborne invasion. The naval base at Rosyth,
with its anchorage for the fleet, lay just to the west of the Forth Bridge,
itself an important link between northern and southern Scotland. The
nation's capital, Edinburgh, was within sight of the Forth's southern
coastline and the whole area was vulnerable to attack from the sea.

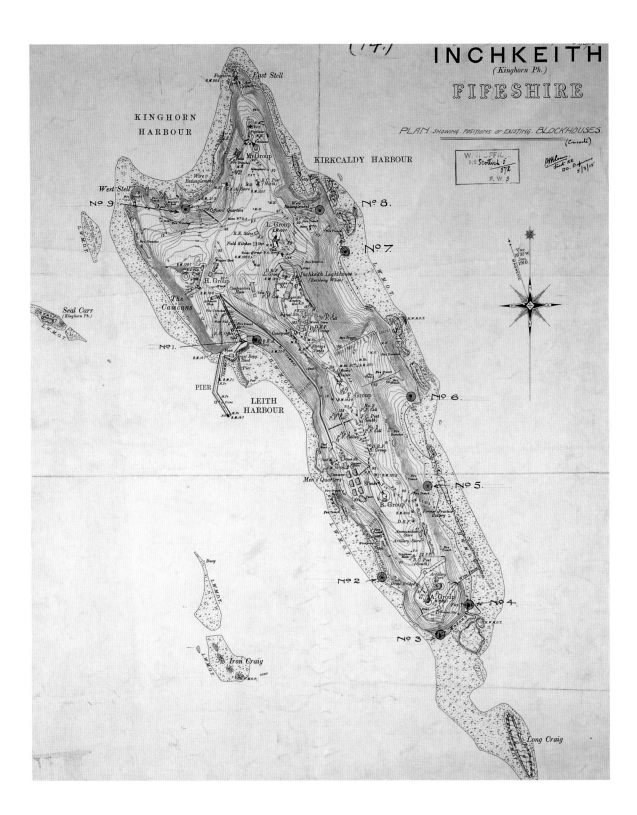

Indeed, for as long as people have had boats, the estuary has offered a natural inroad to mainland Scotland. Both coastlines, together with the islands dotting the river mouth, bear traces of centuries of human occupation. Four of the principal islands of the Forth, known locally as the Inches, have seen varying degrees of settlement and use during the last 1,500 years or so. The largest, Inchkeith, was home to a religious order by the end of the seventh century, having been settled by monks from the island of Iona. It was not until the early eleventh century, however, that this rocky citadel acquired its modern name. Robert de Keth, having fought off marauding Danes on behalf of the Scottish king, Malcolm II, was rewarded with large tracts of land and the title of High Marshal of Scotland. Among the gifts was the ownership of what would become known as Inchkeith. During the reign of James IV, who was to die so tragically at Flodden, Inchkeith became a place of sad exile for Edinburgh's plague victims. The island was to reprise this grim role several times – notably in 1799, when a Russian fleet offloaded many plague-stricken sailors who were subsequently laid to rest there. It has been fortified and refortified repeatedly since the mid sixteenth century, with notable work undertaken by military engineers in the late Victorian period and during both world wars.

The Forth Bridge leapfrogs across the river with the help of Inchgarvie, which provides the foundation for its central span. This rock too bears witness to the preparations for past conflicts: James IV had a defensive tower built here, and the island's dominant position in the Forth's mid-stream was exploited again and again until the end of the Second World War. The twentieth-century military architecture on Inchmickery gives the island the appearance of a huge battleship at anchor, and Inchcolm – home to a community of monks from the mid twelfth until the late sixteenth centuries – also has defences dating to the two world wars.

It was on the European mainland, however, that the principal action focused in September 1939. The period following the declaration of hostilities is often referred to as the Phoney War, though there was little that was phoney about it for those men of the British Expeditionary Forces who found themselves in northern France occupying positions depressingly similar to those that had been abandoned at the end of the First World War. With the swift advance of German forces during the summer of 1940, the Allies were pushed back to the sea and were compelled to undertake the most famous mass evacuation of troops in history: some 200,000 British and over 100,000 French soldiers were

The island was fortified and refortified repeatedly since the mid sixteenth century, with notable work undertaken by military engineers

Opposite **Military O.S. map of the island surveyed in 1919**

German reconnaissance photograph of rail bridge and surrounding area

picked off the beaches around the French port of Dunkirk by vessels manned largely by civilians. With nowhere to run, France capitulated, leaving Germany to contemplate the destruction of the Royal Air Force and the planned seaborne invasion of mainland Britain, codenamed Operation Sealion. With the mighty Luftwaffe looming like storm clouds on the horizon, Britain turned its attention to defence and the fight for survival in the face of appalling odds.

The ancient abbey on Inchcolm

With the mighty Luftwaffe looming like storm clouds on the horizon, Britain turned its attention to defence

On the Firth of Forth, defences installed for the previous war were dusted down and prepared for action once more, and new ones built. Positions on the Inches and along both coastlines were rearmed, and remanned. Airfields were established to provide defences for both the Forth itself – including the bridge and the naval base at Rosyth – and the surrounding regions. An intelligent defensive network was created: rather than operating separately, each element was in communication with its neighbours so that the whole could function as a single entity. The area could reasonably be described as Fortress Forth.

The Firth of Forth and its western counterpart, the Firth of Clyde, have long been special places for Scots. In the early months of the war, the 500-strong garrison on Inchcolm made themselves at home within the halls and cloisters of the ancient abbey. Already a protected ancient monument, it sheltered officers and men until purpose-built accommodation could be provided. They were walking in the footsteps of others who had sought shelter here in past centuries – and perhaps its calm atmosphere, still palpable today, was some comfort to them in those first uncertain days. The men and women of Fortress Forth stood to in 1939 in the sure and certain knowledge that they held the stewardship of an ancient way into the British mainland, and although their defence was barely challenged, it mattered and it was brave.

THE BATTLE

ON 16 OCTOBER 1939, SIX WEEKS AFTER
THE DECLARATION OF WAR BETWEEN
BRITAIN AND GERMANY, THE
LUFTWAFFE CHOSE TO MAKE THE FIRTH
OF FORTH THE TARGET OF ITS FIRST
STRIKE AGAINST THE BRITISH
MAINLAND. THE DRONE OF AIRCRAFT
ENGINES WAS HEARD HIGH ABOVE THE
WATER. THE PLANES WERE TWIN-
ENGINED HEINKEL III BOMBERS,
THOUGH THEIR JOB WAS NOT TO RAIN
DOWN DESTRUCTION BUT TO TAKE
RECONNAISSANCE PHOTOGRAPHS OF
THE NAVAL DOCKYARD AT ROSYTH.

Left Flight Lieutenant George Pinkerton
Right Pilot Officer Archie McKellar

One of the Heinkels, having fulfilled its mission, was reported to be flying over the Forth Bridge on its way home at 1008 hours. But he wasn't going to get away that easily – at 0945 two Spitfires of Blue Section, 602 (City of Glasgow) Squadron, had been scrambled from RAF Drem, just a little to the east of Edinburgh. The senior pilot was Flight Lieutenant George Pinkerton and his number two was Pilot Officer Archie McKellar. Whether they knew it or not, they were flying into history.

The Spitfires headed north-east, their powerful Rolls-Royce Merlin V12 engines pushing them through the sky at over 300 mph. The Heinkel was spotted by the Spitfires as it passed by the Isle of May. Having the advantage of speed and manoeuvrability over the enemy raider, the fighters went into action. Firing their machine-guns in short, controlled bursts, the pilots took it in turns to roll their planes into the attack. The Heinkel's gunners returned fire as its pilot took evasive action. Luck appeared to be with the German crew as the plane disappeared into cloud and broke contact. Who can say whether it made it back to base or what damage the Spitfire's machine-guns had wrought upon it? After returning to base, the armourer informed Pinkerton that he had fired 720 rounds, while his wing man had managed to squeeze off about 1,000. Even though there was no 'kill', the contact was still a landmark. Pinkerton and McKellar had become the first British pilots to take a Spitfire into combat against the Luftwaffe, and they had also fired the first shots in the air war over Britain.

Firing their machine-guns in short, controlled bursts, the pilots took it in turns to roll their planes into the attack

A Spitfire Mk I in flight

1939

But RAF Drem and the Firth of Forth had not heard the last of the Luftwaffe on that fateful day. At 1120 hours, not long after Pinkerton and McKellar had returned from their mission, word came through that another Heinkel had been spotted. Douglas Farquhar, commander of 602 Squadron, was up in the air in minutes, no doubt hungry for a piece of the action. He was soon followed by the planes of Red Section, but to no avail. The Heinkel could not be found and was last seen over the radar masts at Drone Hill. The radar had broken down that morning, and so the fighters were not acting on the most accurate information about the location of the enemy. A potentially fatal blind spot had opened up and for much of the morning and afternoon RAF fighters were sent up to hunt down phantom enemy aircraft.

The Luftwaffe had an important target in mind. They were after HMS *Hood*, the pride of the British Navy. The *Hood*, according to German military intelligence, was heading for the Forth, where she would be easy prey, or so the Germans must have thought. The man selected for the job was Hauptman Helmut Pohl, who had commanded the first Luftwaffe attack on British Navy ships on 26 September. Although this attack had gone badly for the Germans, the experience appears to have stood him in good stead as far as the mission planners were concerned.

With the radar still out of action, members of the Observer Corps spotted enemy aircraft – Junkers this time, not Heinkels – over East Lothian at about 1420 hours and sounded the alert. No sooner had Pinkerton finished his lunch than he was back in the air again. As the enemy approached the Firth, more fighters were scrambled, including the men of 603 (City of Edinburgh) Squadron, based at RAF Turnhouse, which had had just taken delivery of its new Spitfires. As the Junkers reached the Forth Bridge, more sightings were reported from the ground, among them an excited report from the commanding officer of the anti-aircraft battery at Dalmeny Park.

At around 1430 Pohl's lead aircraft was over the bridge, but the *Hood* was nowhere to be seen. What German intelligence had reported was in fact, HMS *Repulse*. Sitting at the dockside at Rosyth, the *Repulse* would certainly have made a worthy target. However, the war was in its early days and the German High Command, still interested in a peaceful solution with Britain, had therefore given Pohl explicit orders to bomb the *Hood* only if she were at a sufficient distance from the docks to avoid civilian casualties. Turning his attention away from the *Repulse*, which he may have thought was the *Hood*, Pohl decided to try his luck on warships anchored in mid-stream, off the east side of the bridge. His first targets were the cruisers HMS *Southampton* and HMS *Edinburgh*.

Several bombs exploded harmlessly in the water, others found their mark. One narrowly missed the bow of the *Southampton*, but the admiral's barge and a pinnace moored alongside were destroyed by the blast. On board the *Edinburgh*, shrapnel injured sailors and damaged the superstructure. The *Southampton* and *Edinburgh* got off relatively lightly, but HMS *Mohawk*, which was escorting a convoy thirty miles to the east of Rosyth, was not so fortunate. Machine-gun fire and shrapnel

HMS *Hood* in the Firth of Forth

Some of the pilots of 602 Squadron in front of the Watch Office at Drem

1939

killed three officers and thirteen men, and the commander, Richard Jolly, was seriously injured, and after guiding the *Mohawk* safely back to dock he died soon after.

The German bombs had taken a toll, but the raiders were not to have everything their own way. The Spitfires from RAF Turnhouse were scrambled and in the skies above Edinburgh they locked on to the bombers' tails and emptied their wing-mounted Brownings into the enemy aircraft. The brass cartridge cases rattled down on to the rooftops as they were ejected from the machine-guns, and years later when gutters were fixed or replaced they were still there, forgotten mementoes of that first battle.

Before the bombs had stopped falling, the anti-aircraft guns of Dalmeny battery, on the north side of the bridge, opened fire, peppering the sky with white plumes of smoke. In addition the *Repulse* brought her guns to bear on the screaming aircraft as they twisted and dived high above the bridge. But it was not only the enemy aircraft which were at risk from the flying shrapnel – a rain of metal began to fall over Edinburgh and the surrounding areas, causing damage to buildings and vehicles but mercifully injuring very few people.

Three waves of bombers had been sent against the Forth and now, with their bombs dropped, the raiders played a deadly game of aerial cat and mouse. Not all of them were successful in their attempts to escape. A lone bomber flying over Cockenzie was intercepted by a group of three Spitfires led by Pat Gifford, and shot down over the sea. Three surviving crew members were picked up by a local fisherman, but the body of the fourth was never found. Pohl himself also fell victim to the Spitfire interceptors. The hail of bullets wrought a terrible toll on his already damaged aircraft. The radio operator was hit and two crew members were killed, their bodies mashed in their seats by the heavy-calibre bullets which raked the length and breadth of the aircraft, though Pohl himself miraculously survived the crash.

It had been a hectic day, and its like was not to be seen again in the Forth, as the Firth of Clyde was soon to become the main Scottish target for the Luftwaffe's bombs. But German planes regularly dropped mines into the Firth or dropped the odd bomb on the towns which skirted these uneasy waters, and over the next couple of months German raiders ran the gauntlet of ground-based anti-aircraft fire and pursuit by fighter interceptors. After being shot down, one German pilot confessed to his captors that the skies over the Forth had become known as 'suicide corner', such was the dread with which the place was regarded by German aircrews.

Inchkeith was also to play its part in these early skirmishes. On the night of 27 May 1940 a German bomber was caught in the beam of a searchlight at Methil. An anti-aircraft battery on Inchkeith opened fire, sending tracer bullets arcing up into the night sky. They found their mark, and one eyewitness reported seeing the plane burst into flames before crashing into the sea.

But the gunners on Inchkeith had their off days too. On 21 February, an Admiralty trawler was passing through the channel off the southern tip of the island, and the gunners on the island noticed the boat was in danger of straying into the minefield protecting the channel. A quick-thinking Artillery officer gave the order for a dummy round to be fired across the trawler's bow to warn the skipper of the danger he was in, and the boat duly changed its course: disaster was averted.

If only the shell had stopped there. Instead of harmlessly sinking, the shell bounced, like a stone skipping over the water. It flew over houses in Leith before crashing through the wall of a tenement in Salamander Street and burying itself in a shed in the backyard. It was a miracle that no one was killed, and the incident is remembered to this day as the battle of Salamander Street.

By mid-1940 the Phoney War had given way to the battle of Britain. The Luftwaffe turned its attention away from the Firth of Forth and

. . . the Forth had become known as 'suicide corner', such was the dread with which the place was regarded by German aircrews

Spitfires on patrol during the battle of Britain

1939

threw everything it had at the south-east of England, bombing London and Kent on a daily basis. With the return of relative peace to the Firth, the fighter squadrons were transferred to the south, where the experience they had gained in fighting off the raiders in Scotland was to serve them well. But the islands and other defences remained in a state of readiness, vigilant against the return of the enemy, until victory in the battle of Britain removed the threat of invasion and permitted several of the ground-based defences to be downgraded and personnel to be transferred to other places. Many soldiers of the Royal Artillery previously based on Inchkeith ended up in North Africa, where the war was a much hotter affair, in more ways than one.

INCHKEITH: AN ISLAND DRESSED FOR WAR

Inchkeith has been a focus for military activity for well over 300 years. The special use to which the island has been put over the years has given it a unique character, which is today expressed by the complex remains of the buildings which cover much of its surface, and even extend deep into its heart.

A Second World War view of Inchkeith: roads, batteries and gun emplacements can be seen clearly

If the island were a person, then Inchkeith would undoubtedly be an old soldier. Like Barry Lyndon, the eponymous hero in Thackeray's great novel, Inchkeith has served in several nations' armies and during that long service has experienced many changes of fortune, all of which have had an impact on the island, clothing it with the various types of fortification.

The island began its military service under the English, who built a fort there after decisively beating the Scots at the battle of Pinkie in 1547. This was a bloody and confusing period in Scottish history. The English continued to wage war in Scotland, where they fought not only the Scots but also the French, while on their own side they employed Italians and even Germans as mercenaries.

When the English fleet departed not long after the defensive works had begun, the island was left with a small garrison of English and Italian troops, whereupon the French, with the full support of the Scots, launched an assault. The fighting was bitter, and it is recorded that an Italian captain called Gaspare had his head removed by a cannonball. Finally the garrison retired to the highest point of the island and were forced back to the edge of a precipice, where they had no option but to plunge to their deaths or surrender. They chose to surrender.

Some idea of the strength of the island's fortress is provided in an English report dated 17 April 1560: 'I think it might be takeable, if we might lie there with 600 men, 3 demi-cannons, 3 culverins, 2 sakers, 2 falcons with 150 shot each piece, and 5 lasts of serpentine powder.' This intelligence report and the failed outcome of an earlier attempt by the English to re-take the island by storm strongly suggest that the French made improvements to the fort after taking over the island. Of course, the French had control of the island for much longer than the English, who appear to have had only a few days to construct defences.

A fresh English force arrived on the outskirts of Edinburgh in April 1560, just after the queen had moved from Holyrood House to Edinburgh Castle, and this time they had Scottish allies, as the Catholic French were proving increasingly unpopular in the Scotland of John Knox, the vociferous anti-Catholic orator. On 7 May the English launched a massive attack on the town but it was not a success, partly due to the fact that the siege ladders were too short.

As it happened, an end to hostilities came about as a result not of military action but of the death of the queen, Mary of Guise, the French widow of James V of Scotland. With Mary's death the French connection was broken and the treaty of Edinburgh between England and Scotland

Manning the guns on Inchkeith during a practice night 'shoot'

was signed shortly after. With the outbreak of peace the island fortress entered a period of retirement from active service, not least because it was recognized that the island had little influence on the passage of shipping into the Forth as it was possible to sail by out of cannon range. The fort was largely dismantled and the island, like a Scottish Alcatraz, was used every now and again as a prison.

Despite some fortification in the Forth during the Cromwellian period, most notably on Inchgarvie, it was not until the nineteenth century that the island was once again pressed into military service. The threat from Napoleon prompted another escalation in fortification construction in the Firth. But it was the 1880s which really saw the island come into its own, with the development of accurate heavy-calibre guns. With Russia replacing France as the most likely threat to the British mainland, a programme of fortification began with the construction of three forts that contained gun emplacements, underground magazines and communication passages, and protected accommodation blocks.

The Victorian forts were never used in anger, but improvements in technology were integrated into the defences. By 1891 the muzzle-loading guns in two of the forts had been replaced by new breech-loaders mounted on disappearing carriages, which made loading and

The island began its military service under the English, who built a fort there after decisively beating the Scots at the battle of Pinkie in 1547

The naval dockyard at Rosyth from German reconnaissance photograph

1939

reloading faster and more secure as it could be done under cover. In the early twentieth century high-tech range-finders were installed. Inchkeith was not the only position modified, and a series of inner defences was constructed at North and South Queensferry.

With the twentieth century came a new threat, in the form of Germany. The construction of the naval dockyard at Rosyth made the Forth a prime target for any potential enemy and so once again the defences were expanded and upgraded. Guns were placed on most of the islands, including Cramond, Inchmickery and Inchcolm as well as Inchgarvie. New batteries were also constructed at Hound Point, on the south shore, and Braehead, on the north shore. Anti-submarine nets were strung across the Forth as a defence against this deadly new way of making war.

But other than a Zeppelin raid on Edinburgh in 1916, the Forth defences saw little in the way of action during the First World War, although the islands did witness the various goings of the Grand Fleet,

including its departure to the largest naval engagement of the war, the battle of Jutland.

From 1938 there was another programme of battery construction and rearming. An important extension to the defences was the addition of anti-aircraft batteries, in response to yet another new type of warfare. Several were placed on Inchkeith and on at least one occasion were responsible for shooting down enemy aircraft. During the early war years the island witnessed military activity like never before, with up to 700 men stationed there. But the end of the island's long military career was fast approaching, and military minds turned to taking the war to the enemy instead of waiting for the enemy to arrive at the gates.

Now the island sits idle, its garrisons long gone, and its uniform of stone and concrete fortifications tattered and worn. The old soldier sleeps.

WEAPONS AND TACTICS

THE COMPLICATED AND CHALLENGING BUSINESS OF DEFENDING A VAST AREA LIKE THE FIRTH OF FORTH MADE A LOT MORE SENSE AFTER WE'D SPOKEN TO NORMAN CLARK, A LOCAL EXPERT ON THE SUBJECT. HE EXPLAINED THAT THE STRATEGIES EMPLOYED IN THE FORTH DOWN THE CENTURIES HAD LARGELY BEEN DICTATED BY THE POWER OF THE WEAPONS AVAILABLE TO ITS RESIDENTS, AND HAD ALWAYS BEEN FOCUSED AROUND INDIVIDUAL POINTS OF TACTICAL IMPORTANCE.

Norman said that in 1549, when Inchkeith was occupied by English and Italian soldiers, their guns were not powerful or accurate enough to threaten shipping in the channels to the north and south of the island. Instead, their strategy was to defend the island from invasion – by Scots intent on evicting the cuckoo in their nest – while at the same time using it as a base for raids up and down the Forth. When the Victorians built their forts on the islands in the 1870s and 1880s, the perceived threat came from the continent, and the challenge was to find a way to make the estuary too hot for invaders to contemplate. Artillery was by then more than capable of targeting shipping effectively, and this shaped the Victorians' strategy for the whole area. Two 10-inch rifled muzzle-loading guns located in the southern fort, facing Leith, and one each in the east and west forts completed the armaments of the island. Similar weapons were installed on the coastline to create a cross-fire capable of covering both channels and making life extremely unpleasant for any ships attempting to pass up-river.

Norman described how the east fort had been the focus of a fascinating experiment in 1884. Unimpressed by their warships' guns during a bombardment of the Egyptian city of Alexandria, the naval top brass determined to find out just how useful their weapons were against weapons on land. With that in mind they brought HMS *Sultan*, a ship that had been involved in the 'policing' action at Alexandria, up the Forth and anchored her just off the coast of Inchkeith. Over the course of two days, the *Sultan* blasted away at the western gun emplacement, which was manned for the occasion by a wooden gun crew. The results were inconclusive but served as fine entertainment for the good people of Edinburgh and Fife, who watched the spectacle from small boats.

Muzzle-loaders of the kind originally used in the Victorian forts had the disadvantage of exposing the gun crews to enemy fire every time they stood in front of the weapon to reload it. This problem was solved with the introduction of breech-loading guns, which allowed their crews to remain under cover while servicing the weapons and had the added advantage of a markedly increased rate of fire. By the time of the First World War, breech-loaders – many of them quick-firing – had replaced all the muzzle-loaders in the Firth of Forth.

Strategy too had evolved and by 1914 the estuary was protected by three concentric lines of defence radiating out from the hub at Rosyth. Developments in the field of telecommunications – the telegraph and the telephone – meant that defensive locations that, out of necessity, had operated independently could now work in concert. Inchkeith served as

Opposite **A 10-inch coastal gun and emplacement on Inchkeith in 1884**

By the time of the First World War, breech-loaders – many of them quick-firing – had replaced all the muzzle-loaders in the Firth of Forth

A 6-inch coastal gun on Inchkeith

1939

a central point in the outermost line linking Kinghorn on the northern shore to Port of Leith on the southern. The central line stretched from Braefoot Point, through the islands of Inchcolm and Inchmickery, to Hound Point on the southern shore, while the innermost line linked Carlingose, the island of Inchgarvie and Dalmeny. The idea was simple: any would-be attacker making for the honey-pots of Edinburgh and the naval dockyard at Rosyth would have to breach each line in succession – not an attractive proposition for any ship's captain.

By the time of the Second World War, the defensive circles covering the Forth had moved further out to sea. Instead of being in the outermost line, our island of Inchkeith now found itself in the central defensive line. Booms to impede ships and submarines were strung between the islands and the coastline, along with minefields. Old gun emplacements were reactivated and new positions prepared. In 1939 the threat from the air was at the forefront of everyone's minds, and the provision of anti-aircraft guns and searchlights was given more muscle. Enemy attacks would also provoke responses from aircraft summoned from airfields at Drem and Turnhouse. It was this steady evolution of the defences that created an integrated Fortress Forth.

Flight Lieutenant George Pinkerton in a Spitfire downing a Ju88 over the Firth of Forth on 16 October 1939

THE AFTERMATH

IT COULD ALL HAVE BEEN VERY
DIFFERENT FOR THE DEFENDERS OF
THE FIRTH OF FORTH. IMMEDIATELY
AFTER THE DECLARATION OF WAR IN
1939, IT WAS ANY BRITISH SOLDIER'S
GUESS WHEN AND WHERE TROUBLE
MIGHT COME. BUT APART FROM THE
EVENTS OF 16 OCTOBER – WHEN THAT
FIRST ENEMY ACTION AGAINST
MAINLAND BRITAIN OCCURRED IN THE
SKIES OVER THE ESTUARY – THE FIRTH
SAW LITTLE IN THE WAY OF ACTION.

Opposite **A Spitfire Mk I of 602 Squadron patrols over the Firth of Forth**
Above **A German Junkers 88**

German planes dropped mines into the river on a fairly regular basis; unused bombs intended for targets on the Clyde were dropped in the Forth now and then by planes lightening their load for their journey home; searchlights scanned the river and sky in search of invasion forces that never arrived; booms curtailed access to the upper reaches of the Firth and kept Rosyth safe from attack by U-boat. The slimmed-down garrisons relaxed while the events that would decide matters involved men and women elsewhere in the world.

And then, at around 11 o'clock on the evening of 7 May 1945 – just an hour before Germany's surrender would bring a final silence – a U-boat ran across its last, luckless convoy close by the isle of May. Two ships were sunk and nine men were killed before the U-boat turned tail and returned to Germany and surrender. Fate had decreed that the first and last enemy actions close to mainland Britain would happen within a few short miles of one another. The Second World War had briefly sidled up to Fortress Forth, only to brush past it like a stranger in a crowd.

the dig

WHEN we turned our archaeological attention to the defences of the Firth of Forth, our first big challenge was presented by the sheer scale of the place. Where should we target our various techniques – examination of historical documents and aerial photographs; topographic and geophysical survey; excavation – to help us understand what happened here?

The reuse of existing fortifications and the creation of new ones ensured that the Firth was protected by a great ring of steel and concrete bristling with guns and searchlights and encircling hundreds of square miles of land and sea. Bigger by far than any single site we had looked at before, Fortress Forth would require us to come up with a very disciplined and precise plan of attack if we were to reveal any of its secrets.

We knew the defences were not seriously tested at any point during the war – that there had never been an invasion attempted here, or even any sustained action – but we were fascinated by what it must have been like for the men and women whose duty it had been to keep the defences in a permanent state of readiness. Our research into the historical background had told us that there had been many centuries of defensive activity in the area, in particular, on the islands of the Forth – the four Inches. The largest of these, Inchkeith, had been pivotal since soon after the battle of Pinkie in 1547, and by 1939 it was the hub of a great wheel. It was for this reason that we decided to focus much of our attention on trying to understand Inchkeith's role at the centre of the Fortress.

A quick look at the island from the air reveals that it is undoubtedly the most dramatic and complex of the military installations that once protected the Firth of Forth. Buildings of stone and brick and concrete, pathways and roads, reservoirs, railway lines – the place is a maze of human occupation. From a distance, it gives

On our way over to Inchkeith

a *Marie Celeste* sensation, as though the occupants have upped and gone just minutes before, leaving doors open and tasks unfinished. Up close, however, the steady decay of decades of abandonment is overwhelming.

We knew that a full survey and excavation of the archaeological remains on the island, including the extensive underground network of rooms linked by tunnels, would be a massive, time-consuming operation and one we could not hope to complete in the few weeks we had available to us. We could see, however, that a focused and limited investigation would shed valuable light on the island's history – and indeed the development of field fortifications and defensive technologies as a whole. At the same time we could provide information that would be invaluable for those tasked with preserving these monuments in the future.

The archaeology of the island exists as a dizzying conglomeration of various periods of building and fortification, and herein lies the first challenge – working out which elements relate to which period. In some cases, architectural techniques and even dated plaques provide a means of identification and enable us to connect specific buildings to a given period of occupation. This is true of the main complex of semi-subterranean

Tony carrying his kit bags

buildings related to defences constructed in 1881, and also of the fortress on the highest point of the island, dated 1564. In many cases, though, such distinctions are not so obvious and this is true even of the gun emplacements that glower over the steel-grey waters from every angle. Some were constructed in the First World War, others in the Second – but which is which? An important aim of our work, then, was to use documentary sources, military expertise and basic survey techniques to separate the Second World War elements from those of earlier periods.

The fledgling fort: Inchkeith in the sixteenth century

The first historically recorded fortifications to be constructed on the island were begun by the English in 1549, but they do not appear to have had time to finish these works before the island was taken from them by the French and the Scots. It was the French and their Scottish allies who built the first substantial fort on the island and it is this which is commemorated in the surviving plaque which includes the date 1549. Very little of this first fort can be seen today, though part of the original defensive structure does survive in the form of a high wall that skirts the top of the cliff on the eastern side of the island.

These remains represent some of the most historically important on the island and their preservation for future generations is obviously of utmost importance. We had no intention of digging anywhere near them, but we did what we call a standing building survey. This involves recording the appearance and condition of upstanding remains, such as walls and buildings, all of which helps bodies like Historic Scotland to decide how best to look after the structure. Standing building surveys are usually done with a total station EDM (electronic distance measurer), rectified photographs and even good old-fashioned drawings, but we had the opportunity to use an exciting piece of new technology, which is basically a 3D measuring system. This gizmo looks like some sort of futuristic robot or a remote-controlled missile-launcher, with a rotating head which spins around and a laser eye which can move in any direction. The business end is connected by cable to a computer, which controls the laser head and also processes the data which it sends back.

Olaf, the machine's operator, explained to our surveyor, John Arthur, how the machine worked. The laser was fired at the wall, with each pulse of light representing a single measured point on the wall. Meanwhile the rotating head moved its roving eye over the wall, taking reading after reading. John was pretty impressed to discover that the machine could take a million measurements in less than ten minutes! All of these laser measurements were then sent back to the computer, where they were processed and turned into an image. Within minutes a 3D image of the wall appeared on the screen, doing in half an hour or so a job that with more traditional techniques would have taken days.

As battlefield archaeologists, we do of course spend much of our time in the field looking for traces of violent conflict – field defences, bullets, arrowheads, fragments of armour and broken weapons. But another

As battlefield archaeologists, we do of course spend much of our time in the field looking for traces of violent conflict

Walking past the cookhouse and Second World War accommodation buildings

intriguing exercise is to look at the more day-to-day aspects of life on the island. Throughout its history as a military installation, the men posted to the island were marooned and isolated, sometimes for weeks at a time. They needed to eat, sleep and relax, as well as performing their military duties, and it is this more personal aspect of life on the island that is the main point of interest for part of our investigation.

Midden deposits were first noted on the eastern side of the island in 1872 by an archaeologist called Grieve. After visiting the island in 1870, he made a cursory examination of what he called a kitchen-midden at the base of the slopes close to the landing pier on the eastern side of the island. A sample of animal bones recovered from the deposit included sheep, pig, cattle, seal, rabbit and horse. Also included within the deposits were various types of marine shell. Although Grieve thought these remains were prehistoric, we thought it more likely that they were laid down much later and may even relate to the occupation of the fort during the sixteenth century.

We were excited by the prospect of investigating the remains of meals possibly eaten by the island's garrison over 400 years ago, but it wasn't going to be that simple. Since Grieve's time, the exact location of this deposit has been lost. Nevertheless we picked our way down the slope leading to the stony beaches on the eastern side of the island and, armed with Grieve's vague description of the site and its location 'within cannon shot of the old landing place', we set about searching for a midden last seen about 130 years ago.

On our way down we came across a pillbox built on a rocky spur. There were gun slits along the walls, which looked down on to the beaches on both sides. But what really caught our attention were the graffiti which covered the walls inside the pillbox. Here, gouged into the brick and concrete, or written in pencil, were the names, ages, regiments and even serial numbers of soldiers who stood guard in this pillbox during the first years of the Second World War. Just as amazing were the carvings of noughts-and-crosses games which those men must have played to while away the long hours of guard duty.

We took some photographs of the graffiti before leaving the pillbox and returning to our quest for the midden. We carried on down the slope, careful not to get speared on the rusty iron spikes that had supported barbed-wire entanglements. At last we set foot on the shingle, very close to a few heavily worn flat slabs. This remnant of paving was all that remained of an early boat slip or quay. We were lucky – this was surely Grieve's landing place. Then we noticed a white slither of something sandwiched between layers of dark earth near the foot of the slope. The white line was made from weathered oyster-shells. Here was our midden!

We rushed to get a closer look. The deposit had clearly suffered from erosion from waves and rainwater, and there must have been much more here in Grieve's time. Apart from the thin deposit of oysters which stretched across the slope for about three metres, there were also some limpets and winkles. More interesting still were the animal bones which protruded from the earth above and below the shell layer. We knew we would have to call on the services of an archaeologist specializing in animal bones, so we took a small sample of shells and bones and took careful notes on the make-up of the midden.

The graffiti we found inside the pillbox

One of the pillboxes we came across on Inchkeith

Before returning we did a bit of beach-combing. We found fragments of white china, and some of these sherds were from mugs and tea cups with the letters NAAFI and the date, 1941 or 1942. NAAFI stands for Navy, Army and Air Force Institutes, established in 1921 to provide catering and retail services to the armed forces.

Dr Catherine Smith, an animal bone expert, looked at our finds from the midden. What we had thought was cow bone, she told us was actually horse, identifying several parts of a lower hind leg, along with pieces of bone from the tail. The bones came from quite a small animal, so it would be more accurate to call it a pony. Grieve's discoveries also included horse bones. We were pleased with this result because we thought the horse bones were in keeping with the sixteenth-

The midden, made from weathered oyster-shells

Finds from our beachcombing: a damaged British mine and a plastic poodle (dropped by seagulls)

century occupation on the island, which the French sometimes called the Island of Horses. Although the bones had no traces of cut marks caused by butchery, we asked Catherine whether the presence of these bones in the midden meant that we were looking at the remains of a French meal. She surprised us by replying that in the medieval and post-medieval period people in Scotland generally ate horses, especially when other food was scarce.

We know from contemporary accounts that food was sometimes scarce on the island, especially during the blockade by English ships. One report from the besieging English, dated 17 April 1560, tells us that 'there are 140 soldiers in the fort, besides 70 women, boys and labouring persons. They have no drink but water, wheat to serve 10 or 12 days, other victual, little or none. Their great relief is oysters and periwinkles, which they get at low water mark in the Isle, and fresh fish with angling rods.' It would not be stretching the evidence too far to suggest that the oysters and winkles we found in the midden were eaten by the beleaguered garrison and their camp-followers during those bleak days of the blockade.

Between a rock and a hard place

Having investigated evidence for the earliest fortification of the island, we then turned our attention to the later defences, beginning with those constructed in the late nineteenth century. Three separate forts were built on the island in the Victorian period, but we were mainly interested in the most southerly of these because it was the easiest to understand as a free-standing defensive work. In the base of two rock-cut ditches that bisect the southern tip, sandwiching the fort between them, we found some very striking stone-built structures. These caponiers – essentially the precursor of the pillbox – were connected to the interior of the fort by tunnels and a stone staircase, which allowed troops to take position under total cover. Today the interiors of these buildings are dark and creepy, their ceilings colonized by large biting spiders which many years ago came over from North Africa as stowaways on ships.

On our first visit to the island we spotted a heavily silted and possibly back-filled trench complex hugging the contours of the cliff-top on the east-facing side. Our excitement rose as we realized that this serpentine depression in the grass might represent what could be literally described as part of Inchkeith's last-ditch line of defence. It was part of a network designed to protect the island from a seaborne assault from the east, and in the event of an enemy invasion Inchkeith's defenders would have sought to hold them at bay from this grim trench-line.

But just precisely which war did the trench relate to? Perhaps the First World War, when a similar fear of seaborne invasion forced the Forth's defenders to prepare for the worst. That war is, after all, the conflict most closely associated with trenches, and trenches are shown on a military map of the island drawn up in 1919, a year after the armistice. It is equally possible, however, that these desperate defences were made ready during the Second World War, when the digging of trenches would not only have provided a valuable additional means of defence, but also have occupied the labour force. We decided to carry out a limited excavation to obtain information on their dimensions, construction and, more importantly, age. Practice drills by soldiers readying themselves for conflict would surely have left tell-tale cartridge cases behind, for instance, and we hoped that these and other forgotten remnants would lie buried and provide us with the evidence we needed.

We picked a likely-looking trench, not too badly eroded, and marked out a strip about two metres wide. The digging was done carefully, each new layer being checked for metal artefacts, and we were always wary of the risk of unexploded ordnance. The front dropped down on to an earth platform, which was stepped into the trench – this was the fire step. Behind this the ground fell away again to the floor of the trench. There was another, wider step at the rear of the trench, which may have supported sandbags to stop it collapsing. The trench wasn't really very deep, just over a metre from top to bottom, but the front was probably given extra height by sandbags, a common practice during the early part of the First World War, before trenches were cut extra deep as protection against artillery. There is also a less dramatic explanation – on Inchkeith the soil is shallow and bedrock was protruding from the base of the trench, so unless they had blasted through the bedrock as had been done in the nineteenth century, the answer was to build a parapet.

The most interesting discovery, though, was evidence for the trench being recut sometime after it had filled with earth, indicating two phases of use. The trench was probably dug during the First World War, and then over time it filled with soil and was possibly purposely back-filled. Then, when the Second World War broke out, the trenches were dug out again and made ready for use. The only objects we found there were the tip of an old pickaxe and a .303 cartridge case from a Lee Enfield rifle on the ground very close to the excavation trench.

In search of a buried machine-gun nest

On the level ground which drops down from the centre of the island to the south, not too far from the most northerly of the rock-cut ditches, we encountered an almost completely buried concrete structure, which we recognized as the lining of some sort of below-ground installation. The inside of this open-topped bunker was filled with soil and had clearly been buried deliberately. At first we had little idea what function it may have

Paul sitting on the edge of the artillery observation post

served, although we guessed it may have been a machine-gun pit, several of which were connected to the island's trench system. The only way to find out for sure was to remove the rubble and dig.

The pit was divided into two by stretching a string across the newly cleared ground. One half was to be dug out while the other would remain in place, thus creating a cross-section through the soils in the pit which would allow us to understand the sequence of burial.

Then began the hard work of emptying the pit. This was not touchy-feely archaeology with trowels and toothbrushes, but required the use of a mattock and shovel: it was like emptying a buried swimming-pool. As

The stencilled notice starts to become clear

the sides of the pit were cleared, splodges of very faint white paint began to appear on the wall of the pit, and then we began to make out writing. It wasn't graffiti, like we'd seen in the pillbox, but a carefully stencilled notice. With cleaning we could read the word TRAINING. With the removal of another layer of rubble and earth more letters and numbers appeared and by the time we had finished cleaning we could make out: TRAINING PRACTICE AREA.

The pit was now well over a metre deep, and at just under two metres we found the concrete floor, which made the pit just deep enough for a man to stand in it to shoulder height. We had to clamber in and out of the pit, the shortest drop being through a small gap between one end of the concrete half-circle and the wall of the bunker behind it, and this is where we found the stumps of metal fittings that had probably belonged to a metal ladder.

But what was the function of our freshly excavated pit? The writing on the wall had given us the tip-off we needed. This was no machine-gun nest, it had been used as an observation post (or fire control post) for artillery training. The pit was positioned directly behind the two large gun emplacements in the south fort and would have provided a clear line of sight out to sea to the east and west. One of the emplacements would fire into area A, the other into area B. The stencilled numbers gave the angle of the arc into which the guns could fire safely during practice. The final clue came from the concrete floor, which was smooth apart from a circular depression in the centre. This is where a range-finding device would have been fitted. It was from here that observers would have monitored the practice fire from the two batteries.

The section cut through the pit showed that it had been deliberately buried, and the concrete chunks

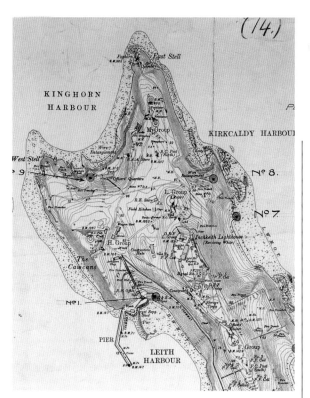

Map of Inchkeith, 1919

the time the map was drawn up. We guessed this must have been where gunners were trained for their craft. What we didn't know was how old these batteries were, what type of guns were used, or how many of them there were. Here was another opportunity to use traditional archaeological techniques. Although the observation post we had excavated was clearly used for practice, it seemed more likely that this related to the two gun emplacements in the south fort rather than to the emplacements stretched across the east-facing cliff.

When we examined this area on the ground during our initial survey, we had little difficulty in finding the half-circular features. These were terraces sitting in the side of the hill at the top of the cliff, with the back of each terrace curving round where it had been cut out of the slope. A series of these terraces had been created, forming a scalloped effect along the contour of the slope. We were interested in finding evidence of the guns that at some point must have been set into these terraces, each of which provided a platform for an individual gun. Our hopes were raised when we passed a metal detector over the ground and got a strong signal from the centre of each terrace, which is where we would expect the gun mounting to have been.

From there it was a simple case of putting a trench across one of the terraces to encompass the area which produced the metal-detector signal. After cutting back the tall grass and nettles we started digging, and it wasn't long before mattock blade hit metal, to reveal a heavy iron fitting with a thick, half-circular plate sat on top of a heavy metal platform set into a concrete slab. The pieces were fitted together by large bolts and screwheads, and were probably left behind when the guns were removed simply because it would have taken

found near the bottom may have come from a roof which was demolished in order to level the structure completely. We have no idea when it was buried, but it does appear on the 1919 military map, meaning that it was in use during the First World War. The fact that the notice on the wall had at some point been erased and replaced might mean that the observation post was brought back into service during the Second World War. So it wasn't a machine-gun nest as we had first thought – excavation had once again proved its worth!

The practice artillery emplacements

The military map of 1919 includes a series of half-circles lining the top of the east-facing cliff, just to the south of where the excavated section of fire trench comes to an end. These features are labelled as 'former practice batteries', suggesting that they had fallen into disuse by

A gun mounting on Inchkeith

too much effort to release them. Around the outside of the metal fitting was a semi-circular concrete trackway, with linear grooves cut or worn into its surface. This would have provided traction for some sort of wheel to allow the gun to be turned on its axis. Thus, each gun would have a limited arc of fire out into the sea in front of it. We drew very detailed plans, and we hope that at some stage an artillery expert will be able to tell us what type of gun sat in this mounting and so perhaps enable us to date the feature. We should, though, be careful of using the date of the gun as evidence for the date of the use of this battery. Guns used for practice were often old models no longer used in active service,

and so the battery may be somewhat younger than the age of the gun. With nothing else to go on at the moment, however, we suspect that this practice battery was used during the early years of the First World War.

How the Second World War was made to disappear

Although most of our work was focused on the island of Inchkeith, we also wanted to investigate the mainland defences. In our initial research we unearthed a fascinating little story hidden on the edge of a modern housing scheme in Dalgety Bay, in Fife.

The smallest archaeological component representing

An aerial photograph showing the location of the pillbox at Donnibristle (circled)

the defences of the Firth of Forth – indeed, the whole of the British Isles – was probably the humble pillbox. Today, examples of these small concrete bunkers can be seen, swallowed up by modern development in formerly strategically important locations all over the countryside. Their gun slits look out over railway bridges, river crossings and potential coastal-landing points, and stand as monuments to a battle that was never fought. There are numerous examples in the vicinity of the Firth of Forth, but one of these sites remains something of a mystery. No longer visible, it is said to have escaped demolition by being completely buried. After hearing this story we examined aerial photographs taken just after the war and, sure enough, a small building stands in the shade of some trees on a hillock.

At the end of a quiet little road called St Bridget's Brae, there is a small area of landscaped ground surrounded by 1960s houses. This peaceful spot is reputed to be the site of the concrete pillbox buried during the landscaping operations that followed the construction of the houses. During the war the pillbox was part of a network of defences protecting the perimeter of Donnibristle airfield.

If you stand on top of the hillock and look down at your feet you can just make out a part of the edge of

. . . it was like
uncovering a long-
vanished tomb,
and we couldn't
wait to get inside

the pillbox, indicated by concrete protruding from the soil. If you use your imagination to clear away the houses and the school further down the slope, you begin to understand that this was a good location for a pillbox – its gun slits would have allowed a clear view down towards the north shore of the Firth.

Having obtained permission to dig from the council, we brought in a small mechanical excavator. We hoped to uncover the entrance to allow us to get inside. Our work caused great interest among the local people, some of whom remembered playing in the pillbox as children. One lady told us that the authorities had tried to demolish it with a bulldozer, but when that failed they had resorted to burying it.

Soon our trench began to reveal one wall of the buried bunker, which appeared to be pentagon in shape, with a long back and four shorter sides. We moved on to the next angle of wall – here was the entrance! Even though the pillbox had only been buried for about thirty years, it was like uncovering a long-vanished tomb, and we couldn't wait to get inside. As more and more soil was removed, we uncovered the gun slits on either side of the doorway, and the excavator shifted the heavy boulders blocking the entrance. Although we had to go in on our bellies, we could stand up once we were inside.

It was pitch black and we needed our torches to see anything. The ground was covered in earth and rubble and old junk like a paint tin and an old sweet wrapper. The price on the wrapper was in decimal money, so we knew the pillbox had been buried after 1971, when the new currency was introduced. There was a gun slit in every angle of the wall, and the wooden frames around them were still preserved, although they were soft to touch, like damp papier-mâché. It was strange to find that bits of glass were still in place in the frames, as we couldn't imagine why a pillbox would have glazed gun slits – perhaps it changed its function when the threat of invasion subsided. Along the walls were the remains of what looked like rifle racks, although they had been badly damaged. The interior was taken up by a Y-shaped concrete wall around which we had to walk to return to the entrance. It was the anti-ricochet baffle, built to protect the men inside from any bullets coming in through the gun slits.

Unlike the pillbox on Inchkeith, there were no wartime graffiti to be seen here. However, we found a few more recent daubings, one of which said, 'Garry O'Mally Rules!' Later we asked a couple of local people about Garry, and were pleased to hear that he is now a plumber and still lives not far from the pillbox he played in as a child!

From its shape and form, with four short walls and a longer back wall, a central doorway and opposing gun slits, we could tell that this was a type-24 pillbox – there were about eight types constructed during the Second World War. After taking photographs and making notes, we covered it up again, but not before we had taken a slip of paper, written our names and the date on it, slipped it into a camera-film canister and left it inside the bunker for future archaeologists to find. Although we had made no staggering discoveries, the exercise had been fun and had informed local people of a piece of their past that many of them did not even know was there. ✿

A German photograph showing clearly the bombing raid on the Firth of Forth

Archaeological Techniques:
Using maps and aerial photographs

ANY archaeologist worth his or her salt will do several things before they even think of putting their boots on and leaving the office for the field. One of these is to look at maps of the area to be investigated – preferably old maps as well as more recent ones. These will give an idea of the terrain, the location of sites of interest and also an insight into the history of the place, as well as the shape and character of the landscape changes over time and from map to map. The other 'must see' are aerial photographs, which, just as the name suggests, are photographs of the ground taken from an aeroplane. Aerial photographs do not show a cartographer's representation of the ground, but the ground itself, and many maps are actually made by referring to aerial photographs.

As we can compare an old map with a more

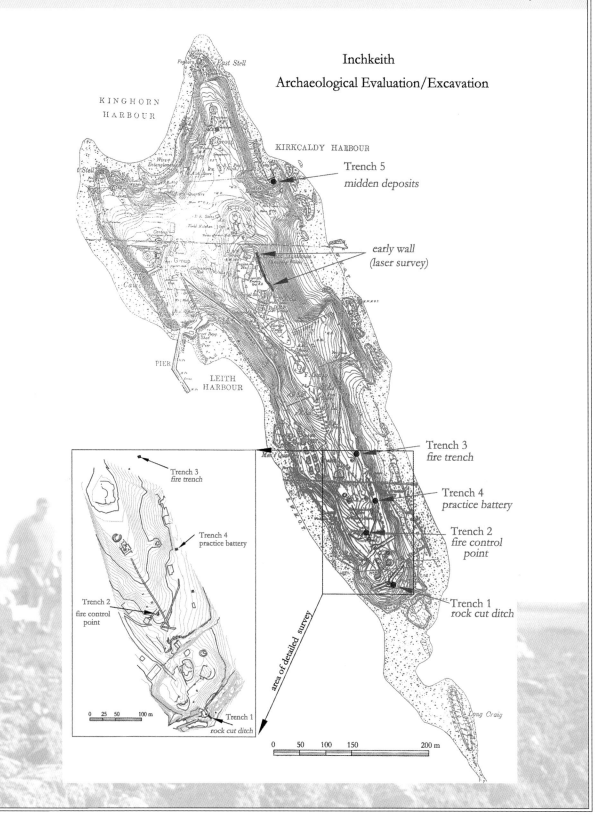

Inchkeith
Archaeological Evaluation/Excavation

KINGHORN HARBOUR

KIRKCALDY HARBOUR

Trench 5
midden deposits

*early wall
(laser survey)*

PIER

LEITH
HARBOUR

Trench 3
fire trench

Trench 4
practice battery

Trench 2
*fire control
point*

Trench 1
rock cut ditch

Long Craig

Trench 3
fire trench

Trench 4
practice battery

Trench 2
*fire control
point*

Trench 1
rock cut ditch

0   25   50   100 m

area of detailed survey

0   50   100   150   200 m

modern one to see what changes have been made to the landscape, so we can compare an older aerial photograph with a more recent one. Our oldest useful photographs, as far as archaeology is concerned, tend to be those taken during and just after the Second World War. The art of interpreting the information contained within an aerial photograph was pioneered by the military during the First World War and refined during the Second. The Firth of Forth itself was photographed on several occasions by German reconnaissance aircraft and one famous photograph shows bombs dropping around the ships anchored near the Forth railway bridge.

Once taken, sometimes at considerable risk, these photographs were examined by experts using magnifying lenses and other instruments. Studying the world from several thousand feet up requires great skill, especially if the enemy have tried to disguise or camouflage their bases or runways. Some of these backroom experts were actually archaeologists before the war, recruited for their skills at observation and interpretation.

We used a photograph taken not long after the war to find our pillbox at Donnibristle. The picture shows some original buildings and even aircraft. The runways are clearly visible, and to the south, just beside a small stand of trees, is a tiny white box. Under a hand lens you can see that it's a small building, but it's impossible to make out any detail. This is our pillbox before it was buried, sitting out in the open on high ground.

Aerial photographs show all the things you would expect of a photograph – houses, roads, hedges, trees and the like – but they also enable us to see things which we would never see from the ground. These are traces of past human activity, and they are most commonly called crop marks. They are so called because this particular type of archaeological feature appears as a result of the differing rates of growth in crops such as wheat and corn. Let's say, for instance, that in prehistoric times a circular ditch was dug around an earth burial mound. Over time the mound itself might be ploughed away and similarly the ditch might be filled with soil and disappear. You may think that the site is lost for ever. But the soil in the ditch will be looser and moister than the soil around it. This means that the crops in the ditch will grow faster and taller than those around them, because of the added moisture. If you take an aerial photograph of this site when the sun is low in the sky, the taller corn will cast a shadow which will show on the aerial photograph as a distinct circle!

But it's not just crops that show up buried features. Very faint lumps and bumps, almost invisible from the ground, will show up as shadow marks when the light is right. Snow may also be a give-away: the snow that drifts into these shallow features may be the last to melt because it is in shadow.

Anyone can get access to aerial photographs from the National Sites and Monuments Records of England and Scotland. Perhaps, though, you do not need to go to that much trouble – a lot of people have aerial photographs of their houses and neighbourhoods on their living-room walls. Another likely place is the wall of a restaurant or a school corridor. Next time you see an aerial photograph, look a little closer, beyond the roofs of houses and the tops of cars – you never know what you may find.

An aerial photograph of Donnibristle airfield

The pillbox uncovered at Donnibristle

Conclusion

Although it ended less than sixty years ago, the physical remains of the Second World War are fast disappearing. Yes, the pillbox in Dalgety Bay showed that some wartime structures are resilient, but many sites have been lost to development and even the straightforward desire to eradicate memories of unpleasant times. It is only over the past few years that sites related to events as recent as the Second World War have been recognized as archaeological sites and an important part of our cultural heritage and many of the military sites in the Firth of Forth have now received scheduled ancient monument status.

We hope that our work in the Firth of Forth has demonstrated that traditional archaeological techniques, such as survey and excavation, can add a good deal to our understanding of the character and role of the Second World War and, obviously, earlier defensive sites. Many sites contain durable structures of concrete and steel, but others, such as trench systems and even concrete features sunk into the ground like our observation post, can disappear from view relatively quickly – we should not forget the deliberate burial of the pillbox here. Only through excavation have we been able to bring these features back to life and begin to provide a fuller picture of how an island like Inchkeith functioned during wartime.

When we talk in terms of archaeology, which may deal with periods hundreds of thousands of years ago, sixty years ago may sound like yesterday. However, the number of surviving Second World War veterans is rapidly dwindling, and those from the First are now an all but extinct species. As we sit on the cusp of living memory, we should do all we can to further the understanding of these key points in our history. We believe it is here that archaeology can come into its own and help us in this duty: remembering those who gave so much and also learning, where we can, from some of the darkest periods of our collective past.

Above Never very far away from their guns, these gunners enjoy a game of football
Below Soldiers at work in an artillery observation post using a range finder

The Battlefields Today

Shrewsbury Today

Viewed from the air, the landscape around Shrewsbury battlefield today presents the patchwork quilt of neatly bordered fields that so typifies our image of the English countryside. Visitors to the site will find it bordered on three sides: by the A5124 road to the south, the A528 to the west and the A49 to the east. A railway line, too, runs north to south, immediately to the east of, and parallel to, the A49. The battlefield is most easily accessible from the A49 north out of the town of Shrewsbury itself.

The main way in which today's view differs from that of 1403 is in the extent to which the landscape is now broken up by field boundaries. These hedges and fences were built much later and give the landscape a smaller, more intimate feeling than it may have had at the time of the battle. Visitors to the site should remember that Henry and Hotspur faced one another across a much more open vista, one in which slight dirt-tracks were all that passed for roads and where land was farmed not in enclosed, regimented fields but in undivided strips of 'rig and furrow' interspersed here and there with hedged fields. Nowadays, the tell-tale traces of this antiquated agricultural practice are best appreciated from the air. When the conditions are just right – when the sun is low in the sky and casting shadows, or when a dusting of snow accentuates the contrast of humps and bumps on the ground – the traces of medieval farming can be startlingly obvious. The practice of rig and furrow – where the 'rig' is the heaped-up strip of ploughed earth on which the crop is planted, and the furrow is the denuded trench left behind by that heaping-up – creates a series of ripples

that march across the landscape like corduroy. Where this was continued over decades and even centuries, the impact upon the landscape is surprisingly indelible.

The main point of focus in the modern landscape of the battlefield is the church of Saint Mary Magdalene, or Battlefield Church. This robust, buttressed building with its square tower sits within an area once bounded by a bank and ditch. Partially visible today, along the line of hedges that enclose the churchyard, this feature was created to mark the site of the mass burial pit which supposedly lies in the church grounds. This enclosure also contained the college that once accompanied the church, and very little, if anything, remains of the buildings, which would have included an almshouse,

refectory and accommodation block. Also discernible nearby are the depressions left by fishponds related to the occupancy of the college.

The town of Shrewsbury can clearly be seen from the top of the ridge, set against the dramatic backdrop provided by the range of hills which separate England from Wales. The town has expanded since 1403, notably towards the north, where the battlefield lies. So far, the site itself has remained relatively undamaged, but only time will determine whether or not this remains the case.

Barnet Today

Of all the battlefields we have visited in recent years, Barnet is the only one that has been accessible via the London Underground! The ground rises noticeably as you leave the platform at High Barnet station and climb the steep slope that brings you out on to the main drag through the town of Barnet itself, with its wide main road, shops and houses.

Visitors in search of the battlefield should continue uphill, towards the north, until the ground begins to level out. A ten-minute walk from the tube station and all at once suburban London gives way to unexpected swathes of green. Ten minutes further on and there is a triangle of village green – Hadley Green. Stand in the middle and you are roughly equidistant between the opposing battle-lines – Lancastrians to the north and Yorkists to the south.

To the east of Hadley Green is the common at Monken Hadley, a sizeable area of ground that is remarkably undisturbed and perhaps the most atmospheric of the battlefield locations at Barnet.

and the road to Kitts End, is the Hadley High Stone. This monument, erected by one Sir Joseph Sambroke in the early eighteenth century, commemorates the battle. It is not, however, in its original location, having been moved further north to allow for the construction of the modern road. To the west of the monument is Old Fold golf club. Ghosting across the fairway of the first hole is the trace of an old hedge line. This fragment conforms to the line of the Enfield Chase boundary hedge along which the Lancastrians are said to have anchored themselves on the morning of the battle.

In all, the site of the battle of Barnet is remarkable for the way in which so much of the open ground over which the fighting raged has remained relatively undeveloped so close to suburban sprawl. Just a half-hour tube-train ride from King's Cross it may be, but a sense of place undoubtedly survives.

Barnet is 25 miles north of London city centre and readily accessible by road or rail.

Flodden Today

The battlefield at Flodden, or more accurately Branxton Hill, is well worth a visit, being one of the most dramatic battlefields in Britain. From Berwick-upon-Tweed, take the A698 to Cornhill-on-Tweed and then turn left at the roundabout on to the A697 to Wooler. After about two miles you will see Branxton village and the battlefield sign posted to the right.

Once in Branxton village, take the sharp right turn along the signposted, hedge-lined road which takes you past St Mark's church. A mass grave was found there in the graveyard in the nineteenth century, and the body of James IV is reputed to have been laid out in the

Noticeable here is the way the ground slopes steeply away towards the east and then up to the north where it meets the common on the plateau. It was down and up these slopes that Gloucester marched his men on the morning of 14 April, still unaware that the misalignment of the two armies had placed him well beyond the end of the Lancastrian left flank. Standing on this high ground – the highest between London and York – it is possible to imagine the ranks of heavily armoured men disappearing into a heavy morning mist.

Further out of town towards the north, in the direction of St Albans and at the junction of the A1000

church after the battle. About 400 yards down the road, to the left, is the Piper's Hill car park.

The monument to the fallen of the battle is accessed through a gate and up a well-made footpath. The path crosses a farmer's field, so don't stray too far from it. Looking south over the field from the monument, which was built in 1910, you get a spectacular view of the ridge of Branxton Hill, with Branxton Hill Farm on its summit. You are standing just behind the English line, and the Scots charged down the steep hill in front of you, with most of the killing taking place in the hollow at the bottom. If you look to your right (west), you will see how the ground at the foot of the hill there remains flat. This may explain why the Scots here had more success than those who charged down directly in front of you: when reaching the bottom of the hill, the latter had to climb again before they could come to blows with the English. You should imagine the landscape much more open than it is today, without the modern field boundaries.

Flodden Hill is around a mile and a half or so further to the south-east. Take the road back into the centre of the village and then turn right up Branxton Hill. Climb the hill, take a left at the T-junction, and after half a mile or so you will see a rough track on the right which goes up to the tree-covered hilltop. This is a public footpath and it will take you to the gun emplacement. Simply follow the track up the hill, bear to the left through the wood and then turn down to the left again when you reach a fork in the track. On the way you will pass the spring which James IV is reputed to have drunk from. The gun emplacement is located in the trees to the right of the track, around two hundred yards after the fork.

Newark Today

The Civil War siege-works of Newark are without equal. Perhaps most noteworthy of all is the Queen's Sconce, her banks towering somewhat incongruously over carefully manicured playing fields and parkland just south of the town centre. What was once the scene of desperate, stubborn resistance is now the domain of dog-walkers and families enjoying days out.

Scattered around the environs of the town are no fewer than nine sites that are instantly recognizable, and the location of a similar number again is known, although more recent development work or agriculture has completely removed any visible trace. The Queen's

Sconce had a twin, known as the King's Sconce, at a location to the north of the town, but sadly this disappeared in the late 1880s to make way for a boiler-works; and of Edinburgh, the Scots' camp to the north-west of Newark, nothing at all survives. Shelford Manor is a private home now, and there is little to be seen from the road.

Newark Castle, while still worth a visit, is a shadow of its former self. One corner and one length of wall are all that can be seen, but the location on a terrace overlooking the Trent makes for an impressive sight, just the same.

A tour of the surviving siege-works of Newark will surely make the visitor wonder at the manpower and skill required for their construction. They were thrown up at great speed in most cases, in weeks rather than months, and yet still they stand, impressive reminders of a time when a war and its bitter aftermath claimed no less a casualty than the king himself.

Culloden Today

Culloden battlefield is located three miles to the south-east of Inverness, which sits next to the A9. Travelling from Inverness, take the A9 south and follow the brown tourist signs for Culloden battlefield, which will take you along the B9006. Other historical sites nearby include Fort George, constructed in the aftermath of the 1745–6 rebellion. Culloden House is today a luxury hotel and after major demolition and reconstruction work in the late eighteenth century bears little resemblance to the house in which the prince spent the night before the battle. Ruthven Barracks, captured by the Jacobites during the rebellion and the mustering-

point for part of the Jacobite army before and after the battle, are some thirty miles to the south of Culloden by road and lie just off the A9 near Kingussie.

The battlefield is owned by the National Trust for Scotland, who have done much to protect the site and provide interpretation for visitors. There is a visitors' centre which, along with a tea room, well-stocked bookshop and audio-visual theatre, has a small museum with a good collection of battlefield artefacts – including a highly decorated broadsword thought to have been carried by Bonnie Prince Charlie.

Until the mid-1980s much of the site was covered by a tree plantation, but this has been removed by the NTS to recreate an open moorland more in keeping with the landscape as it would have appeared in 1746. Well-marked footpaths lead you around the core of the battlefield – but remember, archaeological investigation has demonstrated that the original battle lines extended beyond the points marked with flags and signs, with the location where the Jacobite charge hit the left of the government line lying inside the Field of the English. The action also extended further north into the area of forestry across the road.

Firth of Forth Today

Battlefield archaeologists can learn a salutary lesson from the surviving military installations on the Firth of Forth, and wherever they still exist on the British mainland. Within the lifetime of many of its veterans, the network of defensive and offensive positions that once covered the country has disappeared to the extent that it's possible to overlook the surviving traces altogether.

Visitors in search of the wartime fortifications

around the Forth must keep in mind the idea that the entire area functioned as a whole, and it's helpful to picture Fortress Forth as a single site. For a grandstand view of both coastlines, the Inches and the bridges across the Forth, take the A90 road from central Edinburgh and follow signs for the village of Cramond. A twenty-minute walk across the tidal causeway leads to Cramond Island, itself littered with war remains. Travel west from Cramond and make for South Queensferry. From the pier there, in the shadow of the towering Victorian masterpiece that is the Forth Rail Bridge, visitors keen to venture further can board a pleasure-boat that makes several trips a day to Inchcolm. The journey passes beneath the bridge and past little Inchgarvie, which supports one giant leg of the central span and whose dull, grey wartime buildings seem to have grown out of the rock.

Further downriver, Inchmickery looms into view like the hulk of a decaying battleship, the huts and observation tower mimicking the outlines of a ship's bridge. Most day-trippers come for the abbey. More recent by four or five centuries, the wartime buildings look grim and unloved.

The military installations on all of the Inches were on the receiving end of the Territorial Army's explosives practice in the early 1960s. Nowadays, they are viewed with a more sympathetic eye and there are plans to conserve these priceless relics for display to visitors. The installations on the Forth's northern coastline can be reached by taking the road bridge across the river.

The military complexes remain relatively intact only on the islands – most impressively of all on Inchkeith. Although Inchcolm and Cramond can be visited, with

regular boat trips to Inchcolm from South Queensferry, Inchkeith is in private ownership and access is therefore denied. Relatively secure from the attentions of landscapers and developers in the postwar years, the military installations on the Inches have survived to a far greater extent than on the mainland. Now under the protection of Historic Scotland, they all have a better chance than ever of being looked after for generations to come.

ACKNOWLEDGEMENTS

Two Men in a Trench would like to thank the many people who put so much of themselves into making it all possible. Carrying out six full-scale archaeological projects and turning them into watchable television was never going to be easy – and would have been impossible without the talent, commitment, patience and endless good humour demonstrated by each and every member of the archaeological team and Optomen Television's production team. In addition, we want to thank all those who helped – in many other unique ways – on each of the projects.

Thanks to our friends at Michael Joseph/Penguin: Nicky Barneby, Craig Burgess, Sarah Day, John Hamilton, James Holland, Lindsey Jordan, Marissa Keating, Gráinne Kelly, Catherine Lay, Janette Revill, Keith Taylor, Neal Townsend and Tom Weldon. And a big thank you to Mark Read for all his amazing photographs in the book.

ARCHAEOLOGISTS AND PRODUCTION FOLK

Patrick Acum, Ben Adler, Nick Angel, John Arthur, Dr Iain Banks, Margaret Beckett, Luke Cardiff, David Connolly, Laura Desmond, Paul Duffy, Corinne Field, Richard Herd, Richard Hill, Dr Olivia Lelong, Pat Llewellyn, Louise McAllan, Jennie Macdiarmid, Dave McNicol, Helen MacQuarrie, Ben Motley, Victoria Noble, Rex Phillips, Paul Ratcliffe, Andy Robertshaw, Emily Roe, Lorna Sharpe, Bridget Shaw, Katinka Stentoft, Carolyn Stopp, Linda Stradling, Erica Utsi, Ross White, together with the support staff at GUARD, Jen Cochrane, Chris Connor, Ross McGrehan and Mel Richmond.

SHREWSBURY

Andy Brown, Andrew Freeman, Kevin Hampton, Ernie Jenks, Mark Love, Dr Philip Morgan, Dr Carol Rawcliffe, Simon Rowland-Jones, Jennifer Smith,

Hugh Soar, Dr Paul Stamper, Mike Stokes, Revd Nick Todd, Robin Walker.

BARNET
Dr Juliet Barker, Bill Bass, Clive Cheesman (Rouge Dragon Pursuivant), Jennie Cobban, Alan Dickens, George Georgalla and all at George's Café, Hayden the digger driver, Dr Max Hooper, Sister Janet, Rob Martin, Revd David Nash, Martin Pegler, Dominic Sewell.

FLODDEN
Niall Barr, Dr David Caldwell, Phillip Deakin, Mavis Harris, David Hurell, Helmar Hurell, Lord Joicey and all at Ford Castle, John Logan and all at the Red Lion, Mr Lyell, Phil Moor, Ronald Morrison, Michael O'Donoghue, Alison Parfitt, Patrick Parsons, Alan and Michael Perry, Grant Thomas, Bill and Mavis Walker.

NEWARK
Virginia Baddeley, Phil Beard, Mike Bishop, Christopher Bodkin, Sue Brigham, Roger Chatterton and family, Christopher Duffy, Emma Grant, Jon Humble, David Marcombe, Rene Mouraille, Stuart Murray, John Oxley, Ruth Peterson, D.W. Pickett, Mike Pindar, Alan Smith, Angela Smith, Chris Smith, Richard Tyndall, Matt Vickers.

CULLODEN
Revd Colin Anderson, Mrs Jane Bain, Jim Bone, Mike Fabling, Hugh Gordon, Graham Grant, Annette Jack, James Logan, Dorothy Low, Hugh Dan MacClennan Professor Allan Macinnes, Ross MacKenzie, Len Pentercost-Ingram, Ronnie Scott, Sandy Snell, George Taylor, Robin Turner, John Wood.

FIRTH OF FORTH
Norman Clark, John Dickson, Dave Easton, Sir Tom Farmer, Dr Richard Fawcett, Dr Douglas Grant, Doreen Grove, Nigel Harding, Charlie Knolf, Olaf Kruger, Bill Simpson and the crew of the *Seahunter*, Dr Catherine Smith.

Last, but not least, we would like to thank the members of the following metal-detecting clubs who made such an invaluable contribution: Tyneside Metal-Detecting Association; the National Council for Metal-Detecting; White's Metal Detectors, Inverness; Hertfordshire & District Metal Detection Society. And all the landowners who kindly gave permission for our work to take place.

We can only offer our most sincere apologies to anyone whose contribution we have overlooked here. Thanks to you all.

FURTHER READING

GENERAL

Burne, A. H., *Battlefields of England*, Methuen, London, 1950

Freeman, P. W. M. and Pollard, A. (eds.), *Fields of Conflict: Progress and Prospect in Battlefield Archaeology*, BAR International Series 958, Archaeopress, Oxford, 2001

Keegan, J., *The Face of Battle: A Study of Agincourt, Waterloo and the Somme*, Jonathan Cape, London, 1976

Kinross, J., *Discovering Battlefields of England and Scotland*, Shire, Princes Risborough, 1998

Newark, T., *War in Britain*, English Heritage/HarperCollins, London, 2000

Seymour, W., *Battles in Britain, 1066–1746*, Wordsworth Editions, Ware, 1997

Smurthwaite, D., *The Complete Guide to the Battlefields of Britain*, Penguin, London, 1984

Young, P. and Adair, J., *Hastings to Culloden: Battles of Britain* (3rd edn), Sutton, Stroud, 1996

SHREWSBURY

Bean, J. M. W., *The Estates of the Percy Family, 1416–1537*, Oxford University Press, London, 1958

Bevan, B., *Henry IV*, Rubicon, London, 1994

Fletcher, W. G. D., 'Battlefield College', *Transactions of the Shropshire Antiquarian Society*, pp. 177–91, 1903

Hardy, R., *Longbow: A Social and Military History*, Patrick Stephens, Sparkford, 1992

Morgan, P., *War and Society in Medieval Cheshire, 1277–1403*, Manchester University Press, Manchester, 1987

Priestley, E. J., *The Battle of Shrewsbury 1403*, Shrewsbury and Atcham Borough Council, Shrewsbury, 1979

BARNET

Boardman, A. W., *The Medieval Soldier in the Wars of the Roses*, Sutton, Stroud, 1998

Fiorato, V., Boylston, A., and Knusel, C., (eds.), *Blood Red Roses: The Archaeology of a Mass Grave from the Battle of Towton, AD1461*, Oxbow Books, Oxford, 2001

Haigh, P. A., *The Military Campaigns of the Wars of the Roses*, Sutton, Stroud, 1995

Hammond, P. W., *The Battles of Barnet and Tewkesbury*, Sutton, Stroud, 1990

Lander, J. R., *The Wars of the Roses* (2nd edn), Sutton, Stroud, 1992

FLODDEN

Barr, N., *Flodden 1513*, Tempus, Stroud, 2001

Elliot, F., *The Battle of Flodden and the Raids of 1513*, Pallas Armata, Tonbridge, 1991

Leather, G. F. T., *New Light on Flodden*, Edinburgh, 1937

Mackay Mackenzie, W., *The Secret of Flodden*, Grant and Murray, Edinburgh, 1931

Phillips, G., *The Anglo-Scots Wars 1513–1550*, Boyden Press, Woodbridge, 1999

Smith, R. D. and Brown, R. R., *Bombards: Mons Meg and Her Sisters*, Royal Armouries, London, 1989

NEWARK

Elliot-Wright, P. J. C., *The English Civil War*, Brassey's, London, 1997

Harrington, P., *The Archaeology of the English Civil War*, Shire, Princes Risborough, 1992

Reid, S., *All the King's Armies*, Staplehurst, 1998

Warner, T., *Newark: Civil War and Siegeworks*, Nottinghamshire County Community Services, Nottingham, 1992

Young, P. and Holmes, R., *The English Civil War*, Wordsworth Editions, Ware, 2000

CULLODEN

Barthorp, M., *The Jacobite Rebellions, 1689–1745*, Osprey Men-At-Arms Series, Oxford, 1982

Black, J., *Culloden and the '45*, Sutton, Stroud, 1990

Harrington, P., *Culloden 1745: The Highland Clans' Last Charge*, Osprey Campaigns Series, Oxford, 1991

Prebble, J., *Culloden*, Penguin, London, 1996

Reid, S., *Like Hungry Wolves: Culloden Moor, 16 April 1746*, Windrow, London, 1994

Reid, S., *Highland Clansmen 1689–1746*, Osprey Warrior Series, Oxford, 1997

FIRTH OF FORTH AND THE SECOND WORLD WAR

Jeffery, A., *This Present Emergency: Edinburgh, the River Forth and South-East Scotland and the Second World War*, Mainstream, Edinburgh, 1992

Lowry, B., *Twentieth-Century Defences in Britain: An Introductory Guide*, Council for British Archaeology, London, 1996

Nancarrow, F. G., *Glasgow's Fighter Squadron*, Collins, London and Glasgow, 1942

Simpson, E., *Dalgety Bay: Heritage and Hidden History*, Dalgety Bay and Hillend Community Council, Dalgety Bay, 1999

Wills, H., *Pillboxes: A Study of UK Defences*, Leo Cooper, London, 1985

PICTURE CREDITS

SHREWSBURY 1403

p.14: The Stapleton Collection/Bridgeman Art Library; p.15: The Stapleton Collection/Bridgeman Art Library; p.16: The Art Archive/British Library p.17: Private Collection/Bridgeman Art Library; p.19: British Library/Bridgeman Art Library; p.20: Westminster Abbey, London/Bridgeman Art Library; p.22: Mary Evans Picture Library; p.23: Private Collection/Bridgeman Art Library; p.24: Birmingham Museums and Art Gallery/Bridgeman Art Library; p.26: Border detail from *Battle of Agincourt*, watercolour on paper by English School (19th century): The Stapleton Collection/Bridgeman Art Library; p.30: The Art Archive/Bibliothèque Nationale Paris; p.33: Mary Evans Picture Library; p.34: Hotspur and Prince Henry: The Stapleton Collection/Bridgeman Art Library; p.36: Private Collection/Bridgeman Art Library; p.38: Battle of

Crécy: Bridgeman Art Library; p.39: Index/Bridgeman Art Library; p.40: The Stapleton Collection/Bridgeman Art Library; p.40: The Stapleton Collection/Bridgeman Art Library; p.41: Mary Evans Picture Library; p.57: MS. Laud Misc.748 fol.83v. Bodleian Library, University of Oxford

BARNET 1471

p.76: Battle of Barnet, *The Death of the 'Kingmaker'*: Fotomas Index; p.78: Birmingham Museums and Art Gallery/Bridgeman Art Library; p.79: Fotomas Index; p.79: Private Collection/Bridgeman Art Library; p.81: Bibliothèque Centrale, Ghent, Belgium/Bridgeman Art Library; p.82: Mary Evans Picture Library; p.83: Mary Evans Picture Library; p.83: Mary Evans Picture Library; p.84: Mary Evans Picture Library; p.85: Mary Evans Picture Library;

p.85: Reproduced by courtesy of the National Portrait Gallery, London; p.89: Mary Evans Picture Library; p.90: Fotomas Index; p.91: Lambeth Palace Library, London/Bridgeman Art Library; p.93: British Library/Bridgeman Art Library; p.94: *Queen Margaret of Anjou Taken Prisoner after Tewkesbury*, painting by Sir John Gilbert: Guildhall Art Gallery, Corporation of London/Bridgeman Art Library; p.96: Fotomas Index; p.97: Guildhall Art Gallery, Corporation of London/Bridgeman Art Library; p.99: Maps 175.t.1.(2.) © The British Library; p.104: Bibliothèque Centrale, Ghent, Belgium/Bridgeman Art Library; p.105: © Getmapping

FLODDEN 1513

p.120: The Stapleton Collection/Bridgeman Art Library; p.121: Bridgeman Art Library; p.121 National Trust Photographic Library/Derrick E. Witty; p.123: City of Edinburgh Museums and Art Galleries/Bridgeman Art Library; p.124: Norham Castle: © English Heritage Photo Library/Jonathan Bailey; p.125: Phillips, The International Fine Art Auctioneers/Bridgeman Art Library; p.125: Private Collection/Bridgeman Art Library; p.126: Wolverhampton Art Gallery, West Midlands/ Bridgeman Art Library; p.128: © English Heritage Photo Library/Jonathan Bailey; p.129: Bridgeman Art Library; p.130: *Scottish Army Marches to Attack Norham Castle*: © English Heritage Photo Library; p.135: © The Board of Trustees of the Armouries/II.2; p.140: © The English Heritage Photo Library; p.141: City of Edinburgh Museums and Art Galleries/ Bridgeman Art Library; p.169: © Crown Copyright Reserved/Historic Scotland; p.171: © The Board of

Trustees of the Armouries/VII.104; p.176: *Aftermath of the Battle of Flodden*: © English Heritage Photo Library; p.177: City of Edinburgh Museums and Art Galleries/Bridgeman Art Library

NEWARK 1642–6

p.186: *The Enemy Approaches* by Robert Alexander Hillingford: Private Collection/Bridgeman Art Library; p.187: Mary Evans Picture Library; p.189: Christie's Images, London/Bridgeman Art Library; p.190: © National Trust Photographic Library/Ian Blantern; p.192: Charles I's failed royal coup against parliament: Private Collection/Bridgeman Art Library; p.193: View of Newark,1677: Nottinghamshire Archives; p.194: Fotomas Index; p.196: 'Military and Maritime Discipline' by Thomas Venn, 1672; p.197: 'Military and Maritime Discipline' by Thomas Venn, 1672; p.198: © Skyscan Photo Library/William Cross; p.199: Mary Evans Picture Library; p.200: *The Battle of Marston Moor in 1644*, 1819, oil on canvas by Abraham Cooper (1787–1868): Harris Museum and Art Gallery, Preston, Lancashire/Bridgeman Art Library (HMP 90488); p.204: 'Military and Maritime Discipline' by Thomas Venn, 1672; p.207: Fotomas Index; p.207: Fotomas Index; p.208: Leeds Museums and Galleries (City Art Gallery)/Bridgeman Art Library; p.210: Private Collection/Bridgeman Art Library; p.211: Fotomas Index; p.212: Hannibal House, D.O.E., London/Bridgeman Art Library; p.212: Tower of London Armouries, London/Bridgeman Art Library; p.213: Wallace Collection, London/Bridgeman Art Library; p.213: Private Collection/Bridgeman Art Library; p.214: Mary Evans Picture Library; p.215:

Fotomas Index; p.216: *Cromwell after the Battle of Marston Moor*, oil on canvas by Ernest Crofts: Towneley Hall Art Gallery and Museum, Burnley, Lancashire/Bridgeman Art Library (THA 1983); p.218: Mary Evans Picture Library; p.219: Fotomas Index; p.219: The Board of Trustees of the Armouries IX-1214; p.222: Maps 4670.(1) © The British Library; p.223: Newark Museums Services, Newark and Sherwood District Council

CULLODEN 1746

p.242: © Crown Copyright/RCAHMS; p.243: The Drambuie Collection, Edinburgh, Scotland/ Bridgeman Art Library; p.246: © English Heritage Photo Library; p.247: Philip Mould, Historical Portraits Ltd, London/Bridgeman Art Library; p.247: Courtesy of the Director, National Army Museum, London; p.248: Private Collection/Bridgeman Art Library; p.249: © Duke of Atholl/The National Trust for Scotland Photo Library; p.250: City of Westminster Archive Centre, London/Bridgeman Art Library; p.254: The Royal Collection © 2002, Her Majesty Queen Elizabeth II; p.255: City of Edinburgh Museums and Art Galleries/Bridgeman Art Library; p.256: *Battle of Culloden*, 1746, engraving, 1797, by Laurie & Whittle: The Art Archive/Eileen Tweedy; p.258: Courtesy of the Director, National Army Museum, London; p.259: © The National Trust for Scotland Photo Library; p.261: © The National Trust for Scotland Photo Library; p.262: *The Beheading of Rebel Lords on Great Tower Hill*, 1746, aquatint: Museum of London/Bridgeman Art Library; p.271: © The National Trust for Scotland/Harvey Wood; p.274: ©

The National Trust for Scotland Photo Library

FIRTH OF FORTH 1939

p.288: © Crown Copyright MOD; p.290: Imperial War Museum/H33416; p.294: Imperial War Museum/A1132; p.296: Public Record Office; p.298: Topham Picturepoint; p.299: © Crown Copyright/ Historic Scotland; p.300: A Vickers supermarine Spitfire Mk I: © Hulton Getty; p.301: 602 (City of Glasgow) Squadron Museum Association; p.301: 602 (City of Glasgow) Squadron Museum Association; p.302: Popperfoto; p.303: Imperial War Museum/A1140. NA440; p.304: 602 (City of Glasgow) Squadron Museum Association/Dugald Cameron; p.306: © Hulton Getty p.307: © Crown Copyright/RCAHMS; p.309: Imperial War Museum/H33415; p.310: Imperial War Museum/C5651; p.312: Public Record Office Image Library/WO3962/2; p.314: Imperial War Museum/H707; p.315: © Dugald Cameron; p.316: 602 (City of Glasgow) Squadron Museum Association/Dugald Cameron; p.317: © Bildarchiv Preußischer Kulturbesitz, Berlin; p.329: Public Record Office; p.331: © Crown Copyright: MOD; p.334: Imperial War Museum/C5643; p.337: © Crown Copyright: MOD; p.339: Imperial War Museum/H9061; p.339: Imperial War Museum/5500

Every effort has been made to contact copyright-holders. Any omissions will be rectified in future editions.